TRAINING YOUR RETRIEVER

TRAINING
YOUR
RETRIEVER

BY

JAMES LAMB FREE

COWARD-McCANN, INC.

New York

Published simultaneously in the Dominion of
Canada by LONGMANS, GREEN & COMPANY, Toronto

Manufactured in the United States of America
Van Rees Press • New York

FOR JULIE

I merely wrote it.
She had to read it—
again and again and again.

A new kind of dog book—*by* an impatient man—*for* impatient men—for every duck hunter and gunner of upland game who yearns to own a good retriever—who wants to know how to go about finding and training his own dog, quickly and easily—without spending half his life at it.

ACKNOWLEDGMENTS

I AM DEEPLY INDEBTED TO:

William B. Wenner, who took all but five of the pictures in this book. He worked skillfully and patiently with the black dogs and me, every day for nearly a month. He took more than a thousand pictures in order to get these 120 which were snapped at just the right split second to illustrate clearly each step of training that we wanted to show.

Miss Evelyn M. Shafer of New York, the famous field-trial photographer, for three pictures: Illustrations 11, 119, and 122.

Miss Frances Sterry, for the picture of the litter of Labrador pups, Illustration 13.

The late Percy T. Jones, for the picture of Freehaven Jay used as Illustration 12.

My good friends Thomas W. Merritt, president, and J. Gould Remick, then secretary of The Labrador Retriever Club, for their kind permission to use material from the Club Year Books as the foundation of much of the statistical matter in this book. This saved me much original research work. I also greatly appreciate their permission to reprint the Labrador Breed Description and Standard of Points.

Henry W. Norton, president, and Carlton Grassle, secretary, of the Golden Retriever Club of America, for permission to use the Golden Description and Standard of Points.

Ferdinand A. Bunte, president, and Miss Oleva Groulx, secretary, of the American Chesapeake Club, for permission to print the Chesapeake Description and Standard of Points.

H. D. Bixby, executive vice-president, and Roy Beardsley, field-trial representative, of the American Kennel Club, for patiently supplying much statistical information, and for permission to reprint from the American Kennel Club publication, "Rules Applying to Registration and Field Trials, Amended to October 1947."

All of my many friends in the retriever sport, without whose help and encouragement I never would have tackled and finished this chore.

My imposed-upon secretary, Miss Aileen Morgan, who not only typed several pounds of manuscript, but also did much of the necessary research work.

My durable wife, Julie, who wore out her eyes reading and rereading every draft of every chapter. She edited and blue-penciled ruthlessly, but with such magnificent tact that I rarely even sulked.

—J. L. F.

PREFACE

ACCORDING TO MY BELOVED and long-suffering wife, I am "retriever happy."

This I admit. And here is another thing I will admit: no matter what you have heard or read to the contrary, there isn't so much to training a good retriever. There's nothing to it that a fairly bright moron couldn't figure out for himself, if he had the time. Well, I *took* the time.

If you don't believe it is easy for practically anyone to train these dogs, I will again refer you to my wife. She is a bit weary of retrievers, possibly because at times we've owned a few too many of them, and she claims she was not cut out to be a kennel boy. But she will answer you honestly. She will tell you that for the past ten years I've been training my own dogs, shooting over them, and handling them myself in big-time field-trial competition. Then she'll add, loyally suppressing any hint of surprise in her voice, that I've done all right with them. She will let you draw your own conclusions about my I.Q. rating, as a good wife should.

Actually, it is so easy to get and make a well-trained retriever that I feel any man who likes to shoot waterfowl or upland game is a sucker if he doesn't have one of these superior animals for a hunting companion. I won't go into a song and dance about all the game these dogs conserve. That has been covered thoroughly in everything ever written about retrievers.

I'll just say this: shooting feathered game is twice as much *fun* with a good retrieving dog. Today, I wouldn't go out without one, and I've loved to shoot all my life. But that good dog work is even more fun than the shooting.

And another thing. Probably this isn't tactful, for it is rarely mentioned out loud in talk about retrievers, but these dogs fill your game bag. I often hear "sportsmen" making sneering cracks about "meat hunters." Well, I'm a meat hunter. I like game on my table. And I have mighty little respect for a "sportsman" who kills anything he doesn't care to eat, or who kills and cripples birds and leaves them to rot in field or marsh.

My retrievers put a lot of extra meat on my table. They run down many a crippled pheasant that nothing on two legs could catch. They find my ducks in the heaviest marsh cover. Day after day, they bring me in with limits I'd never get without them. That alone is reason enough for me to hunt with a retriever.

Now in this book I'm going to tell you what I've learned about these dogs. Where and how to find yourself a good one to start with—a dog worth training. I'm going to name names and give addresses.

Then I'm going to tell you how to train your own dog, quickly and easily. How to avoid all the confusion common to the amateur trainer, and all the fumbling mistakes I've made.

I didn't discover for myself all of the training tricks in this book, by any means. During the first few years while this hobby was rapidly becoming a disease with me, I cribbed many of these short cuts from the Hogans. For it was my good luck to stumble into these wonderful dogs and the Hogan family simultaneously. Martin Hogan, the dean of retriever trainers in this country, his daughter Mary, and his famous sons, Frank and Jim. First they trained my dogs, and then they generously tried to train me to train and handle my own dogs. For quite a while they had rough sledding on the latter endeavor. I was unbelievably dumb.

I know now that my approach, like that of most beginning amateurs, was all wrong. I didn't understand the fundamentals of dog training, or try to. I was like an amateur doctor, trying to treat symptoms with patent medicines, and it didn't even occur to me to wonder about the causes. I struggled with many useless dogs. I struggled with, and ruined, some good youngsters because I tried to put them in college at kindergarten age. I spent too much time on my dogs. I wasted a lot of time.

I imposed on the Hogans, and leaned on them too heavily. I would ask them how to get a dog to do so-and-so, and they would show me. I was learning a lot of unrelated tricks, but I wasn't really learning the easy way to train a dog. I was going at it backward.

In this book I'm going to try to tell you how to start right, and do it the easy way.

Part I will give simple and specific answers to such questions as: Where and how can I get a good one—a dog worth training— an easy-to-train dog? What is the best retriever breed for my purpose? Should I get a pup, or an older dog? What are my chances of buying a trained dog, and what would it cost? How important is the pedigree and what can you tell from it?

Part II will give, as simply as possible, quick and easy training methods for amateurs, for impatient amateurs who have very little spare time to waste.

Part III deals with retriever field trials, discusses typical tests to expect, trial procedure, and how the judges evaluate and compare the work of the dogs. Even though you have no interest in going into field-trial competition, the stuff in Part III will help you to understand what you should and should not fairly expect of your gun dog. *There is no difference whatever between getting a dog ready for hunting or for retriever-trial competition.* And don't let any uninformed smart aleck tell you there is.

I've heard this isn't true of the pointer and setter trials—that these have drifted into races between "big-going" dogs, and that few of the good competitors are of much use as meat dogs.

But don't confuse these with retriever trials, which are simply practical hunting tests for the finest working retrievers. I've never yet seen a retriever field-trial champion that I wouldn't give my remaining natural teeth to have with me in a duck blind, or on a pheasant drive.

There are many retriever trial clubs scattered through the East, the Middle West, and the Far Western states—with new ones being constantly organized. Most of them have fairly frequent informal practice trials, to which newcomers are cordially welcomed. There is no better way to give your dog a little extra experience on retrieving shot birds, and to sharpen him up for the hunting season, than to run him in some of these friendly competitions among gun-dog owners in your vicinity. It's fun. And who knows? Your dog might even win a ribbon!

Now then, while this book is aimed squarely at the impatient hunting man who yearns for a trained retriever, I hope it will also be worth the money to the man or woman who simply wants a well-mannered pet or companion dog of any breed. At cocktail parties people are always asking me, "Do Labradors (Goldens, Chesapeakes) make good pets? Are they good with children? Are they good watchdogs? Could my husband use one for hunting, and let the children make a house pet of him at the same time?"

Or, "We have a Collie (Airedale, Dachshund, Scottie, Cocker, Wirehair, or whatnot) and I certainly wish it would behave like your retrievers. How could I teach him to sit, walk at heel, stop jumping up on people, barking at cars, and tipping over the neighbor's garbage can? How could I housebreak him?"

These questions and many more are answered in this book for people interested in dogs of any breed for any purpose. For anyone wanting to *buy* a companion dog or pet, the same principles apply as for the man in search of a good retriever.

And there are no quicker and easier methods of obedience training for any dog than those given in Part II. For a retriever must first be a perfectly behaved dog, before he can be anything more. He must be under absolute and quiet control.

Otherwise he is worse than useless—he is a nuisance in the field.

But he has so much more to learn about his work that a retriever trainer can't waste too much time on the obedience lessons. These have to be learned fast. And it is amazing how fast they *are* learned, by a *good* dog.

CONTENTS

ILLUSTRATIONS

WHICH BREED?

The Golden Retriever

1.

By any standards, the Golden is a beautiful dog to look at.

2.

Tractable, eager-to-please, easy for the amateur to train to obedience.

3.

Handles his birds gently—in fact is tender mouthed almost to a fault.

4.

Has a spectacular nose, and excels at retrieving upland game.

WHICH BREED?

The Chesapeake Bay Retriever

5.

A big, tough, rugged dog—both in body and disposition.

6.

Bred to battle the icy surf of Chesapeake Bay all day, without tiring.

7.

He is sometimes inclined to have a mind of his own, and to need—

8.

—a bit more firmness from his trainer than the Golden or the Labrador.

WHICH BREED?

The Labrador Retriever

9.

An aggressive worker, fast, stylish, equally good on land or in the water.

10.

The leading winner in the trials, he is also most popular with hunters.

11.

It won't hurt your eyes to look at a good specimen of this breed, either.

12.

He is tender mouthed, and very easy for an amateur to train and handle.

13. Don't waste time mooning over the individual pups in the litter.

14.

Instead, study the pedigree. Ask questions about the sire and dam, and the grandparents. Then, if you are satisfied with the ancestors, just shut your eyes and grab a pup.

BUYING
AN UNTRAINED DOG

15.

A dog of 12 months or more should be naturally keen to retrieve. Ask the owner to toss a dummy in light cover.

16.

You want a youngster who fairly sizzles with speed and eagerness as he dashes out after it.

17.

Who hunts fast, aggressively, and persistently in vicinity of the fall.

18.

And who sniffs the breeze, and shows signs of knowing what his nose is for.

BUYING
AN UNTRAINED DOG

19.
That thrilling, heart-stopping splash

20.
—you see when a dummy is thrown

21.
—and a keen young dog hurls himself

22.
—into the water to make the retrieve.

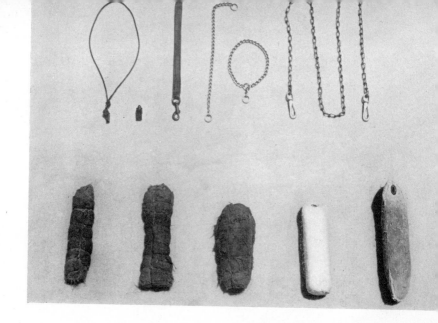

23. SOME USEFUL TRAINING PROPS

Top Row, from left: (1) Small Acme Thunderer plastic whistle, with cord (2) Top view of whistle. (3) Short leather leash. (4) Slip chain collar. (5) Collar arranged to slip over dog's head. (6) Long chain tethering leash.

Bottom Row, from left: (1) 2½-inch burlap training dummy. (2) 3-inch dummy (3) 3½-inch dummy. (4) 2½-inch lightweight floating dummy, filled with cork (5) 3¼-inch heavy floating dummy, filled with sponge rubber.

HOUSING YOUR DOG

24.

Your training job will be much easier if you keep your dog in an outside kennel, and he'll

25.

get plenty of exercise racing up and down a small but properly proportioned kennel run.

OBEDIENCE TRAINING
The Command "SIT"

26.

"Chin up, puppy."
The author's 12-year-old son, Johnnie,

27.

"SIT! Fanny down, puppy."
teaching command to a 2-month-old

28.

"SIT! Ah-ah-ah!"
Labrador pup. If a boy can do it with

29.

"SIT. Good puppy!"
a playful pup, surely a grown man can
(continued on next page)

OBEDIENCE
TRAINING

The Command "SIT"
(continued)

30.

"SIT!"

—*do it with a ready-to-learn dog.*

31.

"SIT! Stern down."

The author giving actual first lesson

32.

"SIT. Careful now!"

to Freehaven Muscles, age 12 months.

33.

"SIT! And stay there."

Elapsed time, five minutes.

OBEDIENCE TRAINING
The Command "CHARGE"
(which means "Lie Down")

34.

"SIT"

Grasp front paws—

35.

"CHARGE!"

and pull them forward.

36.

"CHARGE!"

Steady now, old boy.

37.

"CHARGE!"

Nothing to this one.

OBEDIENCE
TRAINING

The Command
"KENNEL"

38.

"KENNEL!"
Take dog by scruff of neck—

39.

"KENNEL!"
and gently but firmly propel him—

40.

"KENNEL!"
into his kennel, doghouse, or pen.

41.

KENNEL?
Why certainly, boss.

The Command "COME"

42.

This stuff is unnecessary. There is no need to have a struggle, hauling your dog around on a rope.

43.

"COME"

Any young dog will chase you, if you will pick them up and lay them down.

44.

"COME ALONG"

Run away from him briskly, calling "COME" and clapping your hands—

45.

—and also blowing *several* quick blasts on your whistle.

OBEDIENCE TRAINING

The Command "HEEL"

46.

"COME ALONG"

Step out briskly with dog on leash. Pull him up firmly if he lags behind.

47.

"HEEL!"

Walk on, repeating "HEEL" constantly. Hold a stick across his nose if he tries to forge ahead of your knee.

48.

"HEEL!"

At last, take off the leash. Keep patting your leg to keep him coming.

49.

"HEEL!"

No leash, no stick, no hands. After only 10 minutes of this, Muscles HEELS! Well, *almost* heels, then.

SIMPLE CITIZENSHIP

50.

"STOP THAT NOISE!"

Hold dog's mouth firmly closed.

51.

"HIE ON"

Useful for hunting *and* housebreaking.

52.

"DOWN"

Squeeze *front* paws and push dog down.

53.

"NO!—DOWN!"

Stay down. Be a good dog.

STARTING
A YOUNG DOG
RETRIEVING
A DUMMY

54.

Tease him with the smaller training dummy until he is frantic to grab it—

55.

Then throw it, and call HIS NAME, which is the command to retrieve.

56.

When he picks it up, run away clapping your hands and calling "COME."

57.

Keep running away until you can grab dummy from him as he catches you.

TO CURE CHEWING OR PLAYING WITH DUMMY

58.

If youngster has tendency to toss, mouth, chew, or play with dummy— tease him with it—

59.

say "AH, AH, AH"—let him grab it, but hold your hand around it so he can't clamp down on it—

60.

without biting you. Surely, I hope, your own dog won't wish to bite the hand that feeds him. "AH-AH-AH!"

61.

"YOU BE CAREFUL NOW!" He'll quickly understand dummy is to be handled as carefully as a dozen eggs.

BEGINNING TO STEADY A YOUNG DOG

62.

Have him SIT. Hold him by the collar while throwing the dummy, but then send him for it quickly.

63.

Next step: stand in front of dog while throwing, between him and dummy. Make him SIT a bit longer now.

64.

At last, stand beside him. Make him SIT until dummy is down. Then send him by "giving a line" with your hand.

65.

Don't bother with this. Sitting to deliver is unnecessary. Take dummy from him at once when he returns.

INTRODUCING A PUP TO WATER

66.

Never push or throw him in. Don't even toss a dummy the first t'me. Put on your waders, or swimming trunks.

67.

Wade out in shallow water. Call the pup to you with great enthusiasm. Clap your hands. Blow your whistle.

68.

Romp with him in the water. He'll quickly learn he loves it. *Then* lure him to deeper water, and he'll swim.

69.

Now you can toss a dummy from shore, and watch him hit the water with that spectacular, all-out splash.

LEARNING ABOUT DECOYS
The Command "LEAVE IT"

70.

"NO!"

Set out a few decoys, on *land*. There is no need to get your feet wet.

71.

"LEAVE IT!"

Walk the dog through them, back and forth, on leash. Watch him closely.

72.

"LEAVE IT!"

If he tries to grab one, restrain him with leash and command LEAVE IT.

73.

THE LIGHT DAWNS

After 5 minutes: "I get it, boss. You don't want these *wooden* ducks!"

FORCE TRAINING TO HOLD
The Command "FETCH"
(Which means "Don't drop it")

74.

"SIT!"

Force open the dog's mouth. Stuff in the smaller training dummy.

75.

"FETCH!"

When he tries to spit it out, support lower jaw, very firmly at first.

76.

"FETCH!"

Take it from him. Then repeat, supporting jaw more and more lightly.

77.

"FETCH!"

Keep repeating this until finally you can take away hand entirely.

INTRODUCTION TO FEATHERS
(Ounce of Prevention Division)

78.

"AH—AH—Careful, now—"
Use a *dead* pigeon, freshly killed.
Tease dog with it to arouse interest,
but protect it with your hand.

79.

"FETCH—Careful, now—"
Place it gently in his mouth. Have him
hold it a moment. There is no excuse
for having a hard-mouthed dog—

80.

"FETCH—Easy, boy—"
—if you just take this precaution
before a bird is ever shot for him.
He gets the point quickly.

81.

"FETCH it up"
Now back away, call him to you, and
receive the pigeon from him. Then
toss it out for a short retrieve.

INTRODUCTION TO SHACKLED DUCKS

82.

"Good grief! What *now*, boss?" Run through the same routine as with the dead pigeon, but using a *live* duck—

83.

—with wings and legs securely tied. This introduction also teaches dog to take proper body hold on a big duck.

84.

Now toss duck for *short* retrieve in *shallow* water. Get out there quickly if he offers to play with it. But no!

85.

No need for wet feet. Dog takes firm but gentle hold, delivers to hand. Happy man, happy dog, happy duck.

WORKING FROM
A BLIND

86.

Lead dog into portable blind with side wings (type used in trials). Have him SIT, well forward—

87.

—facing hole. Then toss dummy through hole, to land on *ground*, just in front of blind. Send dog at once.

88.

He'll jump through hole to retrieve it before he has a chance to shy at this strange contraption. Repeat this.

89.

Then throw dummy out in water. Dog should go out for it through hole, but may *return* around side.

TO SPEED UP
A DOG ON LAND
AND WATER

90.

Have him SIT. Walk away, a little farther each time, finally 100 yards or more. Wait until he is fairly frantic to come to you—

91.

—then call him, blowing *several* whistle blasts, and just watch him come! Excellent for a dog which has a tendency to putter coming in.

92.

Have him SIT on shore, while you go out in boat. Give him plenty of suspense before you call him. Soon he'll be hitting water with a fine splash.

93.

Row around a few minutes, and let him follow the boat. This further develops his liking for the water, as well as his swimming muscles.

TEACHING
HAND SIGNALS
(Baseball Diamond
Method)

94.

Use a lawn or yard with no cover to hide dummy. Starting from imaginary home plate, walk with dog at HEEL—

95.

—out to pitcher's mound. Give command SIT, followed by *one* sharp blast on whistle, meaning STOP and SIT.

96.

Then toss the dummy toward second base, being sure the dog sees it, and that it lands in plain sight.

97.

Keep commanding SIT, followed by *one* whistle blast, as you leave dog out there, and return to home plate.

(continued on next page)

HAND SIGNALS
(continued)
The Command
"GET BACK"

98.

Make overhead arm signal like a *girl* throwing a ball toward second. Call his NAME and shout "GET BACK."

99.

Dog will probably hesitate, remember the dummy, then turn his head, see it, and GET BACK to retrieve it.

100.

The instant he picks it up, encourage him with *several* quick whistle blasts to come in with it fast—

101.

—all the way to home plate. After only 10 minutes of this, he should be ready to proceed the next day to—

(continued on next page)

HAND SIGNALS
(continued)
To RIGHT and LEFT

102.

—Hand signal to right. Walk dog out to pitcher's mound. Blast whistle, say "SIT," toss dummy to *first* base.

103.

You return to home plate. Call dog's *name* to send him, and throw your arm straight *right* from the shoulder—

104.

—at the same time swaying your whole body to *right*. Whistle him in. Work on this for a full 10-minute lesson.

105.

The next day, work on *hand signal to left.* Use same routine, in reverse. This time, toss dummy to *third* base.

(continued on next page)

106.

You return to home plate. Make arm signal to LEFT, call dog's NAME *only* if this still necessary to send him.

107.

But by now he should be well on his way to associating these arm signals with the direction of the fall, and—

108.

—with *permission to go* and retrieve. Work him only to *left* for 10 minutes. Then try *right*, and *get back*.

109.

As soon as he is smartly obeying all three signals, without your calling his NAME, it is time to move to—

(continued on next page)

110.

—a field with sufficient cover to hide the dummy. Toss it to second base. Dog should no longer need aid—

111.

—of seeing dummy on bare ground. Call "GET BACK" and give overhead arm signal. If he takes it—

112.

—then work him to LEFT and RIGHT, mixing them up. After 10 minutes of this, you should be able—

113.

—next day to start real blind retrieves. Plant dummy without dog seeing it. Direct him to it with hand signals.

RETRIEVER
FIELD TRIALS
Land Tests

114.

Good judges make a good trial. They plan the tests carefully, trying to give each dog an equal opportunity.

115.

Experienced amateur handlers usually are good judges. They are sympathetic but they see every move of every dog.

116.

The birds should be thrown *high*. And *both* gunners should always shoot, no matter how good they think they are.

117.

In land tests, a retriever must sit quietly on the line until his number is called by one of the judges.

RETRIEVER
FIELD TRIALS
Water Tests

118.

In water, the older dogs work from a "blind," and over decoys. *Over* is the word. See that Labrador take off!

119.

A shot is fired as a dead or shackled duck is thrown from a boat. Sometimes live ducks are released and shot.

120.

Dog must deliver duck to his handler in the blind. But in the informal training stakes for younger dogs—

121.

—the judges sometimes dispense with blind and decoys. Here a keen young Golden hits water with enthusiasm.

RETRIEVER
FIELD TRIALS
Gallery Scenes

122.

Scene at 1947 National. At the trials you meet a nice bunch—all sorts of people from various walks of life.

123.

Especially at the "picnic" trials in California, informal—you might even say *exotic*—costumes are in order.

124.

According to trial etiquette, gallery should applaud only *after* each dog has completed his whole performance.

125.

And *please* don't fondle, pet, talk baby-talk to, or feed a ham sandwich to another man's dog. Very bad form.

PART I

HOW TO FIND AND BUY YOUR DOG

Chapter 1

THE GREAT SECRET REVEALED

IF YOU ALREADY own a retriever—or any other kind of dog for that matter—you may as well save your eyes and skip this stuff about how to go about buying a good one. For unless you have more sense than I had when I acquired my first retriever, you're going to take a whirl at making something of the dog you have before you'll even consider turning him in on a new model. And it's entirely possible you are luckier than I was, and that you stumbled into a dog worth training. I'd say it's about a fifty-fifty chance. I believe about half of the purebred Labradors, Goldens, and Chesapeakes in this country are worth training. The bench breeders (meaning those who breed for bench shows *exclusively*) haven't had time to ruin them yet, and that's more than you can say for many of the sporting breeds and most of the other breeds that have become too popular with the bench show "fancy."

Now please don't start telling me about your dog—how he fetches your newspaper, and wows your guests by retrieving a kippered herring out of the icebox. You can't win if you start that kind of a bull session with me. For I have owned some of the most charming and utterly useless dogs you ever saw. I can and will retaliate by boring you for hours about my first retriever, old Nell, whom I dearly love to this day.

Nell was beautiful to look at, a true bench-type Labrador. She would do all sorts of parlor retrieving tricks. She was affectionate, as long as she had her own way. But—she was as hardheaded as a mother-in-law. For instance, I never did persuade her to deliver a duck to hand, and I spent many—too many—weary and frustrated hours trying. Invariably she would spit out the duck as she came ashore. If I wanted it, I could darned well walk over to the edge of the water and get it for myself. She was an incorrigible shot breaker. Also, I never succeeded in curing her of her conviction that it was more important and much more pleasant to run a rabbit than to retrieve a pheasant.

My old hunting partner, Nate Lord, used to laugh until he cried at some of the races he witnessed. A fast field would disappear over the horizon, with the rabbit leading old Nell by half a length, and with me running third but closing fast on the black bitch, screaming unprintable words. It is astonishing what speed a no-longer-young man with a slight paunch can make, even in heavy hunting boots, if sufficiently inspired and pumping plenty of adrenalin.

There were many other essential lessons Nell refused to learn. But I was nearly as stubborn as she was, and struggled with her three years before it dawned on me that she was really not worth fooling with. At that, it broke my heart to let her go. But I finally had enough sense to sell her to a kindly hunter who wanted a bargain dog, and let him cut his retriever teeth on her. I believe he is now a wiser man, also.

So don't tell me about your dog. Just go ahead and start training him, if he's old enough, and you'll find out shortly how good he really is. I hope you're lucky, and that he's eager to please, and quick to learn. But if he doesn't respond very fast to those ten-minute daily lessons, then it would pay you to come back here and read the rest of Part I.

I've read a lot of books on dog training in my life, and tried to follow their instructions, with very poor success. Most of them had me licked before I got fairly started, by assuring me I must have *patience*, a quality I do not possess, in order to teach anything to a dog. It took many years of useless struggle with a procession of lovable but hopeless mutts before a great and simple truth slowly penetrated my thick skull. This, I am now passing on to you, and you'll save yourself a lot of grief if you'll just take my word for it.

For any ordinary mortal to train a dog, *you've got to have a decent dog to start with.*

That looks assinine in print, it seems so obvious—and yet, believe it or not, that is the theme, the "message," of this book. That is the great secret.

Most Americans, including me, are born with a sentimental and unrealistic attitude toward dogs. During childhood years this attitude is further developed by a procession of pets. A boy takes in a stray cur. He feeds it. The mongrel wags his tail and licks the boy's face. From then on, that dog can do no wrong. It is the smartest, the best dog in the world. The chances are it never actually performs one useful function in its life, before being killed chasing a car, shot by an angry farmer for killing chickens, or poisoned by a neighbor weary of replanting his garden. But to the boy that is a wonderful dog. It's *his* dog.

In later years the boy is further misled by the more commercial bench show racketeers and the back-yard breeders. They sell him a "pedigreed" dog, and along with it the false impression that a dog is necessarily worth something because it has a pedigree.

Before you set out to buy an intelligent, easy-to-train pup or young dog, the most important thing for you to do is firmly determine to skip the sentiment, and try to get into a realistic frame of mind. A working cowpuncher takes good care of his horse. He feeds and waters it before he will sit down to his own chow. Sometimes he gets very fond of a top pony. But don't believe what you see in the Western pictures. He doesn't croon "Old Pal" ballads to his mount, walking over a ridge at sunset. And he doesn't waste much feed on a pony that doesn't earn it doing his job.

A dog is a domesticated wild animal. Each breed was originally developed to perform a definite service for man. Many of them have now degenerated under the tender mercies of the kind of bench show breeder who selects and breeds mainly for looks and conformation, and does not bother much about intelligence, or working qualities. If a dog can win a blue ribbon merely by walking around a ring on a leash, and being posed by his handler, why worry about brains or tractability?

But all dogs, at one time, were bred and selected for one common trait: *eagerness to please a man.*

And that is the first and most important trait you want to look for in the dog you buy—in the dog himself, *and in his immediate ancestors.*

If you want to have a trained retriever quickly and easily, there is just one way to begin. Spend a little time choosing your dog, instead of letting the dog choose you. Get a pup or young dog that is intelligent, eager to please the man, easy to train, a dog that has been bred and selected for these qualities—as well as for the natural instincts of hunting and retrieving game—for many generations. Get yourself one of these, and his training will take no more than ten minutes a day.

He eats no more horse meat than a brainless, contrary, hammer-headed, although possibly lovable mutt. And here's another great discovery I've made:

It's just as easy to love a good one.

⊔⊔⊔⊔⊔⊔⊔⊔⊔⊔⊔⊔⊔⊔⊔⊔⊔⊔⊔⊔⊔⊔⊔⊔⊔⊔⊔

Chapter 2

BARGAIN DOGS

SO LET'S ASSUME you're sold on my "message." You want to
end up with a well-trained, useful retriever, and you don't want
to waste a lot of time reaching that goal. You're willing to take
my word for it, and start out with the best material you can
find. You're ready to buy, and you want to know where and how
to go about it.

Well, the first thing to do is to loosen up. Most of us are in-
credible cheapskates when it comes to buying a dog, and we get
just about what we pay for and what we deserve. And when you
pause to figure out the economics of owning a dog—which few
dog owners seem to do—it is obviously downright silly to be
bargain hunting.

So now we come to secret number two, another simple but very
important truth:

A cheap dog is the most expensive in the long run.

The only worse thing than a bargain dog is a *gift dog.* You
have about the same chance of getting a good one this way as
you have of making a seven-horse parlay. If you like to play odds
like those, go ahead, chum. Go ahead and take a dog as a gift.
One of two things happens. You lose a friend, the donor, when
you finally harden your heart and get rid of the beast. Or else
you lose a *lot* of friends by keeping an unruly mutt for the rest
of *his* life, and a good chunk of *yours.* He will alienate your
shooting partners, running wild and flushing pheasants out of

range. He will ruin every hunt for everybody. And he will eat you out of house and home for at least eighteen years. All gift dogs seem to bear charmed lives, and achieve a very ripe old age.

If you want a dog worth training, you've got to think of the original cost as unimportant. Whatever it is, it constitutes only a small down payment on the over-all cost of owning a dog and maintaining it properly over the years of its life. The price of a dog is like the price of a safety razor. They get you on the blades.

At today's prices of horse meat and supplementary feed, it costs at least fifteen dollars a month to properly nourish a dog the size of a retriever. One hundred and eighty dollars a year. If you keep him ten years (which you probably will) his feed costs you eighteen hundred dollars. This does not include your original investment in a small kennel and wire-enclosed run, to keep him properly confined. Nor does it include such things as distemper shots, and occasional veterinary bills. And of course it includes no professional training, at forty to sixty dollars per month. I'm assuming you'll train the dog yourself, right from the start.

If you go about it right, you can buy a *good* retriever pup for as low as a hundred and fifty dollars. You can probably find a bargain, from unproven breeding, for fifty, and kid yourself that you're saving a hundred dollars. You'll keep this little long-shot ticket at least a year, trying to make up your mind about him. Feed cost: a hundred and eighty dollars. A smart deal. Additional losses: one year of your life; possibly a somewhat shortened life, due to hardened arteries acquired in attempting to train a meat-headed pup.

Starting with a good pup at age three months, it takes at least a year to have him in shape to take hunting. It wouldn't take this long to train him, but after all the pup has to grow up. So if you're sufficiently impatient you might want to try to find an older, trained dog, a proven performer.

But, brother, if you want to buy a finished retriever, you'll really have to get the fishhooks out of your pocket. When people ask me what they would have to pay for such a dog, my favorite answer is the gag about J. P. Morgan.

Some upstart had just made a killing in Wall Street, and approached Mr. Morgan for advice. He was wondering if he could afford to own a yacht.

"Young man," replied Mr. Morgan, "if you even have to ask that question, you can't afford it."

You might as well concentrate on finding a pup or a young untrained dog, unless you're prepared to pay as much as five hundred dollars or more for a trained retriever worth owning. You might get a reasonably good, trained shooting dog for that. If your ambition is to own a field-trial winner, a really superior animal, proven in competition, you'll dig a lot deeper. These—depending on their records of wins in trials—change hands at prices of one thousand to five thousand dollars.

But you don't need a potential field-trial champion to have a perfectly satisfactory shooting dog and companion, and these, when available, can be had at prices ranging from five hundred to a thousand dollars.

There is a man I know in California who thinks he has been trying intelligently for at least six years to get himself a good retriever. He doesn't want to wait for a pup to develop. He wants a finished performer, right now. He's been wanting it for six years, and still wants it.

Now this character makes a lot of money, and he spends it freely. He'll wrestle your arm off in a night club, trying to pick up and pay a hundred-dollar check. But he won't pay a decent price to get a decent dog. He has a policy. Someone told him once that no dog is worth more than two hundred dollars. So that's his ceiling price.

He is an ardent hunter, and has the kind of job that allows him plenty of time for shooting everything that flies—quail, pheasant, doves, wild pigeon, sage hen, ducks, and geese. He belongs to a fine duck club, and shoots there every week in season. He takes several hunting trips to other states, and after everything is closed in this country, he goes gunning down in Mexico through the winter. He must spend at least two thousand dollars a year on hunting—on his club and his numerous trips.

He loses an enormous number of killed and crippled birds that he can't find without a good dog. He hates this. He's a sportsman, and a conservationist, at heart. He also enjoys bringing home the meat. If anyone ever needed a real retrieving dog, he's the man. He's always asking me to find him a good one.

The first time I bit. I wrote a lot of letters, and finally located a breeder friend of mine near Chicago, who was willing to part with a good four-year-old bitch, a Labrador. She had proved disappointing as a brood bitch, and my letter hit this breeder at just the right psychological moment. He was willing to let her go for five hundred dollars. I had shot over her, seen her place in a few junior stakes in trials, and knew her well. She would have been perfect for my California friend, and she was more than worth that price.

But do you think he bought her? No.

Instead he bought another two-hundred-dollar bargain from some back-yard breeder. So far, to my knowledge, he's had eight of these. None of them worth keeping. But I will say this for him. He doesn't keep these hammer-heads long. He writes them off, gets rid of them, sells them for what he can get, or gives them away to anyone who is sap enough to take them. Sixteen hundred dollars he has spent for these bargains. He could have had that one good bitch all these years, enjoying her, for five hundred dollars. A very smart guy. A close man with his dog dollar.

One day last fall he called me in great excitement. He had hit the jack pot at last. One of his long shots had finally come in, this time from somewhere in Missouri. A fine-looking Labrador emerged from the crate. It was bold and keen and eager to retrieve. In the yard it handled perfectly for its new owner, marked well, did a very fast and stylish job of retrieving training dummies.

This dog got me an invitation to a good duck club, anyway. We rushed up there. I was to see the living proof that a superior retriever can be bought by mail for two hundred dollars. I was due for quite a ribbing.

The dog was well behaved, and sat quietly in the blind. Presently a pair of mallards circled our decoys.

"Take them," whispered my friend, and I got lucky and made the double. Both fell far across the pond in heavy tules. Now if you haven't seen California tules you don't know what rugged cover is. A man without a retriever doesn't even bother to look for a bird that falls in them. And it needs a really top-notch dog to cope with them. A powerful dog who can force his way through them. A dog with guts, to take the cutting punishment they give him about the eyes and nose. And a dog with a real nose to smell and find a bird amid the stench that invariably rises from a stagnant tule marsh.

But this dog marked those difficult falls perfectly. When sent, he tore through those tough tules like a wounded boar making his charge. Very quickly he emerged with the drake in his mouth. He started back toward the blind. The water in the pond was too shallow for swimming, and the clinging adobe mud was two feet deep, but it didn't bother *this* dog. He plowed through it so fast he didn't have time to get mired. He looked like a field-trial champion. I was getting my mouth set to eat a large dish of crow.

Suddenly, halfway back to the blind, he came to a small island in the middle of the pond. He climbed up on it.

Then he sat down, and proceeded to eat that duck. He ate it calmly, and very thoroughly, while his disillusioned owner screamed and cursed and blasted on his whistle. The dog paid no attention. He ate everything but the feathers and the feet.

Then he arose, licked his chops, stretched, and went back into the tules for the hen. He remembered that fall perfectly, and he ate her, too. There was nothing wrong with his appetite.

Now "hard mouth" is still a rare fault to find in a Labrador. The better breeders eliminate for this ruthlessly, and in all the retriever trials I've seen and judged, I can recall only one of the black dogs that was clearly guilty of this blackest of all retriever crimes.

But my bargain-hunting friend managed to find one.

Whether it's a retriever you're after, or a trainable, intelligent dog of any breed for any purpose, it pays to loosen your purse strings before you start, even if it kills you.

If you honestly can't afford to pay the price a reputable breeder asks for an older, trained dog, then content yourself with a pup or a young untrained dog.

If you can't afford to pay the price for the pup, you can't afford to keep him anyway.

If you're just plain tight, to hell with you.

Chapter 3

THE TRUTH ABOUT PEDIGREES

THIS CHAPTER WILL win me no friends among the more commercial elements in the dog racket. But if you're to buy a decent dog, you must first understand the plain unvarnished facts about so-called "pedigreed" dogs.

I'm always meeting someone who tells me proudly about the big price he paid for his pedigreed dog. And usually he doesn't know any of the names in the pedigree—not even the names of the sire and dam.

Now the sad truth is that merely because you loosen up and pay a good price for a purebred—or pedigreed—dog of any breed whatever, this is no guarantee that the dog is worth anything. It is no guarantee that the animal has any of the easy-to-train qualities you want—intelligence, tractability, eagerness to please, or even a decent disposition.

In fact, many pedigrees, if you know how to read them, virtually guarantee qualities that are just the reverse—stupidity, stubbornness, and a generally ornery nature.

Some of the more venal bench breeders, along with some careless and ignorant back-yard breeders, have for many years peddled and publicized a whopper to the general dog-buying public. I mean this fiction that just any "pedigreed dog" is somehow a mysteriously superior and desirable critter.

"Pedigree:" says the dictionary, "a table presenting a line of ancestors; a genealogical tree."

13

And that is *all* it is.

You could provide a pedigree for any mongrel, if you wanted to take the time and trouble to trace down his ancestors for three generations or more, and write down their names on a piece of paper.

It is simply easier to get the names of the ancestors of a pure-bred dog, because they are recorded in the studbook of his particular breed. *But this doesn't mean any of them necessarily had any desirable qualities to transmit to their descendants.*

To say, "This is a pedigreed dog," means little or nothing.

Yet the *right* pedigree means so much.

The immense popularity of bench shows in this country in my opinion has ruined many fine breeds of dogs, and has greatly added to the confusion of the ordinary mortal who wants to buy an intelligent, easy-to-train pup. To win ribbons in bench shows, a dog needs to take no real obedience training. (To forestall the angry mail from the bench show "fancy," I hasten to except those dogs that are entered in obedience classes and tracking tests at some of the shows. They have to *do* something, at least. But these are a very small minority of the show dogs benched.)

Most of the ribbons in these shows are won by dogs who have to do nothing but submit to being led by a leash—sometimes dragged—around the ring by their handlers. I've seen some pretty unruly specimens become bench champions, judged purely on such things as general appearance, physical conformation, coat, and color. Some breed standards recommend "a kindly, intelligent eye," which is all right as far as it goes. But hell's bells! What is a kindly, intelligent eye? In hiring people, I've looked into the kindly, intelligent eyes of plenty of humans who turned out to be horrible nincompoops when it came to doing a job of any kind.

Now I'm not saying physical conformation isn't important. It is. You need a strong healthy retriever to be able to do his useful work. And surely part of the pleasure of owning any sort of dog is being able to look at him without nausea.

Most good breeders of working dogs try to conform to the breed standards as closely as possible. Many somehow find the time to prove their stock in *both* field trials and bench shows, and for these I have nothing but respect and envy. Some day I hope to have sufficient leisure to show some of my working dogs myself.

But to be a top-notch worker, a dog *has* to be a pretty good physical specimen, automatically. And, unfortunately, the reverse is not true.

My only quarrel with the bench shows is that they have become too popular with people who care nothing about what's inside a dog. The so-called bench "fancy," which blithely ignores the innate qualities, instincts, and tendencies that govern what a dog *does*. The best way to judge a man, or a dog, is not by the way he looks, but how he *acts*. You can't do that in the bench show ring. And neither can the judges who award the ribbons.

If you lump all breeds of purebred or pedigreed dogs, the vast majority now descend from generations of strictly bench-show stock—from ancestors who had to do nothing useful to earn their keep. Fortunately the retriever breeds have as yet been relatively less spoiled by the bench shows, and by indiscriminate and careless breeding, than any other breeds in America. But even with the retrievers, a pedigree as such is apt to mean nothing, and you should examine *any* dog's pedigree with a bilious eye.

Let me throw in a few fast statistics here for the reader who may be thinking of some other breed, but who wants a pup easily and quickly trained to obedience.

During 1947 (the last year for which these records are available) the American Kennel Club registered in the AKC Stud Book 235,720 individual dogs. This does not include litter registrations.

Of these, 96,414 were of the so-called sporting breeds. But 78,000 of those were Cocker Spaniels, which have become so enormously popular for bench shows and as pets that a very tiny percentage are bred and used as shooting dogs today.

So let's subtract all the Cockers, which leaves a total of 18,414 in all other sporting breeds. These include Irish Setters, most of which are now bench dogs, and English Setters, half of which are probably bred for bench exclusively. In fact, I feel sure it is conservative to estimate that less than half the dogs of the remaining sporting breeds come from recent generations of trained workers.

Certainly, not more than 10,000 individual dogs were bred to be trained for useful work, including not only the sporting breeds, but also the small number of guide dogs, guard dogs, and sheep and cattle dogs of other breeds. Only 10,000 out of a total AKC registration of 235,720! Thus 96 per cent of the registered dogs are from bench-show stock.

During 1947, 144,139 dogs were entered in AKC bench shows; 28,098 were entered in AKC field trials; 7,730 were entered in AKC obedience trials.

Of the grand total, 80 per cent of these dogs competing for ribbons were being judged largely on *how they looked*.

Only 20 per cent were judged *by their actions*.

So the chances are 4 to 1, if you're puzzling over the pedigree of an AKC registered dog, that you're looking at the names of a lot of ancestors who were bred and selected for bench standards, rather than ability to take training and perform useful work.

I might say here that the *American Field* of Chicago is the recognized authority on pointer and setter trials, and most of the good *working* pointers and setters are registered in their studbook, *The Field Dog Stud Book*. Many of these are not registered also with AKC. So if you're looking for a pointer or setter, an *American Field* pedigree might easily mean more than one from the Kennel Club. It is more likely to mean the dog came from field-trial stock.

But the AKC has everything else pretty well sewed up, including not only the bench shows, but the retriever and spaniel trials. All serious breeders of working retrievers and spaniels register them in AKC. Some also register their dogs with the *American Field,* but not many as yet.

I hope this clears up a common source of confusion. Many people think a registered dog is a registered dog, and don't know about the two studbooks. It boils down to this: if you're buying a *working* pointer or setter, or want a pup from working ancestors, your chances are better if it is registered in the Field Dog

Stud Book. If you are buying any other breed, it should be registered in the American Kennel Club Stud Book. And if you are buying a retriever, I would definitely insist that it be registered in the AKC. This has a substantial effect on the value of any pups it might sire or whelp in the future, and on the value of the dog if you should ever want to sell it. Of course, there is no harm in a dog's being registered in both studbooks.

Now then, what does all this stuff about registration and pedigrees mean to you in achieving your objective—an easy-to-train dog with such other working instincts and qualities as you want?

If you are buying a mature, trained dog, his work can be demonstrated to you, and you can base your judgment to a considerable extent on just what he *does* as an individual. But his breeding is still important, also, and I would not buy an individual dog, no matter how impressive his work appeared at the moment, unless he also had some good working ancestors close up in his pedigree. He might be a sport, a throwback. If you ever bred him, the chances of his transmitting his accidental good qualities to his pups would be fairly poor. And also, if a young dog, he might have latent bad qualities himself that would crop up later.

And, of course, if you are buying a puppy at any age up to nine months or so, you are almost entirely dependent on his pedigree. But cheer up. The whole secret of reading a pup's pedigree is really quite simple.

You merely want to know, from sources you feel you can trust, just who were his mammy and pappy, and secondarily his grandparents. What did they do? Were they trained dogs? Did they take training easily? Were they used for hunting? If so, *who* shot over them, and what does *he* say about the way they worked? Were any of them field-trial dogs? If so, what were their field-trial records? Were any of them field-trial champions?

Some back-yard breeders whose only interest is selling pups will show you a five- or six-generation pedigree, point a grimy finger at a famous name or two on the right side of the page, and give you nothing but doubletalk about the unknown individuals on the left, or close-up side of the family tree. Now it's fun to brag to your friends about Glenairlie Rover or Blind of Arden or some other great field-trial champion being the great-great-grandfather of your Labrador. But if that's *all* you can boast about in the pedigree, it means very little.

To find out why this is true, we don't need to go into a long-winded discussion of Mendel's Law. We just need to realize this:

Sire and dam (two individuals) each contributed 50 per cent to the traits, instincts, and make-up of your dog.

Grandparents (four individuals) each contributed 25 per cent.

Fourth generation (eight individuals) each contributed only 12½ per cent.

Fifth generation (sixteen individuals) only 6¼ per cent each.

If you will think about this for a moment, you'll readily recognize how silly it is to buy a pup on the strength of one great dog's appearing in his pedigree in the fourth or fifth generation. Yet how many people do it! A fifth-generation ancestor contributes only 6¼ per cent. The other fifteen in that generation contribute 93¾ per cent. If they are unknown quantities, your only safe assumption is that most of them weren't much good. What chance have any of the great qualities of that one illustrious dog to filter down to your pup, if his parents and grandparents are also unknown quantities?

And remember, *bad qualities are inherited,* just like the good ones. Sometimes to a conscientious breeder they seem to be the dominant ones, as far as transmittal is concerned.

So all you want to see is a three-generation pedigree. But you want to know all you can learn about *every* individual in it. The sire and dam, and the grandparents. That's enough. You want to know not only that these six dogs all were easily trainable and intelligent workers, but also that *none of them had serious faults.*

Now, let's clear up one more small but important item in the reading of pedigrees. When the prefix "Ch." appears before the name of a dog, it means *bench champion*. It means only that the dog has won enough points in bench shows to be awarded that title by the AKC. It doesn't necessarily mean the dog could *do* anything, except stand up and walk around the ring.

"Ch." means only that this was a good-looking animal, according to the current standard of that particular breed club. It is no assurance that he had a brain in his head.

There is just one exception that I know of. In 1939 the Labrador Retriever Club incorporated a rule in its constitution and by-laws that no *member of the club* shall use the title "Ch." until a dog, having won a bench-show championship, shall receive a working certificate or better at a field trial. This has been interpreted by the officers of the club to mean that any Labrador entered in a field trial licensed by the AKC, which has satisfactorily completed both a land and a water series in the same trial, is deemed to have obtained a working certificate.

So *if* you're looking at the pedigree of a Labrador and *if* you're dealing with a member in good standing of the Labrador Club (the rule of course is not binding on other Labrador breeders) and *if* the title was acquired since June 1, 1939, then the prefix "Ch." before a dog's name means a little more. It means that dog had to take a certain amount of training, enough to go successfully through two series of a regular licensed trial. It means he had to be steady, to sit quietly on the line and in the blind. And it probably means he had to find and retrieve at least two pheasants and two ducks, and do a satisfactory job of it.

If more sporting-breed clubs would adopt similar rules, it would do much to halt and even reverse the sad downward trend of these dogs on the bench.

But until they do, the wise man looking for an intelligent dog to train pretty much ignores that "Ch." on a pedigree.

The nuggets to look for are dogs with "F.T.Ch." or "Fld. Ch." before their names. Both abbreviations mean Field Trial Champion, and, brother, that means plenty.

Any retriever that has earned that title has *done* something, and he's done it against top competition. He has clearly demonstrated his great intelligence, his desire to work for his handler, his capacity for taking training. You can count on it. He is at least *one* worthy parent or grandparent for the dog you want, and you need inquire no further about *him*.

Well, that's enough about pedigrees. Let's just sum it up.

The man who says proudly, "My dog is pedigreed," is merely exposing his ignorance.

If he says, "My dog is by So-and-so out of Such-and-such," naming two outstanding *working* individuals of the breed, he's beginning to make sense.

If he then tells you about all four grandparents, he's cooking with gas.

For our present purpose—finding an easy-to-train pup—pay no attention to "Ch." on a pedigree (unless it's a Labrador with a working certificate, or you otherwise know it was also a trained dog).

But pay plenty to "F.T.Ch." or "Fld. Ch."

Look no further than second and third generations. But take a *good* look at *all* of those six dogs—both parents, and four grandparents.

If you want an easy-to-train, lazy man's pup, avoid strictly bench stock of any breed like the plague.

And if you want to learn some new unprintable words, just show this chapter to a bench breeder.

Chapter 4

WHAT BREED?

PEOPLE ARE ALWAYS asking, "What is the best retriever breed for a shooting dog?" or, "Which is best just for a pet for my kids?"

Now I hate to see a potentially good gun dog wasted as a house pet. It is like putting Cleopatra in a hash house instead of a harem. Her natural talents would be largely unused. Yet she would be easier on your eyes, and no doubt on your digestion, than some haggard slut of a waitress slinging your food at you.

In a moment of slightly alcoholic enthusiasm, a fellow retriever nut, a breeder, once said to me, "These dogs are much too good for the common people."

The retriever-happy fraternity feels this way about these remarkable dogs. It amounts to a special brand of snobbishness, which has nothing to do with money or social position.

In the Midwest Field Trial Club of Chicago, in which I was active for many years before moving to California, one of the most prominent members was a Chicago cop. And as far as the dogs were concerned, he was one of the greatest snobs. He simply hated to see a well-bred working retriever get into the hands of anyone who would not fully appreciate it. And he would never think of selling one of his pups to anyone but a gunning man.

When you stop to think of it, this attitude is understandable. If a man has devoted years of his life, plus a good deal of money, to the improvement of a working breed, carefully selecting for superior dogs with many valuable qualities, he naturally wants to see *all* of those qualities used. If the youngsters from his kennel are not used for hunting or in field trials, he can't be sure his breeding program is right. For the only way to prove a sire or dam is by keeping track of what his or her progeny *do* in the field.

So here's a tip, for anyone trying to buy a retriever pup just for a house pet, from a serious breeder of working dogs. You'd better forget what you learned in Sunday School. You'd better tell a lie, and tell it pretty convincingly. You'd better look him in the eye, and tell him you'll train the pup and use it, at least for hunting. Even that may not be enough, with some breeders. You may even have to act interested in field trials, to get your hands on a pup of particularly good breeding.

The above is treason, and won't increase my popularity with my retriever breeder friends. But if the truth is told, the best working retrievers *do* make wonderful pets. They can't be beat as easy-to-train, intelligent companions.

But from here on we'll discuss these breeds in terms of their working qualities, for the man who wants a shooting dog or a field-trial prospect. The house-pet seeker can ride along, knowing that the same qualities that make a dog a great worker make him a superior companion for a lazy man.

Hold your hats and here we go.

What is the best breed of retriever?

Well, this is supposed to be a democracy. Let's start by determining which breed is the most popular—which gets the most votes from retriever owners.

From 1931 (when the AKC started registering retrievers) through 1947 the total registrations of the six recognized retriever breeds in the American Kennel Club Stud Book are as follows:

AKC REGISTRATIONS

Year	Labrador Retriever	Chesapeake Bay Retriever	Golden Retriever	Irish Water Spaniel	Curly-coated Retriever	Flat-coated Retriever
1931	40	51	—	—	—	—
1932	58	36	20	17	—	1
1933	84	70	28	10	1	3
1934	121	103	32	24	—	3
1935	126	178	35	18	4	2
1936	174	167	68	31	7	3
1937	277	200	65	58	12	6
1938	283	267	120	57	9	7
1939	392	298	147	43	10	8
1940	473	327	171	43	1	7
1941	523	323	183	46	2	2
1942	460	350	185	46	5	5
1943	362	221	153	31	4	—
1944	515	172	248	44	1	—
1945	956	427	511	59	2	—
1946	1736	780	994	95	2	—
*1947	2035	787	1187	99	1	1
Totals	8615	4757	4147	721	61	48
being	(47%)	(26%)	(22%)	(4%)	(.5%)	(.5%)

of the Grand Total, all retrievers...................... 18,349

* The last year for which these figures were available.

From the above we might reasonably conclude that among the owners of purebred, registered retrievers in this country, the Labrador is:

Nearly twice as popular as the Chesapeake;

More than twice as popular as the Golden;

Twelve times as popular as the Irish Water Spaniel.

There are so few Curly-coated and Flat-coated Retrievers in this country that we may as well forget them, as your chance of finding a good one for sale is very remote.

Now then, which breed has done the most to prove itself *in action*? Which has done best in retriever field-trial competition?

Here is a summary of placings won in open all-age stakes or limited all-age stakes (which count points toward the title of Field Trial Champion) in trials open to all breeds of retrievers, covering the years 1931 through 1948.

PLACINGS BY BREEDS 1931-1948

Per Cent of Retrievers	First Places	Second Places	Third Places	Fourth Places	Total Places
Labradors (47%)	178(75%)	159(70%)	149(66%)	141(66%)	627(69%)
Goldens (22%)	43(18%)	45(20%)	52(23%)	43(20%)	183(20%)
Chesapeakes(26%)	16(7%)	21(9%)	22(10%)	29(13%)	88(10%)
Curly Coats(½%)	0	2(1%)	1(½%)	2(1%)	5(½%)
Irish (4%)	0	0	3(¼%)	0	3(¼%)

The above table covers all the years since retriever trials have been held in this country.

Labradors, comprising 47 per cent of the registered retrievers, won 75 per cent of the first places in championship stakes open to all retriever breeds. They won 69 per cent of all the placings.

Goldens were next, barely holding their own, as 22 per cent of the dogs won 18 per cent of the firsts and 20 per cent of all places.

Chesapeakes didn't do so well, 26 per cent of the dogs winning only 7 per cent of the firsts and 10 per cent of all places.

The number of Curly Coats and Irish Water Spaniels entered, and the number of their placings, were so small that the percentages don't mean much.

Now what is the current trend? Let's take a look at the placings for 1948 only, at this writing the last year for which complete records are available.

PLACINGS BY BREEDS—1948 ONLY

Per Cent of Retrievers	First Places	Second Places	Third Places	Fourth Places	Total Places
Labradors (47%)	34(94%)	30(86%)	22(63%)	25(72%)	111(79%)
Goldens (22%)	2(6%)	2(6%)	10(29%)	7(20%)	21(15%)
Chesapeakes(26%)	0	3(8%)	3(8%)	3(8%)	9(6%)

Irish Water Spaniels, Curly Coats, and Flat Coats won no placings during 1948.

You can decide for yourself whether this reveals a trend, or just a lucky year for the Labradors.

At any rate, the record shows that 47 per cent of the retrievers won 94 per cent of the first places and 79 per cent of all places.

The Goldens, with 22 per cent of the registered retrievers, won only 6 per cent of the first places and 15 per cent of all places.

The Chesapeakes, 26 per cent of the dogs, won no first places in 1948, and won only 6 per cent of all places.

FIELD-TRIAL CHAMPIONS

Since 1931, through 1948, a total of seventy-six retrievers have been awarded the title of Field Trial Champion.

Of these, fifty (66 per cent) were Labradors.

Seventeen (22 per cent) were Goldens.

Nine (12 per cent) were Chesapeakes.

During 1948 only, there were 7 new Field Trial Champions crowned. Six of them were Labradors, and one was a Golden.

Now all this does not necessarily mean you should grab your hat and rush out to buy yourself a Labrador. True, it is the most popular retriever, judging from AKC registrations. And it has proven itself the best in action, in retriever trials. But there are plenty of splendid Goldens and Chesapeakes, too. Before making your decision, you should do a little thinking as to which of these three breeds might best suit your particular purpose and your temperament.

Let me briefly compare the average qualities of these three leading breeds, based on my experience with them in the field, in the blind, competing with them in trials, and judging them in trials.

Before I start, I'll confess for my own purposes I prefer the Labrador. My friends who are Golden and Chesapeake enthusiasts sometimes accuse me of prejudice, and I have trouble convincing them that I love any good dog, regardless of his color or breed. For instance, I was one of the three judges at the first National Championship Trial, in 1941, who gladly and unanimously awarded the coveted title to a wonderful little Golden, King Midas of Woodend. He competed for three solid days with the best Labradors and Chesapeakes in the country, and for those three days he was the best dog. And he was a dog I would be proud to own, and to shoot over under any conditions.

Anyway, I'll do my best here to give you my honest observations on the relative advantages and disadvantages of the three breeds, as objectively as possible.

THE GOLDEN RETRIEVER
(See Illustrations 1-4)

To most people, the Golden is by far the prettiest dog to look at, and he is a beautiful animal by any standards. If I were just looking for a pet for myself or the kids, I would go no further. The Golden is very affectionate, being in disposition much like a setter or spaniel. One of the good ones is always tractable. He is the easiest of the three breeds for an impatient amateur to train to obedience and manners.

Usually he can't take much corporal punishment for his misdeeds, without the danger of becoming cowed and crawling on his belly. Therefore, if you're apt to lose your temper with a dog, I wouldn't recommend a Golden. On the other hand, he's so eager to please, he doesn't really need any severe treatment to stay in line.

A Golden from good working stock is hard to beat as a retriever on land, for any kind of upland game. He has a splendid nose, often winding game from distances up to forty or fifty yards. He has a very tender mouth, and will never damage your game.

He is usually inferior to the Labradors and Chesapeakes in water. His ancestors were not natural water dogs, as the others were. He is often reluctant to take the water at first, and needs more careful handling to get him to enjoy swimming. Also, his long wavy coat is a distinct handicap in this element. He is like a man going swimming in a coonskin coat. In spite of this, I've seen some Goldens that became great duck dogs. But they are the exceptions, not the average. And the best Golden is never as fast or powerful a swimmer as just a good average Labrador or Chesapeake.

If I did most of my hunting on land, with very little duck or goose shooting, I would seriously consider a Golden, particularly if I did most of my gunning in lighter cover, free from cockleburs. It *can* get to be something of a nuisance, after coming in from a hard day in the field, to spend a couple of hours extricating the tangled wads of burs from the long silky hair of a Golden.

THE CHESAPEAKE BAY RETRIEVER
(See Illustrations 5-8)

Of the three breeds, the Chesapeake stands at the other extreme from the Golden in comparing most qualities and traits, with the Labrador somewhere in between. The Chesapeake is a big, tough, rugged dog, in body *and* disposition.

If most of your hunting is duck and goose shooting, and particularly if much of it is in salt water, you'll make no mistake by getting a good Chesapeake. He was originally developed and used by the market hunters around Chesapeake Bay, where he had to battle all day and half the night through the icy surf. For generations he has been bred and selected to take the severest punishment in the water, and he is really a *tough egg*.

Compared to the Golden and the Labrador, he is not so easy for an amateur to train. He is apt to be a bit hardheaded. But a good one is intelligent, and knows when he's licked; if you're a fairly hard-boiled character yourself, you can train one all right. You have to keep ahead of him, and insist on obedience at all times. When he defies you, as he may occasionally, you'll have to be willing to give him a good old-fashioned thrashing, and not with a hairbrush, either. A hickory hoe handle, laid on with vigor, won't do him any permanent damage, and an implement of that caliber is sometimes needed to penetrate his thick hide and convince him you aren't just playing.

At this point I can hear indignant screams, not only from the ladies of the SPCA, but also from some of my Chesapeake-owning friends. Sure, there are exceptions to anything. I've seen some representatives of the breed who never needed a licking in their lives. But on the average a Chesapeake is a rugged individualist, about as tender and sensitive as a Mack truck.

This has one important compensation. The Chesapeake requires a firm and sometimes even a heavy hand from his trainer, and I don't enjoy chastising a dog any more than you do. But it is almost impossible to cow him. I've never seen one crawl on his belly, after the most severe punishment. Indeed, he's more likely to give you a playful nip if you turn your back on him.

Now here's another thing that must be said, that will bring more yelps from the Chesapeake people. Some individuals of the breed show a tendency to hard mouth—the one unforgivable fault in a retriever. If a dog eats your game, or merely crushes it so it's unfit for the table, he's of no use whatever.

In retriever trials I've seen several clear-cut cases of hard mouth among Chesapeakes. I have seen only one Labrador unmistakably guilty of this crime, and no Goldens.

I think many of these cases could have been avoided if these dogs, when young, had been properly and carefully introduced to feathers in the first place. But the fact remains that Chesapeakes seem to have this tendency a little more than the other retrievers; if you get a young one, you must be very careful to avoid letting the fault get started.

Chesapeake enthusiasts will argue that their dogs take a good firm hold on their birds, and seldom drop them. And that many Goldens, and some Labradors, are tender mouthed to a fault, taking sissy holds on big ducks and pheasants, constantly dropping them and stopping to fiddle around, rolling the birds in the mud, stopping to get a fresh hold on the way in. Well, they have a point there, too.

But I believe it is easier to teach a tender-mouthed dog to take a sufficiently firm hold than it is to dissuade his opposite number from flattening his birds. In fact, most professional trainers say it is virtually impossible to cure a really hard-mouthed dog, once this vicious habit is firmly entrenched.

This book is primarily for the impatient man, the busy man, or the just plain lazy man, who wants to know the quickest and easiest way to end up with a well-trained retriever. For him, I'd be inclined to advise against a Chesapeake.

Now please don't misunderstand. This is all comparative, and some of it may even be hair-splitting. The Chesapeake from working stock is still much easier to train than the average dog of *any* breed that has been bred for bench shows rather than useful work. But of these three wonderful retriever breeds, you may as well know he is apt to be the least tractable, the least eager to please, the most inclined to be hardheaded, and even hard mouthed.

THE LABRADOR RETRIEVER
(See Illustrations 9-12)

We have said that the Golden is the easiest of the three breeds for an amateur to train to obedience. But on that score, the Labrador runs him a fairly close second.

There are a few hardheaded Labradors, but the great majority are very tractable. A good one is easy enough to train. If I can train one—and I've trained a good many—anybody should be able to do it.

I suppose there are some pansies in the breed, too, but personally I've never seen a Labrador crawl on his belly. He's not likely to need it, but if necessary the average Lab can stand up and take a well-deserved licking. On him, you can usually make a sufficient impression with a leather strap instead of a hoe handle. Even the toughest of the Labradors is not apt to defy you and need a walloping more than about once a year, for basically he wants to do the right thing. After punishment, he's more likely to jump up and lick your face, as if to say, "Okay, boss, you win," than he is to take a bite at your leg.

If you think you might want to have some fun with your dog in retriever trials, as well as using him for hunting, the records say your chances of picking up some ribbons are best with a Labrador.

And for the man who takes his hunting where he can find it, shooting everything that flies, over land or marsh or water, the Labrador is in my opinion the best all-round choice.

He has an excellent nose, perhaps not quite as spectacular as the Golden's, but plenty of nose to find all the upland game you can shoot for him. He'll trail a crippled running cock pheasant a mile, and bring it to bag. His short straight coat sheds burs, which at times saves you a lot of work and a lot of cussing. In addition to retrieving, he takes naturally to working like a spaniel, quartering close in ahead of the gun to flush upland birds. He is rugged and tough enough to go all day in the heaviest and most punishing cover. I've never seen a Labrador wear out or quit in the hunting field.

He loves the water, his ancestors having been natural water dogs. When sent, he hits the water with a great splash that is a joy to see. He is a fast, strong swimmer. His short, oily coat is no drag in the water. He is not quite as rugged as the Chesapeake for battling icy surf all day, but you'd have a tough time ever drowning a Labrador under the worst conditions, at that. For the ordinary duck hunter's needs, he is all that can be desired.

Personally I like to see a dog *or* a man who seems to love his job. And the average Labrador seems to have this quality even more than the Goldens or the Chesapeakes. In the trials, the fastest dogs are the Labradors. They go at a sizzling run, not only until they find the bird, but they come in with it almost as fast as they go out. Too often you see the Goldens and Chesapeakes coming in at a slow trot, or even at a walk. Perhaps this is a minor point. But part of the pleasure of watching a good dog work is found in the style with which he does his work, whether in trials or in the hunting field.

Now a word about color. Most of the Labradors, and virtually all of the best ones, are black dogs. Out of the 50 Labrador field-trial champions, only two were Yellow Labradors.

At one time several breeders in this country earnestly tried to develop the Yellow Labrador. One of them, a friend of mine, devoted years to this enthusiasm. He spent much time and money, and never did produce a single yellow dog that could compete with the black ones in trials. But he was a hard man to discourage, and we often debated far into the night over the desirability of a yellow versus a black coat on a duck dog.

His argument, of course, was that the yellow coat blends with the dead grass color of a duck blind, or other available cover to hide a dog from waterfowl. (The Chesapeake and Golden enthusiasts use the same argument in favor of their dogs, which have coats ranging from light yellow to golden to dark brown.)

My contention was, and still is, that this is of no practical importance, because ducks pay no attention to a black dog anyway. I've hunted all kinds of ducks under all sorts of conditions, using black Labradors to retrieve them. More often than not, I don't even have the dog in the blind with me, but set him out in the open, right on top of a muskrat house, or on any other dry spot available, where he has a better opportunity to mark falls in any direction. Even the wariest mallards, which flare and shy off if they see so much as a tip of *my* ear, will come straight in to the decoys with a black dog sitting right out in plain sight watching them. I have never had ducks flare, nor lost an opportunity for a shot, because they saw a black dog, whether he was in the blind or out of it.

I have discussed this with dozens of other duck hunters who have had the same experience, and have yet to hear firsthand testimony for a single case where ducks have shied from a black Labrador.

Therefore, it seems silly to me to struggle to produce a recessive color trait. Black is the dominant color in the Labrador breed. If you breed a yellow dog to a yellow bitch, you will usually get some yellow pups, but you are almost certain to get some black ones also. And if you try to improve the other important qualities, as you should, and breed a superior black stud to a yellow bitch, you might get two yellow pups out of a litter of eight. Then, if you're really belligerent about this thing, and destroy all the black ones, the chances are good that you're destroying the only worth-while dogs in the bunch.

In fact, it seems to me that trying to breed and select yellow-coated Labradors comes too close to committing the same sin as the bench breeders—worrying about a color that has no *practical* importance, instead of the really important qualities such as intelligence, tractability, nose, eagerness to hunt, boldness, guts, speed, and style.

WHICH IS THE BEST ALL-ROUND DOG?

People often ask which breed makes the best combined hunting dog, pet, and watchdog.

We've pretty well covered the first two categories. Now how do the three breeds stack up as watchdogs?

Well, if I were the postman, I'd have no fear of a Golden or a Labrador as I went about my legitimate business, but I would give a Chesapeake a wide berth.

If I were planning to burgle a house with no people but a dog in it, I wouldn't tackle one containing either a Chesapeake or a Labrador, but would be fairly confident of my ability to make friends with a Golden, or bluff him into submission. I would not attempt to break and enter a house containing a man with a gun *and* a Golden, for the dog would probably give the alarm. He is not apt to bite, but he will bark, and that's really all you ordinarily need in a watchdog.

To sum up this whole discussion:

For just a pet, I recommend the Golden.

As a specialist on upland game, in fairly light cover, with no burs, the Golden is hard to beat.

For retrieving ducks and geese under rugged conditions, you can't beat a Chesapeake. But you have to be *willing* to beat him if necessary, to show him who's the boss and who's the dog. And I can't recommend him for a pet. He's too inclined to bite the wrong people, and he's relatively hard to train.

For a versatile dog on land and water, for the average hunter, the Labrador is the best bet.

The man interested in field-trial competition definitely wants a Labrador.

And for a combined hunting dog, pet, and watchdog—an all-round dog—your chances of finding the individual you want are much better in choosing a Labrador than from the other breeds.

Now let me repeat—the forgoing generalities apply to the *average* representatives of the *top half* of these three wonderful breeds. They apply to the dogs from *close-up working ancestors,* not from bench-show stock. And even among the top half, there are exceptions in each of the breeds—outstanding and poor individuals. I favor the Labradors, but I've seen plenty of these to which I would not now give kennel space. Remember this when you set out to find your retriever.

You are going to buy one individual dog—a *good* dog—not a breed of dogs.

Chapter 5

HOW TO FIND YOUR DOG

ALL YOU NEED to do is to find *the* reputable breeder who has available the pup or dog you want, and this is easy if you go about it right.

First, dash off a few penny postcards.

If you want a Labrador, send one to:
> Howes Burton, Secretary
> The Labrador Retriever Club
> Meadow Farm Road
> East Islip, L. I., New York

Ask him for the names of a few of the breeders closest to you, who might have available pups (or young trained dogs) from *proven working* stock.

For a Golden, send a similar request to:
> Carlton Grassle, Secretary
> Golden Retriever Club of America
> P. O. Box 226
> Rochester, Minnesota

If you've decided on a Chesapeake, write:
> Miss Oleva Groulx, Secretary
> American Chesapeake Club
> 3301 Franklin Boulevard
> Chicago 24, Illinois

In the past the secretaries of these parent breed clubs have been very durable and long-suffering people, and the chances are the above names and addresses will be the same for several years after this book is published. But if after a reasonable time you receive no answer, then write:

The American Kennel Club
221 Fourth Avenue
New York 3, New York

Ask for the name and address of the secretary of the breed club in which you are interested.

And, if you haven't been able to make up your mind as to which breed you prefer, write all three of the clubs, and be an opportunist. Look at whatever is available in all three breeds, and buy the pup or dog you like the best, whatever he is. You can't go too far wrong, if you get a really good individual, from proven breeding, from any of these three retriever breeds.

The next thing to do is to locate and go to a retriever field trial, if this is possible or practical. This will serve a double purpose. Watching these dogs perform in competition will help you decide which breed you want, if you're on the fence, or will confirm or possibly cause you to question the decision you've already made. And it will enable you to meet the leading retriever people in your territory, including possibly the breeder who has the dog you want.

Owners and handlers at retriever trials are a splendid bunch of people. There you will find a melting pot, from all walks of life—wealthy sportsmen who are captains of industry rubbing elbows with clerks and laboring men, held together by their great enthusiasm for these dogs which they consider "much too good for the common people."

Most of them are very friendly to interested newcomers, and many will talk your arm off, giving you a great opportunity to listen and learn. Try to meet the president and the secretary of the club, and any of the other officers you can. These leaders are usually amateur sportsmen who love the dogs for their own sake, and they will steer you right.

You might even stumble into a good young dog, whose work you see yourself at the trial, that can be bought for one reason or another. This won't necessarily happen at your first trial, but it could. And if your object is to buy a trained dog, sooner or later you'll find one available around the trials.

Most of the people active in this sport are in it for fun, and because they are "retriever happy." But in any group you'll find a few poor losers. Sometimes you can buy a superior dog from one of these if you're right on the spot to make an offer when the dog has had a poor series and is out of the stake. The greatest dogs in the world have their off days, but some of these characters who care only for winning don't realize this, and will impulsively sell a fine young dog at the moment he loses out in a trial.

How do you locate the nearest retriever trial?

In Part III of this opus you will find a list of the names and addresses of the secretaries of all of the clubs (at this writing) that put on one or more trials per year, licensed or sanctioned by the American Kennel Club. The chances are there is one right in your vicinity, or at least in your state. Pick out the closest one, write to the secretary, and ask him to advise you of the dates and location of the next trial.

It is possible there may be a new man in the job by the time you read this book. So if you get no answer in a reasonable time, then write the American Kennel Club, and ask for the name and address of the secretary of the nearest club putting on retriever trials.

New clubs are springing up every year, all over the country. If in my list you don't find one close enough to you, it would be worth blowing a postcard to the American Kennel Club to find out if a new one has been started in your vicinity.

Now most of these clubs have two big licensed trials each year—one in the spring and one in the fall—but also a good number of informal practice trials in between times. For instance, the Southern California Retriever Club is currently having some kind of a trial every four weeks. So the chances are you won't have to wait very long before taking in a trial.

Between your postcards to the parent breed clubs, or your

contacts made at a local retriever trial, or both, you should have no trouble locating several reliable breeders not too far away for you to visit them. And let me repeat once more what I mean by a "reliable" breeder. For your purpose, in buying your first retriever, you want to be very fussy. You want a man who not only has a reputation as a square shooter, but who has other visible means of support than just *selling* dogs. And preferably a man who proves his own stock in field trials. You want no truck with breeders for bench shows *only*, back-yard breeders, or pet shops.

Now just a word to explain what the term "back-yard breeder," uttered in a scornful tone, means among the enthusiasts for good working dogs. It means the man or woman who does not hunt, who has no interest in these dogs for their working qualities, who sees an opportunity for profit in selling pups. These people know nothing of bloodlines, field-trial records, or scientific breeding, and care less. Usually they start by buying the cheapest bitch they can find, so long as it is a pedigreed—meaning only registered—representative of the breed.

Then they breed her to the dog with the cheapest stud fee they can find, and sit back and pray for a huge litter. Retrievers often whelp ten or more pups, and breeders of this ilk try to raise and sell them all. Too often the result is that *all* the pups get a poor start, and are never really strong, healthy dogs for the rest of their lives. Few bitches can give more than eight pups a decent start, and personally I've never had much luck trying to raise that many. Now I seldom try to raise more than six. And I would never buy a pup out of a litter of more than eight, raised on one bitch. Of course, some good breeders will take the trouble to get a foster mother, and put part of a large litter with her, and that is quite another matter.

The type of back-yard breeder I'm talking about usually advertises pups for sale at bargain prices in the classified columns of the local newspaper. Many of them are women. They erect cheap and inadequate pens and runs in the yard, and the pups are often raised in filth. It is impossible to rear strong healthy pups under such conditions.

However, there are some fine pups occasionally raised in back yards, by sincere enthusiasts, hunters, or field-trial people, who have a fine bitch, breed her correctly to a great stud, and raise the litter carefully under sanitary conditions. They will tell you all about the sire and dam, the grandparents, their *working* qualities, and their field-trial records. I don't call those people backyard breeders, simply because they live in a city, town, or suburb instead of out in the country. In fact, you're quite likely to have one or more of these on your list, as well as some of the larger breeders with country kennels.

After you have located your breeders, it will save your time and theirs if you write or phone them first, inquiring if they have anything available to suit your needs, before going to see them. Usually the best dogs or pups are obtained from the least commercial breeders, men and women who are doing their bit to improve the breed, purely as a hobby. Although they charge good prices for the occasional pups and dogs they sell, very few make anything but a substantial annual loss on their kennels. They have a big investment in sanitary kennels and runs. They feed their dogs the best food obtainable, and plenty of it. They raise small litters, assuring the pups a good start. They reluctantly but firmly have the poor specimens put to sleep—instead of selling them for what they can get.

Many of their pups they keep themselves for field-trial prospects. Others are earmarked for friends in the game, people they *know* will appreciate and do right by a worthy pup, and give him an opportunity to show what he can do in trials. So don't be disappointed if breeders of this type don't have a pup you can buy and take home whenever you happen to drop in.

But the law of averages says that from your list, you'll find at least one good breeder with something available. If you impress him as honest, and as a man able to appreciate a real dog, he'll probably let you have the pup or dog on approval for a few days, and return your money if you return the dog in good health. Some will even go so far as to guarantee their dogs unconditionally, allowing you to return them at any time, if you don't like them. You won't find any back-yard breeders or pet shops doing that. This privilege could be horribly abused, of course, but if you're the kind who would do so, such a breeder wouldn't sell you a dog, anyway. He's interested in placing his animals with the right people.

By the time you've located your breeder, you've probably decided whether you want a male or female, but perhaps we should have a little discussion of this before you make your selection.

MALE OR FEMALE?

You sometimes hear it said that a female makes the better hunting dog. I have not found it so. I've had some wonderful bitches I've used as shooting dogs, and some wonderful males, too. If you have no strong preference either way, perhaps you'll do best by being an opportunist on this score also—buying the best available retriever you can find, whether it is male or female.

The drawback to a female, of course, is that she does come in season twice a year, and you have to be careful at those times to have her confined in a stout pen that she cannot get out of— and that dogs cannot get into. Some astonishing feats of climbing can be accomplished at such times, for love. Freehaven Jay once went over three nine-foot fences, believe it or not, in order to fix us up with an unplanned litter from a bitch who was that way.

But this is not such a serious problem if you plan to use your bitch only for hunting. Many times I've taken a bitch in season out shooting with no trouble. There are several preparations on the market that can be doused on her, which effectively fool the farm dogs, and even male shooting dogs in the same party.

However, if you are interested in competing in trials, or think you might be, then you want a male. You cannot enter a bitch in season in a trial. It is unfair to the dogs, and it is definitely against the rules.

If you think you might be interested in becoming a breeder, then of course you want a female.

Sometimes you hear people say a female is better, because she doesn't wander away like a male—stays close to home. This is perfect nonsense. Nobody in his right mind will allow a valuable retriever—male or female—to roam at will, to be stolen, killed by a truck, poisoned by an angry neighbor, or just to accumulate bad habits that ruin it for any good use. So if the dog is kept properly confined and under control, this question is beside the point.

Chapter 6

SOME NAMES TO SEEK IN PEDIGREES

FROM THE THREE leading breeds, there are 238 individual retrievers that have *placed* in open all-age or limited all-age stakes in trials licensed by the American Kennel Club from 1931 through 1948.

In this chapter, I'm going to list them all: 112 Labrador dogs; 47 Labrador bitches; 24 Golden dogs; 13 Golden bitches; 34 Chesapeake dogs; and 8 Chesapeake bitches.

Look for these names in pedigrees. These are the candy kids, the ancestors you want for *your* dog. And you want at least a couple of them in the second or third generation.

For your convenience in checking pedigrees, the names are arranged alphabetically, along with each dog's AKC registration number, year of birth, year in which each field-trial champion won his title, and total number of championship points.

Prior to July, 1947, placings in open all-age and limited all-age stakes earned points as follows: First place, 5 points; second place, 3 points; third place, 1 point; and fourth place, no points. Only since July, 1947, has fourth place earned ½ point.

Thus there are a number of dogs listed that have placed fourth in one or more trials, but are credited with no points. Don't sell them short. Any dog that has gone clear through an open stake to place fourth is quite a dog. Veteran field-trial handlers are very happy to get a fourth.

Of course you want to find the available dog or pup with the *most* of the *best possible* ancestors, as close up as possible in the pedigree.

In a general way, the dogs and bitches that have become field-trial champions and then gone on to amass a much larger point total—being the most thoroughly proven performers—have also been the greatest sires and dams, and have produced the most outstanding progeny. There are many exceptions, of course. But you can't go far wrong if you buy a pup whose pedigree is well sprinkled with the names of the big point winners.

These are not too easy to find, but you may as well set your sights high. A man can dream, can't he?

To win a Field Trial Championship, a retriever must win a total of 10 points. However, he must win first place and thus acquire 5 of these points in at least one all-age stake open to all breeds of retrievers, and not more than 5 of the required 10 points may be acquired in a trial open to only one breed.

Thus you will note a few dogs in the list having 10 or more points that still are not field trial champions.

On the other hand, you will find dogs that are champions many times over: Little Pierre of Deer Creek with 68½ points; Black Panther with 68½; Glenairlie Rocket with 63 points; the immortal Golden, Rip, also with 63; Freehaven Jay, 60; Shed of Arden, 59; Tar of Arden, that wonderful bitch, 53; and 32 more great dogs and bitches that have 20 or more points.

Now one more thing before getting on with the list. A few of the dogs have no registration numbers, which means for one reason or another they were not registered in the AKC studbook at the time they last placed in a trial. A purebred but unregistered dog can be entered in a trial by paying an extra "listing" fee.

These were included in our list because it is quite possible some of them have been registered since, or that some of their descendants have been successfully registered, by going through the necessary red tape, tracing down their ancestors, getting affidavits, and supplying evidence to satisfy completely the AKC of their purebred origin.

However, if you run across any of those names on a pedigree, you should make very sure the pup or dog you are considering is eligible for AKC registration. If the breeder can show you the litter registration certificate, or the registration certificates of *both* sire and dam, that's all you need to see. If not, you'd better buy the dog only subject to his AKC registration.

ALPHABETICAL LIST OF RETRIEVERS THAT HAVE PLACED IN ALL-AGE STAKES 1931-1948

Labrador Retriever Dogs

Name	AKC No.	Year of Birth	Year F.T.Ch. Awarded	Total Points
Andy of Upham	A520630	1940		3
Banchory Night Light of Wingan	893641	1932	1937	21
Banchory Varnish of Wingan	A61030	1933	1937	15
Bancstone Buck	A173495	1936		
Bancstone Turpentine	A646119	1942		1
Banks of Arden	A159963	1937		6
Bard of Arden	A793995	1944		
Bengal of Arden	A998454	1944	1947	35½
Black Jack	938783	1934		
Black of Scottswood	None			
Blackjack of Barrington	A591103	1941		1
Black Major	A884765	1944		5
Black Market of Audlon	A745195	1943		1
Black Panther	A853111	1944	1947	68½
Black Prince of Sag Harbor	S184395	1946		6
Black Roland of Koshkonong	A582260	1941	1946	22
Blind of Arden	965612	1933	1936	47
Boar Ranch Nip	None	1941	1944	29½
Bracken's Sweep	A997169	1943	1946	50½
Brignall's Gringo	S231197	1946	1948	22½
Brignall's Nick	None	1946		½
Buck of Monona	A398698	1938		4
Bugla Brant	944816	1933		1
Captain Jiggs	A605940	1941		1
Carbon of Barrington	None	1943	1947	10
Carl of Boghurst	799955	1929		8
Chum of Canton	A586684	1940		1
Cliff's Patrick	None	1944		6½
Crevamoy Pride	None	1943		1
Cumshewa Sinbad	S44905	1944		3½
Dela Winn's Tigh	None	1944		½
Dell's Park Tag	None	1942		2
Drinkstone Pons of Wingan	905777	1931		6
Diver of Trab	S30665	1944		5
Dunottar Plush	A360928	1939		1
Earlsmoor Moor of Arden	A159966	1937		

Name	AKC No.	Year of Birth	Year F.T.Ch. Awarded	Total Points
Firelei's Hornet	A749743	1943	1946	44
Flair of Shedstone	A719601	1943		4½
Freehaven Again	A473727	1940	1945	16
Freehaven Jay	A240811	1937	1939	60
Gabriel of Cram	A508375	1940	1944	10
Glenairlie Blackjack	A378726	1939		1
Glenairlie Rocket	A239815	1937	1939	63
Glenairlie Rover	A90631	1933	1937	17
Glenmere Jack				½
Glenmere Joe	768170	1929		
Glenmere Monarch	768169	1927		5
Good Hope Angus	A641461	1941		1
Grangemead Precocious	S127563	1946		5
Grangemead Solomon	A489250	1940		3
Grouse of Arden	A7166	1934		2
Grouse of Trabington	S128563	1945		½
Gun of Arden	A268628	1938	1943	33
Hi-Tail of Wyandotte	A885452	1944	1948	13
Hi-Water Pete		1944		½
Hiwood Mike	A382739	1935	1941	41
Hiwood Nero	A386573	1938		3
Jerry of Grant's		1944		½
Jock Dhu	A196869	1935		
Laddie of Rockingell	A431662	1938		5
Ledgeland's Donne	977680	1934		3
Ledgeland's Sambo	A330485	1938		4
Little Pierre of Deer Creek	A776978	1943	1946	68½
Lorrendon's Lulu Duke	A953782	1943		5
Major of Stonegate	A884971	1944		1
Malarkey's Okanagan Pat	A876934	1944	1948	16½
Marvadel Black Gum	A975648	1945	1947	36½
Matchmaker for Deer Creek	S45265	1946		6
Meadow Farm Night	A169876	1936	1941	26
Michael of Glenmere	A150354	1935	1941	14
Ming	A285385	1933	1940	16
Mint of Barrington	A509320	1941		
Moose	None	1927		½
Mott Place Captain	A853503	1944	1948	13
Mully Gully Goo	A963683	1944	1948	13
Nelson's Black Prince	A789610	1944		7
Nigger of Barrington	252208	1931	1938	43
Nig of Swinomish	None	1945		½
Nith's Double	757643	1926		
Odd's On	811077	1928		3
Orchardton Dale	A440958	1938	1943	17
Orchardton Dorando	A440957	1938	1943	23

Name	AKC No.	Year of Birth	Year F.T.Ch. Awarded	Total Points
Patrollman of Timber Town	A539683	1941		3
Peconic Pyne of Arden	A43615	1935	1938	12
Pons Jr. of Wingan	960053	1934		2
Raffles of Earlsmoor	957536	1931		1
Rip of Holly Hill	None	1946		4
Rip of Wake	S73709	1946		6½
Rock River Jack	A859748	1945		½
Rodarbal Black Magic	A852992	1943		3
Sab of Tulliallan	757642	1922		1
Saglek	None	1935		5
Sam of Arden	981723	1929		4
Sam of Woodend	A698809	1942		1
Sand Gold Terry	A432378	1939	1943	20
Schmidt's Okanagan Joe	A876930	1944		3
Scoronine of Deer Creek	A607057	1942	1946	11
Seaborne's Black Prince	A322164	1938		13
Shadow's Ebony Bob	A390827	1939	1945	12
Shed of Arden	A330767	1939	1942	59
Sir Jock	A511359	1941	1945	34
Smudge of Allen Winden	814009	1930		1
Son	A434553	1939		
Spider of Kingswere	S61672	1946		6
Timber Town Clansman	A128842	1936	1940	21
Todd's Tartar	S230799	1945		8
Trowbridge Topper	A740474	1943		5
Tyke of Barrington	None	1935		11
Tyke of Woodend	None			
V-Day For Deer Creek	A975104	1944		4½
Vestals Norge	None	1937		10
Yodel of Morexpense	A473730	1940	1945	14

Labrador Retriever Bitches

Name	AKC No.	Year of Birth	Year F.T.Ch. Awarded	Total Points
Black Magic of Audlon	A745194	1943	1945	24
Bracken's Jill	None	1943		1
Bracken's Peggy	S40038	1943		1
Braes of Arden	A159960	1937	1943	14
Bramble of Timber Town	A416362	1940		1
Buddha of Arden	A557014	1941		3
Cinar's Tulle	A350469	1939		
Confusion at Deer Creek	A776977	1943		9
Decoy of Arden	965611	1933	1936	17
Earlsmoor Marlin of Arden	A330770	1939		6
Echo of Arden	A7165	1934		1
Firelei of Deer Creek	A509058	1940	1946	17

Name	AKC No.	Year of Birth	Year F.T.Ch. Awarded	Total Points
Freehaven Darkie	A460413	1940		5
Freehaven Molly	A367504	1939		4
Garscube Meg	None	1928		5
Gilmore's Peggy	A947141	1945	1947	34½
Glenairlie Eve	A448267	1939		8
Goldie of Goldieland	A675679	1939		8
Gorse of Arden	A159961	1937	1942	13
Honey Chile Trixie	A977320	1944	1947	12½
Jade of Sandylands	A125387	1936		4
Jewel of Sandylands	A123299	1936		
Joy of Arden	A82221	1936		12
Keith's Black Magic	S3052	1944	1946	37½
Kilsyth Goldie	A251342	1937		3
Kingdale's Ink Spot	S51248	1946		½
Krystolida's Dynamite	A780075	1943		½
Ladies Day at Deer Creek	S54266	1946		½
Ledgelands Dora	995266	1934	1940	10
Lorrendon's Nylon	S31061	1945		3½
Marvadel Cinders	A351115	1939		
May Millard	703064	1927		½
Miss Madison	A400964	1938	1946	11
Orchardton Doris	905779	1930		3
Peggy of Woodend	A210293	1937		
Penelope Jane	None	1940		
Sandlake Hornet	S104480	1946		1
Sky Pilot's Judy	None	1939		1
Star Girl	A568530	1941		
Tar of Arden	A210256	1937	1941	53
Trabington's Black Witch	None	1945		5
Trevrchamp Marsey	S4014	1944		4½
Tri-Stada Gun Moll	A806669	1943	1948	13
Victory Joy	A980567	1945		5
Wardwyn Welcome	A816283	1944		½
Whitecairn Wendy of Wingan	934280	1932		9
Wingan's Daily Double	A104408	1936		

Golden Retriever Dogs

Name	AKC No.	Year of Birth	Year F.T.Ch. Awarded	Total Points
Apache Trigger	A732880	1943		2
Bingo of Yelme II	A833289	1944		½
Bushaway's Golden Rocket	A648775	1942		1
Cresta Chip	A994048	1948		3½
Gold	A708145	1942		1
Golden Kidd	S20621	1945	1948	11½
Goldwood Frisco	A872638	1944		10

Name	AKC No.	Year of Birth	Year F.T.Ch. Awarded	Total Points
Goldwood Tuck	A205346	1937	1940	31
H.R.H. Timothy	A584049	1941		
King Midas of Woodend	A207518	1937	1941	17
Kingsdale Buck	A843397	1943		7½
Michael of Woodend	A327770	1939		
Nero of Roedare	A112862	1936		13
Peter of Woodend	A569148	1939		8½
Pirate of Golden Valley	A507433	1941	1943	33
Ready Always at Marianhill	None	1946		5
Rip	A86933	1935	1939	63
Royal Peter Golden Boy	A616198	1941	1945	36½
Royal's Royal of Stonegate	A814479	1945		6
Stilrovin Rip's Pride	A561185	1941	1946	10
Stilrovin Nitro Express	A396107	1940	1942	49½
Stilrovin Super Speed	A396108	1940	1942	34
Whitebridge Wally	A226373	1937	1941	28
Zipper of Lakeview	A979798	1945		1½

Golden Retriever Bitches

Name	AKC No.	Year of Birth	Year F.T.Ch. Awarded	Total Points
April Showers	A532502	1941	1945	12
Banty of Woodend	A299293	1938	1941	12
Bonnie of Golden Valley	A507427	1941		3
Golden Beauty of Roedare	A246295	1937	1942	15
Kingdale's Goldie	A843396	1943		3
Patricia of Roedare	A300261	1937	1944	14
Shelter Cove Beauty	A487805	1941	1944	26
Shirayuki	A975510	1945		½
Stalingrad Express	A642163	1942		5
Stilrovin Katherine	A396109	1940	1946	12
Stilrovin Vee	A598386	1942		3
Susie Q. of Deer Creek	A316352	1939		1
Tonkahoff Esther Belle	A793606	1944	1946	10

Chesapeake Bay Retriever Dogs

Name	AKC No.	Year of Birth	Year F.T.Ch. Awarded	Total Points
Babylon Captain Brownie	None	—		1
Bayle	A789367	1944	1946	17½
Big Chief	A293230	1937		
Blemton Just Ted	A72985	1935		3
Bob of Montauk	A78768	1936		5
Brewster's Laddie	A1597	1934		1
Brookhaven Gep	None	1930		1
Buddy Brown	A753055	1940		6

Name	AKC No.	Year of Birth	Year F.T.Ch. Awarded	Total Points
Bud Parker Bang	881831	1931		3
Chesacroft Baron	A177853	1936	1945	20
Chesacroft Bob	A68453	1934		1
Chesacroft Newt	934526	1933		1
Chesdel Happy Joe	A350334	1938		1
Delshore Duke	A897745	1944		3
Dilwyne Chesabob	A78769	1936		7
Dilwyne Montauk Pilot	A63115	—	1937	26
Flood Tide Pete	960003	1933		
Guess of Shawong	A410126	1939	1942	19
Gunnar II	A323445	1938		7
Howe's Bonnie Laddie	894667	1930		
Howe's Pal	A68389	1930		
Ingham Hill Laddie	None	1929		
King of Montauk	None	1923		8
Laddie's Rowdy	A783993	—		7½
Lakewood Ben	A600708	—		5
Michael of Deerwood	A678562	1942		1
Nelgard's Brown Bomber	A983621	1945		1
Pride of Montauk	None	1926		1
St. Jones Chief	S23403	1945		
Shagwong Chief	203853	1932		
Skipper Bob	984475	1931	1935	26
Sodak's Gypsy Prince	831195	1931	1936	14
Sodak Rip	A277831	1938	1941	14
Storm Cloud	900447	1932		

Chesapeake Bay Retriever Bitches

Name	AKC No.	Year of Birth	Year F.T.Ch. Awarded	Total Points
Blemton Binnacle	A445723	1940		
Delmonte Ginger	A548269	1940		1
Dodel Fusty	A333257	1938		1
Princess Anne	892089	1933		4
Shagwong Gypsy	A63979	1935	1939	28
Shinnecock Belle	A42949	1935		6
Tiger of Clipper City	A734222	1943	1946	27
Tops	None	1933		6

Chapter 7

SELECTING YOUR DOG

NOW LET'S ASSUME you've found your breeder, decided on the breed and sex you prefer, and whether a pup or an older dog.

HOW TO PICK A PUP
(See Illustrations 13-14)

Many retriever-happy people, including me, get to kidding themselves that they can pick the best one out of a litter of young pups. We all have different systems, and go through our own sets of motions.

But actually, with pups up to three or four months old, you're almost entirely dependent on the pedigree. Given a litter of good healthy pups, with the right breeding behind them, you're about as well off to shut your eyes and reach in and grab one, as to go through all the nonsense I do.

Many times you'll be given no choice. The breeder will point out one particular male, or a female, and tell you that is the only one available. He is keeping the others, or they are already spoken for by other people. Well, if you're dealing with the kind of breeder you'd better be, go ahead and take the pup that's left. He wouldn't sell it to you if there was anything wrong with it. And you'll have just as good a chance as he has—maybe better—to end up with the prize of the litter. Arnold Rothstein did pretty well, just betting that the wise guys were wrong.

49

Anyone who raises a litter of pups, and sees them every day, is bound to pick some favorites as he goes along—and even the most experienced dog men will often pick them for foolish reasons, or no reasons. Pups change so fast, even from day to day, it is impossible for anyone to look into a crystal ball and know exactly what a pup will turn out to be when it grows up.

So spend your time studying the pedigree, and asking questions about it, instead of mooning over the individual pups. Exactly who were the father, mother, and the four grandparents? What did each of them *do?* In field trials? As shooting dogs? What were their dominant good qualities? What faults, if any? A good breeder will know these answers, and will tell them to you quite frankly.

After you are satisfied with the breeding behind the litter, go ahead and grab yourself a pup out of it, and take it home.

Of course, you want a healthy-looking pup, with good bone, and reasonably straight legs. If it's a Labrador it should be black. A spot of white on the chest only is permissible, but not on legs or feet or anywhere else. There's a good practical reason for this stern suppressing of white spots in the breed. If it were allowed to degenerate into a lot of black and white spotted dogs, these *might* be a bit too conspicuous for duck shooting companions. Also, the lovers of these coal black animals just don't care to have them lose their identity, and be confused with coach dogs or pointers.

But if you're in the hands of a good Labrador breeder, there will be no weak, sickly, or deformed pups, and none with excess white to choose from. All these will have long since joined their ancestors in canine heaven, wearing small extra halos for having done their bit toward maintaining and improving the standard of the breed.

Now I'm going to include right here the complete descriptions and standards of points that have been established by the three parent breed clubs. These are used as guides by bench-show judges. Read them if you like, but for a new retriever enthusiast trying to buy his first pup, these detailed standards may prove more confusing than helpful.

They apply mainly to grown dogs—not immature puppies. Puppies are like babies—they are apt to grow in sections, and at a given moment nobody can tell for sure what their conformation will finally be.

THE LABRADOR RETRIEVER

Description and Standard of Points

(Adopted by The Labrador Retriever Club, Inc., and Approved by The American Kennel Club, July 10, 1945)

General Appearance. The general appearance of the Labrador should be that of a strongly built, short-coupled, very active dog. He should be fairly wide over the loins, and strong and muscular in the hind quarters. The coat should be close, short, dense, and free from feather.

Head. The skull should be wide giving brain room; there should be a slight "stop," i.e., the brow should be slightly pronounced, so that the skull is not absolutely in a straight line with the nose. The head should be clean-cut and free from fleshy cheeks. The jaws should be long and powerful and free from snipiness; the nose should be wide and the nostrils well developed. Teeth should be strong and regular, with a level mouth.

The ears should hang moderately close to the head, rather far back, set somewhat low, and not be large and heavy. The eyes should be of medium size, expressing great intelligence and good temper, and can be brown, yellow, or black, but brown or black is preferred.

Neck and Chest. The neck should be of medium length and powerful and not throaty. The shoulders should be long and sloping.

The chest must be of good width and depth, the ribs well sprung and the loins wide and strong, stifles well turned, and the hind quarters well developed and of great power.

Legs and Feet. The legs must be straight from the shoulder to ground, and the feet compact with toes well arched, and pads well developed; the hocks should be well bent, and the dog must neither be cowhocked nor be too wide behind; in fact, he must stand and move true all round on legs and feet. Legs should be of medium length, showing good bone and muscle, but not so short as to be out of balance with rest of body. In fact, a dog well balanced in all points is preferable to one with outstanding good qualities and defects.

Tail. The tail is a distinctive feature of the breed; it should be very thick toward the base, gradually tapering toward the tip, of medium length, should be free from any feathering, and should be clothed thickly all round with the Labrador's short, thick, dense coat, thus giving that peculiar "rounded" appearance that has been described as the "Otter" tail. The tail may be carried gaily but should not curl over the back.

Coat. The coat is another very distinctive feature; it should be short, very dense, and without wave, and should give a fairly hard feeling to the hand.

Color. The color is generally black, free from any rustiness and any white marking except possibly a small spot on the chest. Other whole colors are permissible.

Movement. Movement, or action, is the crucial test of conformation. The Labrador's legs should be carried straight forward while traveling, the forelegs hanging perpendicular and swinging parallel with the sides, like the pendulum of a clock. The principal propulsive power is furnished by the hind legs, perfection of action being found in the Labrador possessing long thighs and muscular second thighs well bent at the stifles, which admit of a strong forward thrust or "snatch" of the hocks. When approaching, the forelegs should form a continuation of the straight line of the front, the feet being the same distance apart as the elbows. When stationary, it is often difficult to determine whether a dog is slightly out at shoulder, but, directly he moves, the defect—if it exists—becomes more apparent, the forefeet having a tendency to cross or "weave." When, on the contrary, the dog is tied at the shoulder, the tendency of the feet is to move wider apart, with a sort of paddling action. When the hocks are turned in—cowhock—the stifles and feet are turned outward, resulting in a serious loss of propulsive power. When the hocks are turned outward, the tendency of the hind feet is to cross, resulting in an ungainly waddle.

Approximate weights of dogs and bitches in working condition. Dogs—60–75 pounds; Bitches—55–70 pounds.

Height at Shoulders. Dogs—22½–24½ inches; Bitches—21½–23½ inches.

The Golden Retriever

Description and Standard of Points

(By Courtesy of The Golden Retriever Club of America)

General Appearance. Should be of a symmetrical, active, powerful dog, a good level mover, sound and well put together, with a kindly expression, not clumsy or long in the leg.

Head. Broad in skull, well set on a clean and muscular neck, muzzle powerful and wide, not weak jawed, good stop. Eyes dark and set well apart, very kindly in expression with dark rims. Even teeth, neither undershot nor overshot.

Color. Rich golden, must not be as dark as an Irish Red Setter or cream color. The presence of a few white hairs on chest permissible, but white collar, feet, toes, or blaze to be penalized.

Coat. Must be flat or wavy, good undercoat, dense and water resisting.

Ears. Small and well set on.

Feet. Round and catlike, must not open or splay.

Forelegs. Straight, with good bone.

Hindlegs. Strong and muscular, well-bent stifles.

Hocks. Well let down, not cowhocked.

Nose. Should be black, but a light-colored nose should not debar from honors a dog that is good in all other respects.

Tail. Should be straight, not curled at tip or carried over the back.

	Points
Head	20
Color	10
Coat	5
Ears	5
Feet	10
Forelegs	10
Hindlegs	10
Hocks	10
Nose	5
Tail	5
Body	25
Total	115

Body. Well balanced, short coupled, and deep through the heart. Loins must be strong, back ribs must be deep and strong with good second thighs; shoulders must be well laid back and long in the blade.

Note. The ideal weights for adult dogs and bitches in good, hard condition should be: Dogs, 65-68 pounds; Bitches, 55-60 pounds. Heights at shoulder: Dogs, 23–24 inches; Bitches, 20½–22 inches.

THE CHESAPEAKE BAY RETRIEVER

Description and Standard of Points

(Adopted by The American Chesapeake Club, July 1, 1933, and Approved by The American Kennel Club, September 12, 1933)

General Disqualifications.

1. Black or liver colored.
2. White on any part of body, except breast, belly, or spots on feet.
3. Feathering on tail or legs over 1¾ inches long.
4. Dewclaws, undershot, overshot, or any deformity.
5. Coat curly or tendency to curl all over body.
6. Specimens unworthy or lacking in breed characteristics.

Head. Skull broad and round with medium stop, nose medium short, muzzle pointed but not sharp. Lips thin, not pendulous. Ears small, set well up on head, hanging loosely and of medium leather. Eyes medium large, very clear, of yellowish color and wide apart.

Neck. Of medium length with a strong muscular appearance, tapering to shoulders.

Shoulders, Chest, and Body. Shoulders sloping, and should have full liberty of action with plenty of power without any restrictions of movement. Chest strong, deep, and wide. Barrel round and deep. Body of medium length, neither cobby nor roached, but rather approaching hollowness, flanks well tucked up.

Back Quarters and Stifles. Back quarters should be as high as or a trifle higher than the shoulders. They should show fully as much power as the forequarters. There should be no tendency to weakness in either hind or forequarters. Hind quarters should be especially powerful to supply the driving power for swimming. Back should be short, well coupled, and powerful. Good hind quarters are essential.

Legs, Elbows, Hocks, and Feet. Legs should be of medium length and straight, showing good bone and muscle, with well-webbed hare feet of good size. The toes well rounded and close pasterns slightly bent and both pasterns and hocks of medium length—the straighter the legs the better.

Stern. Tail should be of medium length: Males 12–15 inches, and females 11–14 inches; medium heavy at base, moderate feathering on stern and tail permissible.

Coat and Texture. Coat should be thick and short, nowhere over 1½ inches long, with a dense fine woolly undercoat. Hair on face and legs should be very short and straight with tendency to wave on the shoulders, neck, back, and loins only. The curly coat or coat with tendency to curl not permissible.

Color. Any color varying from a dark brown to a faded tan or deadgrass. Deadgrass takes in any shade of deadgrass, varying from a tan to a dull straw color. White spot on breast and toes permissible, but the smaller the spot the better, solid color being preferred.

Weight. Males, 65–75 pounds; females 55–65 pounds.

Height. Males, 23–26 inches; females, 21–24 inches.

Symmetry and Quality. The Chesapeake dog should show a bright and happy disposition and an intelligent expression, with general outlines impressive and denoting a good worker. The dog should be well proportioned, a dog with a good coat and well balanced in other points being preferable to the dog excelling in some but weak in others.

The texture of the dog's coat is very important as the dog is used for hunting under all sorts of adverse weather conditions, often working in ice and snow. The oil in the harsh outer coat and woolly undercoat is of extreme value in preventing the cold water from reaching the dog's skin and aids in quick drying. A Chesapeake's coat should resist the water in the same way that a duck's feathers do. When he leaves the water and shakes himself, his coat should not hold the water at all, being merely moist.

Color and coat are extremely important as the dog is used for duck hunting. The color must be as nearly that of his surroundings as possible and with the fact that dogs are exposed to all kinds of adverse weather conditions, often working in ice and snow, the color of coat and its texture must be given every consideration when judging on the bench or in the ring.

Courage, willingness to work, alertness, nose, intelligence, love of water, general quality, and, most of all disposition should be given primary consideration in the selection and breeding of the Chesapeake Bay Dog.

Points

Head, including lips, ears, and eyes....	16
Neck	4
Shoulders and body	12
Back quarters and stifles	12
Elbows, legs, and feet	12
Color	4
Stern and tail	10
Coat and texture	18
General conformation	12
Total	100

Note. The question of coat and general type of balance takes precedence over any scoring table that could be drawn up.

Length head, nose to occiput	9½–10
Girth at ears	20–21
Muzzle below eyes	10–10½
Length of ears	4½–5
Width between eyes	2½–2¾
Girth neck close to shoulder	20–22
Girth of chest to elbows	35–36
Girth at flank	24–25
Length from occiput to tail base ..	34–35
Girth forearms at shoulders	10–10½
Girth upper thigh	19–20
From root to root of ear, over skull .	5–6
Occiput to top shoulder blades	9–9½
From elbow to elbow over the shoulders	25–26

Don't spend too much time worrying over these breed standards, if you're after a pup. Almost any jerk can recognize a reasonably well-put-together pup when he sees one, without studying a table of points. And that's all you want, from an appearance standpoint. Sure, you want a decent-looking dog. But you are mainly interested in what's inside.

I honestly believe with young pups it's impossible to tell which member of the litter has the most desirable stuff inside. Yet, knowing it's a waste of time, I usually toss something for each pup to retrieve, presumably to determine which is naturally most interested in retrieving. This is about the same as trying to decide whether a two-year-old baby might grow up to be a pitcher for the Brooklyn Dodgers, by handing him a baseball and seeing if he throws it.

In many young retrievers the powerful desire and instinct for retrieving seems to lie dormant, and often does not bloom until age eight or nine months, or even a year. This was true of Free-haven Jay, who according to the record is one of the field-trial greats of all time.

He was three months old when I picked him blindly out of a litter sired by the illustrious Glenairlie Rover. I took him home, and in my ignorance was greatly distressed when I could not get him to retrieve or even to chase a ball or a training dummy. He just wasn't interested. At last, in despair, when he was nine months old, I put him in training with Jim Hogan. Evidently, he was just about ready by then to come to life. Also, Jim Hogan was the lad who knew how to wake up his natural instincts, and speed his progress. At any rate, just three months later he won his first stake in a field trial, and from then on was sufficiently precocious, winning the title of Field Trial Champion before his second birthday.

That started me on my "retriever-happy" career. Since then, I've raised and trained many good dogs who weren't much interested in retrieving as young pups.

Another fairly useless thing I do in picking a pup is to try to find the one that is boldest, most alert, and presumably most intelligent. For instance, I run away from them, calling, whistling, and clapping hands—to see which chases me most aggressively. But the little character who yawns, curls up under a bush, and goes to sleep today—might easily be the one who would win the race tomorrow. Puppies are mercurial. They do a lot of napping, between their violent fits of play. At any given moment, trying to pick the brightest of the lot is virtually impossible.

So let's just sum up this matter of picking a pup.

Deal with a good breeder, preferably a field-trial man, but at any rate someone with field-trial stock.

Study the parents and the grandparents in the pedigree. If they had the right stuff inside, you can be as sure as it's possible to be that the pups will have it also. The one you grab may never be a field-trial champion, but after all there aren't many of those, and just who do you think you are, anyway? Your pup is likely to grow up to be the finest gun dog you ever dreamed of owning, at the very least.

BUYING AN OLDER DOG
(See Illustrations 15-22)

In buying an adult dog—a year old or more—you'd better study the breed description and standard of points a bit more carefully—at least enough to recognize a fairly good physical specimen when you see him. You don't need a potential bench champion, but you do want an animal with no serious defects from the conformation standards set up by the breed club, which presumably had practical reasons for most of them.

Then, whether the dog is trained, partly trained, or untrained, you should be just as fussy about the parents and the grand-parents in the pedigree as if you were selecting a young pup. This is important for several reasons. You may not think now you'll ever be interested in using the dog for breeding. Neither did I, when I bought Jay, "just for a shooting dog." Since then he has sired several field trial champions, and I have at times been wading in black pups up to my ears.

Right now you probably are positive you would never think of selling your dog. I was equally sure I would never part with my first retriever. But then Jay gave me the field-trial fever, which led to the incurable disease of breeding. And I have been obliged to sell many dogs to which I was attached. You can't keep them all.

Being human, our ideas are subject to change, and it is smart whenever possible to buy anything, whether it's a dog or a house, with an eye to its resale value. No matter how good an individual retriever may be, an impressive pedigree with well-known working ancestors behind him will make him much more valuable if you want to sell him. And of course the pedigree has an even more important effect on the value of his pups, and the stud fee he can command.

First, let's assume you are buying a young untrained dog of *twelve months or more*. You are satisfied with his pedigree.

Even though the dog is untrained, and priced accordingly (possibly from two to three hundred dollars), by that age you can tell something about his natural traits and characteristics. By now he should naturally be keen to retrieve. Ask the owner to toss a training dummy in cover sufficient to hide it. It doesn't need to be a long retrieve. You can tell a lot just from a bundle thrown in a yard. I like to see a youngster who scorches the ground in his eagerness, going out. If he misses the dummy on the first cast, he should show some persistence about hunting until he finds it. You should see him at least showing signs of discovering that he has a nose, sniffing the breeze, and working his way upwind to the fall. The important things to watch are what he does *until he finds the dummy*. That's what reveals the most desirable of his natural, inherited characteristics. Don't worry too much if he doesn't come right in and deliver to hand, or even if he wants to run away and lie down and play with the dummy. That's just puppy stuff, and easily corrected in the course of training—if he has the right stuff in him.

With a reasonably tractable dog, it is easy to take undesirable things out of him. But it is impossible to put things into him that should be there in the first place. Such things as keenness, fire, desire to hunt, persistence, guts, and a good nose to smell with. When a youngster who has these things goes out to retrieve a training dummy, it doesn't take an expert to recognize him. You'll know. Quality will stick out all over him.

If you're a duck hunter, before buying such a young dog you should also see him go in the water. It doesn't need to be big water, for a long swim. A swimming pool or a small pond will do. When a floating dummy is thrown in, he should hit the water enthusiastically, without hesitation. If he runs up and down shore, trying to make up his mind, and finally tiptoes in as if he hates to get his feet wet, he's not the duck dog for you. By careful training and encouragement, you *might* improve his water work a lot, and you might not. But to do that heartwarming and spectacular job in the water that a good retriever should do, he should be pretty enthusiastic about it to start with. You don't want to spend your life sitting in duck blinds, cussing your dog just to get him to go in the water.

So in buying a young untrained dog you need to see only three things: the pedigree, one land retrieve, and one in the water. You'll know whether he's for you.

But if you're putting out the money for a *trained* retriever, you should see a good deal more. You should see him do all of the retrieving chores that he can *reasonably be expected to do, at his attained age, and at his price.*

Many new retriever enthusiasts, after seeing the open all-age dogs perform in a field trial, make the mistake of expecting a young trained dog to do the same stuff that the hot competitors make look so easy. You wouldn't expect a high-school ballplayer to measure up to big-league standards. No more should you demand that a young retriever be able to do blind retrieves, and take whistle and hand signals like a five-year-old field-trial champion.

In Part III you will find descriptions of the typical tests usually encountered in trials, both on land and in water. In buying a trained dog, it isn't fair to ask the owner to show the dog doing more than he would have to do in a trial.

If the dog is under twelve months, eligible for a Puppy Stake, you should be satisfied to see him do the simple marked retrieves, a single shot pigeon on land, a shackled duck in the water, that are described as the tests to be expected in that particular stake.

If he is a little older—a derby dog—Derby Stake standards should be applied. If he is just about two years old, judge him by Junior Stake tests.

Now if the dog is older than two, and the owner is offering him as a good shooting dog but frankly says he doesn't think he'll ever be an open all-age dog, he will be priced accordingly, and you should judge him by the typical tests of a Non-Winners Stake. That is the stake for the faithful duck and pheasant dogs, the meat dogs, who are wonderful hunting companions but don't quite have that extra something that makes a possible field-trial champion.

Of course if you want a field-trial winner, and are digging down for a price running into four figures, then you want to see that dog do everything he would be asked to do in an open all-age stake. As a matter of fact, before buying such a dog you would be wise to see him compete in one or more trials as well.

Any sincere retriever enthusiast who sells you a trained dog of any age would want to spend sufficient time with you and the dog to be sure you understand how to handle him and get the most out of him.

It is nearly always a mistake for anyone not experienced in training and handling retrievers to buy his first trained dog by mail. In fact, it can be tragic. Many fine dogs have been ruined this way.

Most of the leading retriever trainers use the commands, the hand signals, and the whistle signals given in Part II of this book. But the dog you buy may have been trained quite differently. And the smallest misunderstanding in this respect can be terribly important.

A duck hunter I used to know, an impatient and choleric man, once bought his first and last retriever, a dog I happened to know, a good one. He paid a thousand dollars for it, and it was shipped to him by air. He grabbed the dog out of the crate, and left at once for a duck-hunting trip.

He could not get that dog to retrieve a duck. He would scream, "Fetch," and "Go fetch," and, "Get the hell out there," and everything else he could think of. The dog would just sit quietly in the boat and look at him patiently. The man lost his temper. His companions ribbed him unmercifully about his thousand-dollar dog.

At last, in a rage, he impulsively gave the dog away to his guide. And to this day he is convinced that retrievers are utterly useless.

Now there was nothing wrong with that dog. He had been trained, as most retrievers are, to go in and retrieve *only when his name was spoken.* To him, the command "fetch" meant something quite different, as you will see in Part II.

It is almost impossible for the seller of a trained dog to give you in a letter everything you should know about that dog, the commands to which he responds, his little idiosyncrasies, and the tricks of handling him. Futhermore, a trained retriever is almost human, and instinctively he can spot a greenhorn, and will take perverse delight in playing you for a sucker sometimes, if he can get away with it.

So if you want to put out important money for a trained dog, it is much better to buy your first one at least in person rather than by mail. Then the owner can demonstrate the dog thoroughly, *show* you what you can reasonably expect the dog to do, and *show* you how to handle him properly.

Thus, after you get the dog home, you will know what has gone before in his education, and it will be simple for you to carry on from that point with his training—with no waste motions— enough to keep him improving with age and experience, instead of slipping backward. For a dog, like a man, does one or the other. Which it will be, with a good trained dog, depends on his new owner.

But don't let this alarm you. It takes very little time, and it's easy, to keep a trained retriever in the groove.

PART II

HOW TO TRAIN YOUR DOG
THE EASY WAY

LLLLLLLLLLLLLLLLLLLLLLLLLLLLLLLLLLL

Chapter 8

TRAINING FUNDAMENTALS

OF COURSE, the *very easiest* way to get your dog trained is to duck the job entirely, and send him to a professional trainer. But good retriever men are scarce, and busy. They won't take more dogs than they can comfortably handle, and give each owner his money's worth. At this writing, such men charge prices ranging from forty to sixty dollars per month for board and training—and believe me, they earn every cent of it. Properly to start a twelve-month-old retriever, a trainer should have him at least two or three months, depending on the individual dog and on how fast he can safely be pushed.

If, as is quite possible, you can't find a well-recommended retriever specialist in your vicinity, able and willing to take on your dog, then you'd better do your own training. Don't make the mistake of compromising on a strictly bird-dog trainer. Some of these are very fine men, but unless they have taken the trouble to learn the retriever specialty, and *have done some actual handling in retriever trials*—they can't do as good a job on your retriever as you can do yourself. They don't know how. For the main job of pointers and setters is finding and pointing live birds—on land. With them, retrieving is strictly secondary. And they are rarely asked to retrieve waterfowl.

So your average bird-dog trainer has no idea what a good retriever can and should be asked to do. He seldom has adequate water, or even land cover, to train retrievers at his home kennel at all times of year. And he is likely to be too easily satisfied with sloppy obedience to commands—since this phase of training is not so important in pointer and setter work, and usually is not emphasized with bird dogs as it must be with retrievers.

At the other extreme are the "obedience trainers" to be found in almost every community, who undertake to teach manners to any kind of dog. Some of these will assure you they can train a finished retriever, but unless such a man has had a good deal of actual experience in AKC licensed retriever trials, I wouldn't entrust a good young prospect to him. A trainer of this type probably has even less adequate land and water facilities than the bird-dog man.

He'll teach your dog the obedience commands, all right. That's his business. But he knows even less than the bird-dog man about retriever work. And he's all too likely to slow down a promising youngster, take the steam out of him, and spoil his enthusiasm for his work—by trying to make him *too steady too soon.* He'll take on anything from a Scottie to a Great Dane, and most of the pets he gets aren't really worth training. So to get results, he often has to use very severe methods.

These aren't necessary for a tractable, intelligent young retriever. It's so easy to train such a dog to the obedience commands, you might as well do it yourself. And after just reading this book, and perhaps attending one field trial, you'll know more about training a dog to retrieve than some of these obedience trainers. They aren't much on reading books. They're more inclined to think they wrote them.

Many of the top retriever trainers today are converted Springer spaniel men, who still handle both Springers and retrievers. The spaniels at least are required to do a decent job of retrieving, as well as flushing, and more emphasis is usually put on this part of their training than with the pointing dogs. Even so, the land retrieves in a Springer field trial are mostly short, simple singles—primer stuff to a good retriever. And the spaniel water tests are a joke to a dyed-in-the-wool retriever nut. About all they prove is whether or not the dog is willing to get his feet wet.

So I wouldn't even send a young retriever to a spaniel trainer, no matter how good his reputation in that field—unless he is one of those who also handles a lot of retrievers, and has done well with the latter dogs in trials.

Now even if you are lucky enough to have a *good* retriever trainer start your dog, you still need to understand how to carry on his education. And if you have the professional go on and finish the job you still should know how to keep the dog up to snuff, and how to handle him to get the most pleasure from your educated shooting companion. If you're going to *own* a retriever, you should understand the principles of training.

But with the good trainers so scarce, the chances are you'll have to train the dog yourself, if you want the job done right.

There's nothing to it, and it's fun—*if* you don't start backward, as I did. Before you start, just get a few simple fundamentals firmly ensconced in your noggin. Then it will be a breeze—about as taxing to the brain as learning to play gin rummy.

FUNDAMENTAL NO. 1

Get a decent dog to start with.

We have already harped on this enough. If you're still with me, and haven't angrily tossed this book in the ash can—then I assume you're sold on the principle, in theory, at least. Now then, just how do you determine whether you have a dog worth training?

Here is a very simple and practical yardstick:

If the dog does not respond to his lessons *before you run out of time and patience, and feel like chucking the whole thing,* then he's not the dog for you to train. Get smart, and get rid of him. Write him off. Sell him to a bargain hunter. Or give him to your Aunt Minnie for a house pet. Get yourself another dog.

Yes, I know. This is easy to say, and tough to do. You become attached to *any* dog very fast, and love him in spite of everything. The longer you keep him around, the harder it is to banish a useless dog. But until you bring yourself to do it, you're yielding to sentiment instead of using your head. And that, friend, is your problem. I had to battle it out for myself, and so will you.

FUNDAMENTAL NO. 2

Everything a dog learns depends on his memory, and only his memory.

Contrary to sentimental dog fiction, he has no reasoning power. When we speak of an intelligent dog, we really mean a dog blessed with plenty of memory cells in his brain.

In his obedience training, you put him through an action, and speak a command. You repeat this. He associates the action with the command. The better his memory, the less repetition is required. That's all there is to the obedience training.

In the more advanced exercises, in retrieving, the same principle applies. You arrange it so that when a dog goes through a certain action, a pleasant result occurs. He finds the dummy, or the bird. With a little repetition, he quickly associates in his memory the action and the exciting result. He learns to mark falls. To use the wind and use his nose. To take a line. And finally to take whistle and hand signals to blind retrieves.

He learns all this purely through *repetition* and *memory*. Remember those two words. Paste them in your hat. Keep them in mind, and every lesson in this book will not only make sense, but will seem childishly simple. As you go along, you'll find yourself improvising new stunts and short cuts of your own— based on this principle—to get faster results with your own dog. Remember those two words, and you're already a better dog trainer than *some* of the men who call themselves professionals.

FUNDAMENTAL NO. 3

This principle I call *doubling up, and pyramiding*.

Most of the training books I've read have thrown me for a loss by saying you must teach a dog only one thing at a time. Probably this is sound advice if you're struggling with a stupid mutt. I wouldn't know. I never lasted long enough to train a dog of that type to come in out of the rain.

But for a good young retriever, or any dog with a good memory, this is utter nonsense. It would take forever.

With a *good* dog, in every lesson you can and should work him on two or more commands. This is like teaching the touch system on the typewriter. Each day you keep adding letters, until suddenly the student knows them all. In the advanced retrieving exercises, you'll be working your dog on five or six different things simultaneously, within a ten-minute session. That's the secret of the good professional trainers. That's how one man can do a good job every day on twenty or thirty dogs. And that's how *you* can train *one* dog in an average of only ten minutes a day.

FUNDAMENTAL NO. 4

Don't start the serious training too early.

This is the most common and the most costly mistake of the enthusiastic amateur with his first retriever pup. I've found it the hardest wrong practice to discourage.

You won't gain a thing by starting a pup on the retrieving work before he is a year old. If he happens to be unusually slow to mature, you can do him much harm by starting earlier.

At every trial of our new Southern California Retriever Club, at least one eager newcomer shows up with a four- or five- or six-month-old pup, determined to enter and run him in stakes for older dogs. When, for the good of the pup, we refuse the entry, the owner is vastly indignant.

Quite likely the pup has never retrieved anything but a glove or a tennis ball. He's never seen a pigeon, or a live shackled duck, nor heard a gunshot. We try to explain to the owner the pup is too likely to toss and play with a pigeon, and needlessly become hard mouthed, if he hasn't been properly introduced to feathers before being sent to retrieve his first shot bird.

A big live mallard drake, with only his feet and wings tied, squawking and pecking indignantly as the youngster approaches in the water, can badly frighten a young pup, and even make him permanently cripple shy.

The rude and abrupt introduction to the gun *might* make him gun shy.

But the biggest danger is in requiring the youngster to be steady to shot much too soon.

Now let me emphasize—all this applies to the training in *retrieving*. It won't hurt a good young pup to give him some of the simpler obedience training, whenever you like, if you don't get too tough about it. Never give a young pup any severe punishment. Let him grow out of his diapers before you spank him for disobedience.

However, nearly all well-bred retriever pups can be taught quite easily and painlessly to "sit" on command; walk at "heel"; stop jumping on people when you say "down"; and to go into the pen or leap in the car when you say "kennel." And if a pup does respond reasonably well to these commands, he is much less of a nuisance to have around while you're waiting for him to grow up.

But don't, please, try to *combine* the command "sit" with retrieving. Many pups are ruined this way—by your not only rushing their retrieving, but making them sit and wait before being sent. Some greenhorns go much farther. I recently narrowly escaped a stroke when I saw the new owner of a *four-month-old* pup working him on whistle and hand signals, and blind retrieves. At four months, mind you! You'll better understand the idiocy of this after you've read the later chapters on training. For now, let me say only that what this clown was trying to do was about like putting a three-year-old child in school—and then starting him right out with calculus, before he's had arithmetic, algebra, geometry, and whatever else you need before attempting calculus.

With some pups, more precocious than the average, it is safe to start them doing a few simple retrieves at eight or nine months, *provided you do not require steadiness*. But even with such a pup you will lose nothing, and save your own time, by waiting until he is a full twelve months old. At successive six-month intervals, he'll be just as far advanced—possibly farther—than if you'd started earlier.

The big danger in rushing the retrieving is that of boring the pup—ruining his natural keenness to hunt and to retrieve. And brother, that is important. That quality, you want to keep. *All* of it.

FUNDAMENTAL NO. 5

Give short, frequent lessons.

If you're in a hurry about this thing, it's perfectly all right to give your dog a little work every day—or even twice a day. But don't overdo it at any one time. Don't give him a chance to become bored. A retriever's work should be his fun.

An average of ten minutes a day is plenty, particularly in the obedience training, and the earlier stages of the retrieving work. Now obviously there will be times when you'll have your dog out considerably more than ten minutes, for *some* of the more advanced work. But try to keep that average in mind—ten minutes a day. It's much better to underwork than to overwork a young dog. And if at times you get busy and can't take him out for several days, don't worry about it. He won't lose any ground, and it won't do him a bit of harm to sit in his pen for a few days, thinking how nice it's going to be when he gets back to school.

It's a great temptation, when you get a new young dog and you're full of enthusiasm, to take him out and work him silly. Practically all newcomers to the retriever-happy ranks are guilty of this, to some degree. It is responsible for most of the sloppy, indifferent retriever work that you see.

FUNDAMENTAL NO. 6

Be alone with your dog when you're training.

Tell the kids to go fly their kites, and try to find a place where you can have privacy. For all of the obedience training, and even for the first simple retrieves, the garage is a good place.

Until the youngster is well along in junior high school and his work has become more important to him than anything else and also until you have become firmly entrenched as the boss, you want no admiring audience distracting and confusing him.

Particularly during the early obedience training, be sure to have him in a closed room or small fenced-in yard, where you can easily catch him if necessary. Which leads to:

FUNDAMENTAL NO. 7

Never give a command you're not in a position to enforce.

This seems so obvious it needs no discussion. Yet everyone, including me, is guilty of this mistake all too often. If you do your best to avoid it, you'll save yourself and the dog a lot of useless arguments.

It's a lot easier to avoid letting the dog become disobedient than to cure it after this fault becomes a habit.

FUNDAMENTAL NO. 8

The tone of voice is more important than the words of the command.

Now I've read that you should always speak quietly to a dog. Bunk! At times I find it very useful to holler. And I mean *holler*.

When a dog is cutting up, it is often more effective than a licking, and much less painful to dog and man, to say loudly and sternly: "Aah—*aah*—AAH—"

If you make this sound on a rising tone, and with rising volume, it has a positively magic effect on a dog. If you really give out with it, it seems to say very clearly to your canine pupil, "You stop that nonsense, now. You be careful. You know better than that. I'm fed up, and you'd better behave, bud—or else."

Another favorite of mine, which for some reason seems to give a lot of belly laughs to my hunting partners, is suddenly to bellow at the top of my lungs: "*WHAT* ARE YOU DOING?"

I use this when a dog is at some distance out in the field, fiddling around, hunting mice, or otherwise not tending to business. Or when he ignores the whistle. You'd be amazed at the instant results usually accomplished by this inquiry, when the inflection is just right, and the voice choking with emotion.

Now all this is no doubt very funny to you at first, and possibly even silly. But it will pay you to think it over.

Why do you suppose the Army spends so much time drilling its officers in the "tone of command"—teaching them to bellow orders in a parade-ground voice?

I'll tell you why. It gets results.

It gets results with men, and it gets results with dogs.

Nearly all beginning trainers just sound too damn wishy-washy when they give a command. I don't mean you should yell every time you speak to a dog. Certainly not. But you should always speak with plenty of firmness in your voice, and when necessary, even sternness. You should sound as though you mean it, and as though you expect instant obedience, as a matter of course. You'll get it, if you can put this over in your tone.

Think of it this way. You're not begging a dog to do something. You're not requesting it. You're not even asking. You're *telling* him.

In this one respect, a woman is at a disadvantage in dog training. Her voice is simply weaker, and higher pitched, than a man's. She can't bellow like a top sergeant. But even so, if she really tries she can get that ring of authority into her commands. And when necessary, she can get fine results by throwing away her inhibitions and yelling like a fishwife.

One thing a woman can do as well as any man is to learn to blow the whistle properly, and this is just as important as the voice. When a dog is working at some distance out in the field, you control him entirely with whistle signals and hand motions.

He can hear that whistle at great distances—if he wants to. Many times I've demonstrated this by taking out a wise old retriever, handing my whistle to a greenhorn handler, and telling him to blow it. He trills it sweetly. The dog pays no attention. He doesn't even look around.

Then I take the same whistle. I blast it just once. The dog spins, his ears go up, and his fanny goes down—right now.

He has heard the tone of command in the tone of the whistle.

That sound wave just reaches out, spins the dog around, and pushes his rear end down.

There's nothing much to learning to blow a whistle this way. Just forget your bashfulness, and give it everything you've got. What you want is a note as sharp, abrupt, and high as you can get. Also loud.

Block the opening in the mouthpiece with your tongue. Build up air pressure in your mouth—say about sixty pounds—or until you feel your eardrums are about to go out, or you're going to have a stroke. Then move your tongue aside quickly, and let her blast!

As soon as you get your new whistle, practice this a little, before you try it on the dog. It's a fine way to become unpopular around the house. Even better than practicing on your duck call.

FUNDAMENTAL NO. 9

No tidbits. No tipping.

The other day I was working some young dogs in the yard. A nice-looking old gentleman came along, and hung over the fence, watching. Every time one of the dogs retrieved a training dummy, the old man muttered and sadly shook his head. At last he could stand it no longer.

"When they *do* it," he said indignantly, "why don't you *give* them something?"

I tried to explain that this was not a trained-seal act; that there is no need to throw a frozen fish to a Labrador every time he does the job he was born and bred to do; that a retriever needs and expects no more reward for doing his job than a friendly word of praise, or a pat on the head. But the old man was unconvinced. As he stalked off down the road I could hear him grumbling, "He ought to *give* them something."

Give your dog a cooky every time he does what he's supposed to, if you like. But it's a useless precedent you're starting, and will become a nuisance. If he learns to expect these tips, there will come a time, out in the field, when you run out of tidbits. If you never start this practice, he'll be just as happy without it.

SOME USEFUL PROPS
(See Illustration 23)

The essential training tools you need don't amount to much, and are easily obtained.

1. *Whistle.* The best kind I know is the one used by virtually all professional trainers for retrievers—the *small* Acme Thunderer. This is made of some sort of plastic, and the color is brown. If you can't get it from your local sporting-goods store, you can send for one to Abercrombie & Fitch, New York; or Von Lengerke & Antoine, Chicago. Take the trouble to get this whistle. It is much better than the bird-dog whistles, or any of the larger whistles, whether plastic or metal. It has a higher, sharper note. A dog can hear it farther, and it seems to do something authoritative to his ear.

Put the whistle on a cord, and form the habit of wearing it around your neck, whenever you're training or when you go hunting. No matter how good you think you are at whistling through your fingers or your teeth, I advise you to use an Acme Thunderer anyway. Get your dog used to it. You can get a lot more authority into its tone than you possibly can into any unaided mouth signal you can make yourself. And it will still work, even if your mouth is dry—or you suddenly see someone sucking a lemon.

2. *Short Leather Leash.* The handiest kind, I've never seen in a store. Any harness maker will make one up for you at small cost, using a good piece of harness leather about one inch wide. The finished leash should be about eighteen inches long, the leather doubled and sewed together, leaving a loop for your hand at one end, and sewing in an ordinary harness snap at the other. This is just the right length for leading a big dog at heel. You can wad it up and put it in your pocket. And it's about right to use for corporal punishment, if such should be necessary.

3. *Slip Chain Collar.* The sporting-goods stores have these, but be sure you get a fairly heavy one, and with *welded* rings on each end. Since the war, they sometimes try to unload collars with soldered rings. These are likely to pull apart, and if you leave your dog chained to one, you could lose him. Measure your

dog around the biggest part of his head, and get a collar just large enough to slip over his head comfortably, without much space to spare. Some people call these "choke" collars, and think they are cruel, and that trainers use them to administer punishment by choking a dog. This is nonsense. The collar tightens only when the dog pulls against it, and he quickly learns not to make himself uncomfortable. These retrievers have heavy necks. To keep an ordinary collar tight enough so it can't pull over the head is more uncomfortable than the occasional squeeze from a slip collar. It looks better, too, than a big wide leather affair, and it doesn't wear off as much hair.

4. *Long Chain Leash.* Any sporting-goods or hardware store has these. But get a fairly heavy one, five or six feet long, with a good big harness snap on one end. This will come in handy whenever you take the dog away from home, to tie him up securely and safely. Don't ever depend on a piece of rope, if you're going to leave him even for five minutes. One of these critters will chew through a rope like an ear of sweet corn.

5. *Land Training Dummy.* Make this yourself out of an old gunny sack. For starting a young dog, it should be small enough to that he can pick it up easily without stretching his mouth, but not so small that he might inhale it when he makes a fast pickup, and get it halfway down his throat. Take enough of the burlap to fold and roll into a cylinder about twelve inches long, and from two to two and a half inches in diameter. Tie it up securely with a stout cord, so it won't come apart. No need to tie any feathers on it, or to doctor it with artificial scent. Your hand scent on the dummy will be plenty, by the time the dog gets to using his nose. At the outset, it will be mainly sight retrieving anyway, while the dummy is new. Later you'll need two more dummies, larger and heavier, but the one small one is plenty for a while.

6. *Water Training Dummy.* The best thing I've ever found is a small boat fender, filled with cork, and covered with heavy canvas. You can get these in many sporting-goods and hardware stores, and in any event in marine-supply stores. Get a small one, not more than two and a half inches in diameter, to start off with. These are light, float, of course, don't get soggy, and

have some resilience. Later you'll want two larger and much heavier boat fenders, more like the size and weight of the body of a big mallard duck. You can also buy these, filled with sponge rubber, from three to three and a half inches in diameter. *Always* use the training dummies. *Never* throw a stick in the water for your dog to retrieve. This is a fine way to start hard mouth.

Chapter 9

SPARE THE ROD

NOW WE COME to a very ticklish subject, one that is tactfully ignored in most of the books, pamphlets, and articles about training man's best friend.

Well, here goes my neck. I'm going to devote *a whole chapter* to it. I'm going to discuss it frankly and realistically. And already I can hear the chorus of shrill outraged screams from some of the more hysterical unclaimed maidens of the SPCA.

They'll just have to go ahead and scream. For to anyone seriously interested in training any kind of a dog, this question of punishment is important. So let's haul it out on the table. If you're still with me by now, I assume you're the type who is willing to face the facts of life.

First, let's get this in the record: I'm not a sadist, and I don't enjoy giving a dog a licking. Neither do I enjoy spanking my kids.

But a famous public-opinion poll shows that even today most American parents occasionally spank their children when they persistently misbehave and forget their manners, before they reach the age of reason. These parents feel they are doing their offspring a favor to raise them as decent citizens who are liked, instead of despised as little varmints, by the people around them.

Most modern psychiatrists agree.

Well, remember this: a dog—unlike a child—*never* reaches the age of reason.

When the owner of an unruly dog asks what to do, I like to remind him of that old but good story about the eminent child psychiatrist and the spoiled brat who refused to get off the hobby horse. The illustrious doctor finally whispered in the little monster's ear,"You nasty little so-and-so, you get down off that hobby horse right now or I'll knock your goddam teeth out."

The surprised kid climbed down like a little man.

This gag contains a pearl of psychology for any overindulgent mama, *or* dog owner.

If you convince your dog that you're ready and willing for a showdown, you probably won't need to have one. At any rate, not more than one. But *if he needs it*, a good old-fashioned thrashing won't hurt him a bit, will clear the air, and will save both you and the dog a lot of time and trouble.

Be sure you administer any such needed corporal punishment in private. Most people just don't understand the occasional necessity for it in dog training. A retriever has a hide ten times as thick as the tender behind of a child. Yet a parent who thinks nothing of walloping his kids, if he sees you administering a well-deserved licking to a seventy-pound Labrador, is likely to yell for the humane society, and want to put you in the jail house. You'll be scornfully accused of "beating a poor dumb brute." For some reason, this is considered worse than spanking a human child.

I guess the answer is that many people have devoted some serious attention to properly raising their kids, but none to the matter of training decent dogs. These are the people who tolerate perfectly horrible animals for house pets—untrammeled mutts who bark insanely at friends who come to call, nip their ankles, and jump up on them with muddy feet. Such spoiled dogs chase cars, dump the neighbor's garbage can, dig up his garden, kill his chickens, and generally scourge the neighborhood. They are cordially hated by everyone but their softheaded owners, receive many surreptitious kicks, and end up being shot or poisoned by a fed-up neighbor, or flattened by a truck.

Now I don't think their owners are doing these dogs a favor, any more than those parents are doing their children a favor when for lack of needed discipline they allow them to become juvenile delinquents.

Any dog should be obedient, and should receive whatever kind and amount of punishment is needed to make and keep him so. And of course a working retriever *must* be under perfect and quiet control—or he is worse than useless. A hardheaded, defiant dog in the field is a nuisance, and an imposition on your hunting companions. Unless you're willing to do whatever is necessary to keep your gun dog in line, you're better off without one.

An earnest but misinformed "dog lover" once told me flatly that *all* dog training for *any* purpose is cruel. Also, that all dog trainers are cruel people, who enjoy inflicting punishment on helpless animals.

Obviously this is utter nonsense.

Take the amateur trainers, for instance—the hobbyists. No amateur in his right mind would go to the trouble and expense of keeping and training a kennel full of dogs, unless he really loved dogs. He might keep one meat dog just for practical purposes, but not a dozen.

The same is true of the better professional trainers and handlers. Most of these men could make twice as much money in other jobs or businesses. Why do you suppose they stay in the dog business?

They don't talk baby talk to dogs, and they don't proclaim themselves as "dog lovers." But take my word for it, they love and appreciate a good working dog much more deeply than any spinster lady loves her little yapping lap dog.

Beyond that, common sense tells you that men who know dogs are not going to ruin promising material with cruelty, or too much punishment. A hunting dog who is not keen for his job, and not supremely happy when doing it, is worthless. You can't beat a dog into doing all that a good retriever must do in the course of a day afield. It is impossible. A dog that has been "trained" this way will quit on you every time, when the going gets tough.

Of course, there are skunks in every group, and there are some self-styled trainers who are stupid enough to be too severe with dogs. They don't get any of my dogs, and I don't like them any better than you do.

Your good trainers—amateur and professional alike—administer corporal punishment only to those dogs that clearly need and deserve it, and even then very sparingly. They try never to lose their tempers. When they have a bad day, and are in a foul mood, they just leave the dogs in the kennel.

When it becomes necessary to give a dog a walloping, they do so only when the dog is caught right in the act of disobedience—so that the punishment will be clearly associated with the crime in the dog's memory.

A common mistake of beginning amateurs, when a dog defies a command at some distance out in the field, is to call the dog in and *then* punish him. This is useless, unjust, only confuses the dog, and might even ruin him if done repeatedly. For the *last* thing he did was to come in to his handler when called—a correct, obedient action. And in his memory the licking is associated with that. Next time he is called, he probably will be reluctant to come, and you can't blame him for that.

The only way to punish a dog for a misdeed out in the field is to stir your stumps, *run out to him,* catch him, and thus make him understand that he is getting his medicine for whatever he just did or failed to do. That illustrates an important training principle. In his memory, a dog will always associate punishment with the *last* thing he has been doing.

If your dog ever demands a showdown, apply only as much pressure as needed to win the argument and command obedience. Try first a rolled-up newspaper. Wallop him with it, hard, several times, across the big muscle of the flank. It is impossible really to hurt any dog this way—and a retriever scarcely feels it through his heavy coat. But the rolled newspaper makes quite a startling noise, and one good application oftens gets amazing results even with a Labrador or Chesapeake—and likely is all that will ever be needed with a Golden.

But if your dog is tough, and the newspaper fails to convince him, then you must use a strap, and give him a good housecleaning and get it over with. Use as heavy a strap as you need to penetrate his hide and hair, and have him feel it enough to realize you're not just playing.

Hold the dog firmly by the scruff or collar with one hand, so he can't get away from you, and administer the licking with the other, always on that big flank muscle. There is no possibility of injuring him there, even in extreme cases where a very heavy strap is needed.

Most retrievers can take and like a lot more punishment than they ever need, without any danger of being cowed. But if you should be unlucky enough to get one who *can't take as much as he needs*, and shows signs of being cowed—then you'd better get rid of him at once. He just isn't worth fooling with, unless you like to see a dog crawl up to you on his belly.

At the other extreme is the occasional retriever who just can't seem to remember and profit by a licking—yet seems to have a good memory otherwise, and all the other qualities needed to make a great worker. Such a one is a youngster I'm training now—or perhaps I should say he's training me. His name is Freehaven Muscles, and he is built like a jeep. Also, he can happily absorb as much pounding as a jeep.

There isn't a mean hair in him, and in most ways he is quick to learn. His fault is too much eagerness, to the point of madness. His instinct to go and retrieve is so powerful that I honestly believe he hovers on the borderline of insanity. A slight understatement would be to say he has an obsession. When a gun goes off, and he sees something fall, he's gone—right now. He knows he's supposed to sit until he's sent. He's had plenty of spectacular wallopings for breaking. They don't mean a thing. When that bird falls, he just can't stand it. Whether I'll ever be able to steady him before my right arm wears out is the sixty-four-dollar question.

I wouldn't recommend such a dog for most amateurs to train, including me. As the horse trainers say, he's just too hot. It isn't likely, but if your pup should grow up to be one of these lunatics—unless you're a very determined and rugged character yourself—you'd better do one of two things:

Let a good professional get him under control for you.

Or—you guessed it—get another dog.

But the chances are your dog will be in tractability somewhere between Jay and Molly, and will require little or no corporal punishment. No retriever ever loved his work more than Freehaven Jay. But he is an individualist, and occasionally decides he has a better way of doing it than mine. About once a year he has always tried me out, to see if maybe the boss was going a little soft. And he always found out, promptly. He is a tough dog, and I have really had to lay on that leash a bit, to win this annual debate. There were never any hard feelings. After it was over, he would jump up and lick my face, and you could almost hear him say, "Okay, chief. You win."

Among the retrievers, there are plenty of such splendid, spirited dogs who (like some children) occasionally need a firm hand. But the kind you pray for is an individual like Molly.

The finest working bitch I ever owned or hope to own was Freehaven Molly, a Labrador, strangely enough. She was keen, fast, had everything. I only ran her in three trials, and she placed in two of them. She would easily have finished her field-trial championship if I had not been obliged to retire from competition during the war—and before the war was over a rattlesnake got her. She was a wonderful shooting dog, too—had just as much guts as any Chesapeake in Maryland. But she had more of that eagerness to please than any animal I ever saw. In seven years that we were hunting pals, I never so much as whapped her with a newspaper. She didn't need it, and she didn't get it.

I hope you get one like her.

Now I've devoted a lot of space to this subject of punishment, because it has been largely neglected and avoided. This very silence has fed wild rumors about the cruel methods of dog trainers. It has been the source of much unnecessary hysteria and confusion.

I definitely don't want to give you the impression that if you set out to train your retriever, you're going to be spending all your time beating up on him. The chances are you'll have to deal out very little or no severe punishment, if you get the kind of dog you should in the first place.

The main thing is to sell yourself on being *willing* and *ready* if necessary to administer just punishment. If you make this sale, your dog will know it instinctively. He'll get it from your tone of voice, and from the way you blow your whistle. These retrievers are amazing critters. They know if you're bluffing, and sometimes seem to take great delight in calling your bluff.

But a good one, with plenty of that eagerness to please, if he also feels in his bones that you'll stand no nonsense, won't push you too far. And even one of the tougher individuals, if you offer in a firm tone to knock his teeth out, will usually climb right down off the hobby horse.

Chapter 10

HOUSING YOUR DOG

SO YOU'VE BOUGHT your dog or pup, and you bring him home. The thing to decide right now is—where is he going to live? In the house? Or outside, in a simple kennel?

It is perfectly possible to raise a retriever as a house dog, and still make a good shooting dog of him. But if you're like I am, you're not man enough to do it this way. It is definitely doing it the hard way.

If you're going to train the youngster quickly and easily, you want to deliberately make a one-man dog of him. He will be one naturally, if given half a chance. You want to be his one and only hero. You don't want him to become a tramp—everybody's pal, nobody's friend. While he's in the early stages of training, at least, you don't want anyone else even to speak a kind word to him—much less fondle and pet him, and make a lap dog of him.

This rule is almost impossible to enforce, no matter how tough you're willing to get, if the dog lives in the house. Your kids will play with him, and maul him, until he's just too tired to take much interest when you suddenly come home and take him out for his retrieving lesson. Then too, all guests consider themselves great hands with dogs, and they will toss him tidbits from the table, call him when you've ordered him to sit in the corner, confuse him, and generally undo the obedience teaching you've given him.

As a house dog, he is bound to pick up sloppy habits, and to become confused as to whether his purpose in life is to be a play-boy, or to work for a living at the job for which he was born.

A friend of mine had a half-grown retriever, and while he was away at the office his kids enjoyed, among other things, throwing croquet balls for the pup to retrieve. After awhile they would tire of the sport, and leave the pup in the yard to chew up these solid wooden balls. Now that his serious training has begun, it is still a question whether he can be broken of the notion that ducks are like croquet balls—something to be tossed around and played with, and finally dismantled.

If your dog has the run of the house, you simply cannot control what happens to him while you're away. He will be much better off, at least for a year or so, if you keep him in a proper pen out in the yard—and *keep it locked, with the key in your pocket.*

Contrary to general opinion, you don't need a big place in the country to keep a retriever. There is plenty of room in any suburban or even city back yard for an adequate kennel and run. I live on thirty-four acres, but my dogs live in individual kennel runs that are only four feet wide and twenty-four feet long. These are much better for a dog than being confined in a large yard. He gets more exercise, running up and down a relatively small and *narrow* runway. (See Illustrations 24 and 25.) In a large yard, he'll spend most of his time just lying in a corner.

The best arrangement for a single dog—which is also adequate for two dogs—is a narrow run, roughly four feet by twenty-four feet enclosed with heavy wire fence, and *completely fenced over the top.* You may not believe the wire on top is necessary, but take my word for it. Most retrievers will go over a six-foot fence sooner or later—and probably sooner. It's best to have the fence six feet high, and higher if you're over six feet yourself, so you don't have to bend your neck every time you go in to clean the run. Use wire at least as heavy as hog wire, with a mesh no coarser than two by four inches. You probably won't believe this either, but you'll find out if you use chicken wire that a retriever will eat it like butter.

I like a concrete floor in the run. Today this will cost about fifty dollars, unless you can mix the cement and pour it yourself, but it's well worth it, if you're going to keep a valuable dog. It's much easier to keep clean than anything else, and to keep the dog free of worms. If you don't use concrete, then your fence wire must go down in the ground an extra two feet, to assure that the dog can't dig under.

I've heard some bench-show breeders say they don't like to keep their dogs on concrete, because it tends to spread their feet. Some say it even does something bad to their legs. But I've kept Labradors on concrete for ten years, and have never seen any evidence that it affected their feet *or* legs.

Even if it did spread their feet a bit, I doubt if I could work up much excitement over it. The important thing, it seems to me, is to keep a dog in clean and sanitary surroundings, where it's easy to keep him healthy and free of worms. An earth or even a sand or gravel run is bound to become foul and infested in time, no matter how you try to keep it clean. But with smooth concrete, it's so easy to pick up the stools with a small shovel, and hose down the run once a day. The sun does the rest, keeping it dry and sterile.

The sun is the best medicine for wormy stools, sterilizing them quickly on the hot concrete, and thus preventing the dog from reinfesting himself. Therefore the run should be carefully located so the sun strikes every part of it some time during the day.

But it should also have a moving patch of shade somewhere in it at any time of day, for the dog's comfort during the hot weather. If the long way of the run goes east and west, and there is one small tree near the middle of the south side, this double purpose will be nicely accomplished. If no tree is in the right spot, you may have to cover one small section of the run with a canvas tarpaulin to provide the needed bit of shade.

The only other shelter needed by a retriever is a small dog-house in one end of the run. If you're in a cold climate, this should be just barely large enough for the dog to curl up in comfortably. In the winter, it should have a swinging dog door, to close the opening and keep body heat inside. That's all the heat a retriever needs. He is naturally a cold-weather animal. He'll be much healthier, and his coat will be better, if he is not kept in artificial heat.

Now on the matter of chewing up wooden doghouses, I've had very little experience with Goldens and Chesapeakes, but almost any dog, when confined, will chew on any wood he can get his teeth on. And if you have a Labrador, I can sincerely advise you to protect every exposed corner of a wooden house with tin or galvanized metal. The edges of the dog door should definitely be so protected. If you don't the dog will eat it. And one of these big critters can masticate an amazing quantity of carpentry work in one day.

If you sensibly decide to keep your dog properly confined when you're not with him, you'll have a certain amount of trouble at first. If you have young children there will probably be some tears before you make them understand, and you may even have to go to the pound and get them a mongrel of their own to play with and maul, so they'll let your dog alone. Your sentimental friends won't understand, will think you're cruel to keep "that poor beast" penned up in a "cage," and will scoff at your not allowing them to pet him and make a bum out of him.

Well, they don't expect to paw your wife, and talk baby talk to her, do they? Why should they do it to your dog?

If you explain this, some people will understand. But there is always a smart aleck in the crowd who can't see why it's much easier to train a young dog if he worships only you, and is not expecting a lot of babying from every Tom, Dick, or Harry who comes along. You can save yourself the embarrassment of telling people to let the dog alone—by just leaving him in his pen when unbelievers are around.

Many horrified visitors, seeing my retrievers in their "cages," are firmly convinced that these poor animals never get any love and affection. This of course is nonsense. They get plenty. But they get it from me, exclusively.

Whenever you're at home in the evening, with no guests around, by all means bring the dog in the house. Let him lie quietly beside your chair, while you read your book. Talk to him. Pet him. Take him with you when you go for a walk. Make a pal of him. Just don't let anyone else do it. And when you have him out of his run, *always* keep him under control, pleasantly but firmly.

It is best, at least until you are solidly entrenched as the boss, to feed the dog yourself, if you possibly can. If you travel, or for any reason have to delegate this job part of the time, probably your wife is a better bet than a child or a servant. But whoever does it, you must try to indoctrinate thoroughly—persuade him or her just to give the dog his food, and not try to pet or baby him, or divide his allegiance.

This won't make so much difference after you get to giving the dog his real retrieving work. For he soon discovers that this is even more important and much more fun than eating. And after you once take him hunting, and shoot birds for him, he's your dog—and you're the number one hero, no matter who feeds him.

This is a thing the SPCA ladies will never believe. They are incapable of understanding it. But it's true just the same.

My retrievers, who spend much of their time in their "cages," are far *happier* dogs than any pampered and spoiled Pekingese with no particular purpose in life. Like a good man, a good dog gets his supreme pleasure from doing the job he was born to do, and doing it well. To believe this, all you have to do is watch the dogs competing in a retriever trial. Just show me one of these who isn't getting a bigger kick out of life than any bored and useless house pet, and I'll eat him.

Your dog will get more plain fun out of the high spot of his day—the ten minutes you take him out for his work—than an ordinary pet finds in twenty-four hours of lying around the yard, wondering what mischief he can get into next.

Now if you're still not convinced that you and your dog will both be better off if you keep him properly confined, here's the topper. If he's any good, you have a substantial investment in him. You don't want to lose him.

There is no such thing as a male dog, of any breed, who sooner or later won't wander off in quest of love, if he has the chance. He may seem quite content for a while, at large in a yard with an ordinary fence around it. But eventually he'll turn up missing. And it is just a question of time before he's killed by a car, or stolen by a dog thief.

Some females will stay at home, except when they come in season. But nobody will remember to examine a bitch every day. She'll come in season unexpectedly, and then she'll be gone over the fence, too. *If* she comes back at all, it will be to present you with a litter of mongrel pups—and this is almost worse than not coming back at all.

So never mind Aunt Minnie. Even though she and her friends think you are peculiar, eccentric, and cruel, build a nice tight run in your yard. Put a good padlock on it. Keep your dog in it, *except when you have him out yourself.*

Chapter 11

KINDERGARTEN—SIMPLE CITIZENSHIP

IT IS BEST to have your outside run and doghouse all ready, and pop your dog right in it the night you bring him home. Almost any pup, or any dog of any age, will do some howling and barking his first night alone in strange new surroundings, no matter whether he's in the house, or outside in a yard kennel. So you may as well have his permanent quarters ready, and break him of his noise-making only once, instead of twice.

The first command he must learn, to be a good citizen, is *"stop that noise."* It is also important to have him understand thoroughly what this means, for another reason. Later, when he gets to retrieving, and birds are actually shot for him, he quite likely will have a tendency to whine, or even to bark, from pure excitement, while waiting to be sent. If this is not curbed at once, it can develop into a serious fault.

A dog that makes a racket in a duck blind, just as a bunch of mallards set their wings and come in to your decoys, will obviously spoil many shots for you. This is an easy fault to prevent, right from the start, but a hard one to correct after it becomes established and a dog gets to giving mouth like a hound every time he sees a bird in the air or hears a shot.

For this reason, in the retriever trials the judges are quite severe on a dog even for whining softly on the line or in the blind. They penalize for this, and sometimes even disqualify the dog entirely, in open all-age stakes. The easiest way to avoid this trouble is to make sure your dog understands what you mean when you say, "Stop that noise."

COMMAND: STOP THAT NOISE
(See Illustration 50)

Whether it's a pup or an older dog, the first procedure is the same. When he starts making a racket, try to sneak up on him, and catch him right in the act of howling or barking.

Hold his mouth shut with one hand, waggle a stern finger at him with the other, and tell him firmly, in the tone of command, *"Stop that noise."* Repeat this admonition several times, then go back in the house.

If he tunes up again, as he probably will, go out and repeat the above procedure, and then lock him in his little doghouse for the night. You should of course have a bolt on the door of the house for this purpose. Let him go ahead and howl himself to sleep. The noise will be sufficiently muffled by the house that it won't quite drive you crazy, or be bad enough that the neighbors will bring down the law on you—for a night or two, anyway.

Many young retrievers will be pretty well cured in one night, some will take two or three. Just be sure, until you win this argument, that the dog associates two unpleasant things in his memory each time he sets up a racket. First, having his mouth held shut, and being scolded by the boss. Second, being confined in his house for the night.

This treatment will probably be sufficient for your dog. But if you should draw one who thinks he throws back to a wolf or coyote ancestor, who persists in howling at the moon, and you begin to run out of patience—then it's time to go a bit further. One way or another, "Stop that noise" must be learned.

With a young pup, say under nine months, I would hesitate to apply any severe treatment, but would simply continue the scoldings, and locking him in his house. This is almost sure to win, fairly soon, with a puppy.

But with an older dog, after you know darned well he knows what is meant by "stop that noise," I wouldn't fool around more than three nights before beginning to apply more pressure. I enjoy my own sleep too well to spend very many nights arguing with a noisy dog.

First, try really squeezing when you hold his mouth closed, hard enough to pinch his lip against his teeth, while you're repeating the command. This won't actually hurt him much, but every dog hates it, and this likely will be enough punishment to win the debate.

I can remember owning only one Labrador who needed more drastic treatment, and she was my first one—old Nell. We lived in a Chicago suburb then, and the neighbors were beginning to get pretty tired of her nightly music, after about a week of it.

She knew perfectly well what I wanted when I staggered out there in my pajamas in the middle of the night, pinched her lip, and told her in no uncertain terms to stop that noise. Each time she would pipe down for about half an hour, but just as I was getting back to sleep, the singing would start again, louder than ever. She was rapidly alienating the whole block, not to mention my long-suffering wife. When I locked Nell in her house it did no good. She just howled twice as loudly.

I was still green enough to be pretty squeamish about licking a dog, but at last was driven to a choice between this, a possible divorce, and a quite probable tar and feather party, with me as guest of honor. So at last I went out there with a heavy leather leash, and really gave her a housecleaning—what you would call a good old-fashioned thrashing. She took it in stride, but for the rest of that night she was quiet.

I thought I had won—but I didn't know Nell. Remember—she is the one I struggled with for three years, before waking up to the obvious truth she wasn't worth fooling with.

Anyway, the very next night after her licking, she was at it again, howling like a zombie. And then, in desperation, I invented my Bomb. I strung together, on a long strong cord, a nest of assorted tin cans. I suspended this on a small pulley just above the spot at the end of the run where she liked to sit and do her nocturnal singing to the moon. I secured the other end of the cord to the railing of a sleeping porch just outside my bedroom.

That night when she started the music, I leaned out the window and shouted, "Stop that noise." As usual, she paid no attention. I waited five minutes, smoked a cigarette, then crept out on the porch, untied the cord, and dropped the Bomb. The tin cans landed right beside old Nell, on the concrete run. In the quiet of the night they made an unearthly racket. It scared hell out of her. She scuttled into her house, and was quiet for the rest of the night.

I was only obliged to drop the Bomb once more, and then Nell was convinced that it paid to heed the command. After that, when she would occasionally try a couple of tentative yips, it was enough to shout "stop that noise." She would scurry for her house, sure that the Bomb would follow.

If your dog is stubborn about this command, another useful stunt is to shout it out the window first, then turn on a light that the dog can see—a yard light, back-porch light, or even some light inside the house. Wait five minutes, and *then* go out to administer the licking, or drop the Bomb, or do whatever unpleasant thing you're going to do. After that, it will usually be sufficient just to turn on the light to quiet the varmint. He'll associate this with the punishment, and figure that's coming next.

But if you have to resort to these severe measures, and it takes more than two or three nights for the dog to respond to this command, the chances are you have a hardheaded individual who will be just as stubborn in all his later training—and your best bet is to get rid of him and get another dog. At this early stage, you probably won't do it. But, friend, you'll find out—just as I did.

HOUSEBREAKING

I'm going to include here what I've learned about housebreaking not only retrievers, but all the miscellaneous house pets we've been guilty of harboring and cherishing.

Even if your retriever lives in an outside kennel, as he should, you'll have him in the house with you at times. Also, you don't want him messing up hotel rooms when you have him on hunting trips. Hotel and motel keepers are inclined to be ugly about this.

I think I've tried most of the recommended methods for house-breaking. A very common one is training the pup to do his business on a newspaper. This is easy to do, but I don't see much sense in it. Every dog I've ever trained this way, sooner or later, when I was taking my ease of a Sunday, with the paper strewn comfortably around the living-room floor, would fix up the sporting section before I had a chance to read it.

Even if your family is neater than mine, and you never have papers on the floor except the one the dog is supposed to use, it is still a damn nuisance to have to bundle up these savory little packages and dispose of them several times a day. In my opinion there is only one sensible place for a dog to relieve himself, and that is outside.

And there is only one way to teach that. During the first few days you have the dog in the house—*never give him a chance to make a mistake*. Until he understands he should never do it in the house, someone must be watching him every minute. The instant he starts sniffing around, acting as if he has to go, take him out immediately. Take him to the same place, every time, right from the start. You don't want dog messes all over your nice lawn, or flower garden. Take him behind the garage, or to a vacant lot next door, or to some place he can use as a toilet area without being a nuisance to *anyone*.

Don't let him start doing it on a neighbor's lawn or garden. This is likely to start a feud that will make the Hatfields' and the McCoys' little squabble seem like a mild disagreement between boy scouts. You think it's silly to mention this? You'd be surprised how many thoughtless dog owners are guilty of this imposition on their neighbors.

Always, when you take him out to the proper place, give the command "hie on." (Rhymes with *lie*. See Illustration 51.) Then say, "Be a good dog." Say this in a cheery, encouraging voice. You'll be surprised how quickly he'll get it, and it will speed up his performance, and save you a lot of standing around and waiting.

This command comes in particularly handy when you have him on a hunting trip, and take him out of your hotel room to a strange place to do his business. If he understands then what you mean by "be a good dog," he'll get down to business with much less preliminary sniffing of bushes. You'll be able to get back to your highball that much faster, and to explaining to the gang just how you happened to miss that cock pheasant you needed to fill your limit.

Now it's a nuisance, especially if—tsk—you keep your dog in the house all the time, to have to watch him every minute he's awake during the first two or three days. But this is the only real way to housebreak him, and in the long run it's by far the easiest way. In addition to taking him right out whenever he shows signs of having the urge, you should take him out anyway at regular intervals, whether he wants to or not. With a young pup this should be every two hours. With an older dog, every three hours is often enough. If you simply don't give him the chance to start the habit of doing wrong in the house, you'll be amazed at how quickly he'll form the good habit of doing it in the proper place outside. Dogs are such slaves to habit, and form them so quickly, that he'll soon be reluctant to do his business anywhere but at the regular specified place.

Quite likely you yourself can't be there to watch the pup constantly for the first few days he's in the house, and if so you have to delegate the job part of the time to a servant or another member of the family. Someone has to do it. And whoever has the duty, it is his fault if the dog is permitted to make his first mistake.

If this should happen, there is nothing to do but show him the crime, scold him sternly, say "no" several times, and then take him right out to the proper place, and tell him to "be a good dog." I've never accomplished anything by rubbing a dog's nose in a mess he made in the house. It seems to be much harder on the rug and on me than on the dog. This is ineffective as punishment, and sometimes leads to depraved appetite, getting a pup started eating his own stools.

After a very few times of doing his stuff at the correct place outside, the dog prefers to do it there, and will start telling you when he wants to go out, either by whining or by scratching at the door. When he once starts this, you can begin relaxing your vigilance. But for several weeks, as a precaution, he should be taken out at least two or three times a day, whether he asks or not.

Now nobody in his right mind is going to get up to take a dog out every two or three hours, all through the night. And fortunately this isn't necessary, even with a quite young pup.

A good retriever, or any dog worth keeping of any breed, is naturally clean, and instinctively will not foul the place where he sleeps. So, until he is thoroughly housebroken, all you have to do at night is to tie the dog on a short chain, not over four or five feet long—wherever he is to sleep. This serves a double purpose. In addition to housebreaking him to hold everything through the night, it also gets him in the habit of sleeping where you want him to, whether it's in a corner of the kitchen, the basement, or the master's bedroom. But the minute you get up in the morning, take him out instantly to "be a good dog."

If you should be unlucky enough to draw a dirty individual, who will persistently foul his own nest, then you will have to do one of three things:

1. Resort to severe punishment, including walloping if necessary.

2. Give up, and keep him outside in a kennel run, where he really belongs anyway. This will save you all this trouble about housebreaking, because even the dirtiest dog will eventually learn he's more comfortable if he doesn't foul the small house where he sleeps, and will finally get to using the run. He will housebreak himself, in effect. Then, when you take him hunting, if you tie him short in a corner of your bedroom, you'll probably have no difficulty. He will have taught himself not to foul his nest.

3. Or—yes—get rid of the dog.

Before we leave the kindergarten stuff, just a few words for the people who are always asking how to train a dog to stop chasing cars, tipping over the neighbor's garbage can, biting people, and being a general neighborhood nuisance.

CHASING CARS

If your dog is properly confined, this problem will never come up, and that is the best solution. But if you're going to be knuckleheaded about this thing, and insist on trying to give your dog the run of the place; if you claim he never leaves the yard *except* to chase cars—and you want to cure that—there's only one way I know or have ever heard of.

That is to set a trap for him. Get a friend to drive you up and down the street in front of your place, in a strange car. Conceal yourself on the floor, in back. When your dog gives chase, have the driver slam on the brakes and stop quickly. You come roaring out of the car, and chase the dog home. Try to give him the surprise of his life. If this doesn't work the first time, then make yourself a tin-can bomb, and hurl this at the dog, from the car. As a last resort, jump out, catch him, and give him a walloping he'll remember the rest of his life. It may require very severe treatment to cure this craze. It's up to you whether you want to dish it out, or keep the dog penned up after all, or let him ultimately die under the wheels of an automobile.

RAIDING GARBAGE CANS

If a dog gets to roaming the neighborhood and becoming a nuisance, he is automatically accumulating many bad habits that will utterly ruin him as a working retriever. But if you don't care about this, and are keeping him just as a pet, and if you are determined to give him his "freedom," then you'd better try to cure him of his more offensive tricks. If you don't, the problem will be solved anyway. You will lose the dog. He will be poisoned, or shot.

Did somebody else's dog ever get to raiding your garbage can? If so, you know how annoying this can become. A dog who forms this habit invariably tips over the can, spreads the contents all over your yard, and paws through it for selected delicacies. If a dog keeps coming back to yours, night after night, I suppose it's a nice compliment to the quality of your garbage. But it gets to be something of a nuisance, cleaning up the mess every morning, and can finally bring a man to a pretty violent frame of mind.

If a neighbor should complain that *your* dog is doing this to him, you'd better take steps to stop it, fast. If you like, you can try setting another trap. If you're silly enough to lose all the time and sleep, go ahead and stake out in the neighbor's yard— try to catch the dog in the act, and punish him severely. This may mean many hours, or even nights of waiting. Personally I don't have that much time to waste on any dog. And even a severe licking may not cure this nasty habit. It probably will relieve that particular neighbor. But everyone has a garbage can. The dog will probably start working a different one the very next night.

A friend of mine had this problem with his dog. At last in desperation he bought an air rifle, loaned it to the currently ag-grieved neighbor, and authorized him to use it on the dog—with certain specified precautions.

They moved the garbage can from the back porch to the rear of the yard, and carefully stepped off the distance. It was a good 150 feet—50 yards—from the house. The neighbor, a hunter and a careful man with a gun, agreed to shoot from his bedroom win-dow only when the dog was presenting his stern as a target, to avoid any possibility of hitting an eye.

That same night the dog found the can in its new location with no trouble at all. The neighbor heard the clatter as it went over. He crept to the bedroom window with the air gun.

In the bright moonlight he could clearly see the dog, with his head down among the pork-chop bones, and his south end presented temptingly toward the house. *Target for tonight!* He let the dog have it. The shot was a beauty, a bull's-eye on the big muscle of a rear flank.

It produced instant results. With a startled yip the dog leaped high in the air. He came down running. He went away from that dangerous garbage can, but fast.

Of course at that distance he couldn't really be hurt by a B-B gun. The pellet didn't even break the skin. But it stung enough to startle and frighten him, and to implant in his memory a mighty unpleasant association with the business of raiding garbage cans.

My friend claims this permanently cured the dog of the garbage-can craze. He says it was better for the dog to be carefully shot by a B-B gun than eventually to have his head blown off with a real weapon, by some less forbearing neighbor.

Such a solution is a bit risky at best. And it depends on your dog's locating a co-operative garbage-can owner, who is also a good shot.

Personally I would prefer just to keep the dog at home nights, in his pen, where he belongs.

BITING PEOPLE

Most retrievers have no meanness in them, and you rarely find one who will bite unless greatly provoked. But occasionally even one of these gives his owner a great surprise. Often it is the mildest-mannered dog—of any breed—around home, who is most dangerous to other people when he roams.

The only really painful dog bite I ever received was from an Irish Setter, a mild-mannered breed if there ever was one. This was a beautiful dog, with limpid brown eyes. But in his soul he was no good. He was a wandering mutt, a spoiled and pampered pet.

When I was working in my garden in my own back yard, he would come in there, and bark and snarl at me, insanely. I was naturally a bit annoyed, but would always chase him out by tossing a clod of dirt at him, and think no more about it. One day he changed his tactics. Without making a sound, he sneaked up behind me, and sunk his teeth in my leg. This was too much.

I carried him home by the ears. When his owner saw and heard us coming, he was greatly indignant over my method of returning his pet. He wanted to make something of it.

Speechless with rage, I showed him my bleeding leg. He simply didn't believe his dog did it.

He shouted, "You're crazy. Rex never bites. He wouldn't bite anybody."

For some reason the dog owners who neglect their pets most are always the surest they can do no wrong. Naturally, a sneak like Rex won't bite anybody when his master is around. But the so-and-so bit me, without provocation. And in my own yard. That, I didn't like. I told his owner so. I told him if it ever happened again, I thought Rex's dark red hide would make me a nice rug. Such conversation doesn't help neighborhood relations.

Nobody has the right to keep a dog and allow it to become a nuisance to others. If you don't know where your dog is, you don't know what he's doing. And the chances are, whatever it is, it isn't good. If he starts wandering, there is only one decent thing to do—and one safe thing for the dog himself.

That—once more—is to keep him confined except when you are with him.

Chapter 12

GRADE SCHOOL—OBEDIENCE TRAINING

WITH ONLY EIGHT basic obedience commands you can keep your dog under easy and quiet control, whether he's a working retriever or a house pet of any breed.

Before you start teaching these, it is best to wait a few days after bringing home a new dog or pup. Give him a chance to get over his shyness, and to become accustomed to his new surroundings. If you have much argument over "stop that noise," wait until he's reasonably happy about that before going on with his further schooling. Try to feed him yourself during this period. Pet him, and talk to him, and build up his confidence in you. This will take very little time, and will make the whole training job easier.

After you have become well acquainted, you can start teaching these obedience commands any time you're ready—to a pup of three months or more, or to a dog of any age. Contrary to popular impression these commands can even be taught to a very old dog who has been spoiled, if he has a reasonably good memory, and an inherent desire to please a man.

Obviously it may take a bit longer for a young and playful pup to grasp them, but a dog of twelve months or so, if he's worth training at all, should be responding within *two weeks* at the most to these eight commands. Furthermore, you can accomplish this magic result in only ten minutes a day, through the simple principle of *doubling up* and *pyramiding*.

Most people just can't believe this. But I've done it myself, many times, and so can you. Ten minutes a day for fourteen days—a total of two hours and twenty minutes of your valuable time—is all you need to spend to have a dog with perfect manners, and to convince your astonished friends and family that you are one hell of an animal tamer.

There is just one catch. Don't expect these fast results if your dog is exhausted by play, or just plain bored, when you take him out for his first lesson, or any lesson. If you insist on making a house pet of him, then you should pen him up or tie him up on a short chain, and allow nobody to go near him, for at least two hours before you try to teach him anything.

Any decent retriever—even a young pup—should then be able to take a ten-minute stretch of intensive training without becoming indifferent or sulky. If he shows signs of wanting to quit on you too soon, he may be sick, and you should have a good vet examine him. But if he's healthy—and isn't keen enough to take ten minutes of serious work a day—then he isn't worth fooling with.

1. THE COMMAND: SIT
(See Illustrations 26–33)

This command is now used by virtually all retriever trainers in this country, and is preferred to the old country command, "hup." I've never discovered how the latter word originated, what it meant, or why it was used. But many English trainers still use it.

If you should import a trained dog from England, and he just looks blank when you say "sit," see what happens on "hup." If he responds, I would recommend switching him over, teaching him "sit," anyway.

Why? Because it is almost impossible to say "hup" quietly, and still make the sound convey authority. If the dog is trained to "sit," you can eventually have him sit by just hissing through your teeth—making an "s" sound. This comes in handy in the blind, when ducks are coming in, to be able to remind your dog to be steady without making a big racket. And it is *mighty* useful if you ever handle him in a field trial. The judges can scarcely hear a little soft hissing, and they won't penalize the dog for unsteadiness unless they hear you making a lot of noise, loudly nagging at him for the apparent purpose of keeping him steady.

To teach your dog "sit," just hold him by the scruff or the collar with one hand, and push his fanny down with the other. As you do this, say "sit!" in a firm tone.

If you have any trouble pushing his hindquarters down, use a rocking motion from fore to aft, exerting rearward and downward pressure simultaneously. This way you can easily tip a big dog over into a sitting position, without having to force him to bend his hind legs.

Keep repeating the command "sit," while you hold him firmly in the sitting position for a few seconds. Then release him. Praise him and pet him for a moment. Then repeat the whole routine two or three times. By now he should begin to associate the command with the simple action. Try it, without touching him.

Speak the command firmly, at the same time holding up one hand with extended index finger. (See illustration.) This admonitory hand signal will come in handy later at times, if right from the start the dog associates it with the command to sit. There will be times when he is far out in the field with a strong wind blowing, when he can't hear the whistle, and then it's useful to be able to stop him with the motionless upstretched arm.

If he doesn't sit at once on the spoken command, push him down again. But a good dog should be doing it without help, before the first ten-minute lesson is over.

The first few times he does it, make him stay in the sitting position only a few seconds. Then release him by jumping up, moving a few steps away, clapping your hands, and calling "come." He'll be delighted by his release, bound after you, and thus make a start also on learning the command "come," within the very first brief lesson. Each time after he *sits*, then *comes* a few steps to you, pet him and make a fuss over him, and tell him he's a fine dog.

After the ten minutes are up, put him back in his kennel, no matter how much fun you're having. If you're determined to cram the obedience training into him, it's all right to take him out again the same day for one more ten-minute lesson—*but only after an intermission of several hours*. And actually, you'll get fast enough results to satisfy anyone with just one lesson a day.

The next time you take him out, tell him to sit at once. If he's at all slow about it, remind him by pushing him down. Keep at it until he obeys at once, without help.

A dog should know darned well what the command means after that first lesson. But if he's a little slow, give him the benefit of the doubt, and continue during the second and third lessons just to push him down, if necessary.

After that, I wouldn't fool around much. If he is slow at all about putting it down, whack him on the fanny with the flat of your hand. This should be enough, unless—unhappy man—you should be struggling with a hammerhead like old Nell. I finally had to resort to the strap, even to convince her it was a sound idea to *sit* when I suggested it.

Every time you take the dog out, after that first lesson, start out by having him sit, before going on with the main business of the day. Gradually increase the time you require him to stay in that position, without moving, until you have him up to a minute or so.

When he seems quite steady, move back a step or two, holding up that finger and telling him firmly to sit, as you move away. Keep gradually increasing the distance, until you can move ten or twelve feet away from him. If he chisels or moves at all, put him back on the exact spot where he belongs—scold him, and sternly tell him to "sit." *Never* let him get away with chiseling.

This can develop into a bad fault. Sometimes you see an itchy retriever who can cover an astonishing amount of territory without ever lifting his fanny off the ground. This is a nuisance when hunting, and very bad in field trials.

2. THE COMMAND: COME
(See Illustrations 42–45)

The dog should sit well enough at the beginning of the second lesson so that you need only devote two or three minutes to this, and can bear down for the rest of the session on "come."

Have him sit for a few seconds. Then suddenly turn, run *away* from him, clapping your hands and calling "come." (This is the conventional command. I use "come along," myself. Either is perfectly all right, and you can take your choice.)

It is the natural thing for any young dog, or young puppy, to chase you when you run away from him. This should be all that's necessary to teach him to "come." I've never yet had to resort to forcing methods on any Labrador I've trained, even including Nell.

However, some trainers tell me they occasionally have to resort to the rope—and we may as well include this method here—just in case you should be unlucky enough to need it. If the dog simply won't chase you when you run away, get yourself twenty or thirty feet of clothesline. Tie a harness snap on one end of it. Lay the line on the floor, across the room. Have the dog sit. Quietly attach the snap to his collar. Move away, and get the rope in your hand.

Then clap your hands, and call "come," enthusiastically. If he doesn't respond, give a light jerk on the rope. Don't haul him in, hand over hand. Keep giving smart jerks, calling "come" each time, until you have moved him up to you. He'll soon give up, and come under his own power. Then pet him, and praise him, and make a fuss over him.

Now try it a few times, attempting to confuse him as to whether the rope is attached or not. Have it laid out on the floor, but do some sleight of hand with the snap, sometimes attaching it to his collar, sometimes not. You can teach the dumbest dog to come this way, if you want to bother with it. Personally, I don't.

The chances are this won't be necessary, if you are careful to be alone with your dog when you are teaching him to "come," so here's nothing else for him to do but chase after you when you run away. If there is a large admiring audience, any pup might be distracted, and run around sniffing all the nice people, instead of paying attention to his new boss's antics.

Each time you run away, stoop down quickly just as he catches up to you, take him in your arms, and pet him and praise him. After he has done this three or four times, try calling "come" and clapping your hands—without running away. But be ready to jump up and start moving away, if he slows up or stops before he gets clear up to you.

He should be coming to you fast, on command, within two or three lessons at the most.

As soon as he is responding well to the spoken command, begin also using the whistle. Say "come," clap your hands, and quickly blow *two or more* fast blasts on the whistle. Be sure you *never* blow just one blast to have the dog come. Most handlers blow *four* times, in quick succession.

Later, when your dog is ready to learn to take directions from your hand signals, you'll be teaching him to stop and *sit* when you blow just *one* whistle blast. So you can avoid later confusion between the two uses of the whistle by being careful right from the start to use the correct whistle signal for "come."

To a properly trained retriever the sound of the whistle means just one of two things:

1. Several quick blasts mean *come* right now, and fast.

2. One sharp blast means stop and *sit* instantly, and look at the boss for further directions.

3. THE COMMAND: KENNEL
(See Illustrations 38–41)

This command means, "Go in your kennel; or, jump in the car; or, get in the duck boat."

There is no need to devote any separate lessons to this. Every time you put him away, have him *sit* before the door of his house, or the gate to his run. Then point to the opening and say "kennel." The first two or three times you'll have to take him by the scruff or the collar and heave him in. But he'll learn what this command means very quickly, and after that you should insist on instant obedience to it every time. Sometimes a dog will want to stall on this one, like a child procrastinating about going to bed. A whack or two on the rear end with a rolled newspaper should be enough to convince him that when pappy says "kennel," he means it.

The first time you want him to get in the back of the car, or into a shipping crate, or a boat, or any strange place or conveyance, have him sit first, then point where you want him to go and say "kennel." Toss him in, if necessary. He'll soon learn to get into any place or any thing, when you give this command.

This is easy to teach, yet for some reason it makes a spectacular impression on people when they see a dog smartly obey this simple command.

4. THE COMMAND: HEEL
(See Illustrations 46–49)

If you are right handed, train your dog to walk at heel on your left side, so there will be no danger of accidentally shooting him when you carry your gun under your right arm. If you shoot from the left side, of course, you'll want him to "heel" on the right side.

Actually on this command he should walk along smartly, his head held high, with his nose beside your knee, neither forging ahead nor lagging behind. Insist on perfect performance to this command, and don't allow him to start getting sloppy, wandering away from your side to sniff bushes. This can be a nuisance to you, and also very dangerous to the dog when you're hunting heavy cover—particularly if there is a trigger-happy member of your party who shoots at rabbits on the ground.

As soon as your pupil is responding reasonably well to "sit" and "come," you can start teaching "heel"—surely by the fourth or fifth lesson.

Let him out of his kennel and have him *sit* for a moment. Then move away, and have him *come*. (In this and all succeeding essons, give him a quick refresher course in all the commands he *has* learned, before going on with the new one.)

Now attach your short leash to his collar. Get him on your left side, pat your left leg, and step off briskly—saying "come." Try, through repeating this command, and plenty of encouragement by patting your leg, to get him coming along beside you without even realizing he is under the restraint of leash and collar.

But if he doesn't get it this easily, and pulls back against the leash, don't then start dragging him around the yard, choking him with the collar. Any young dog is likely to be somewhat panicky the first time he feels the restraint of leash and a tightening slip collar, and may plunge around, fighting it, like a calf on the end of a cowpuncher's rope.

Don't let it get this far. If he pulls back, hold him there just long enough for you to get to him. Then release the pressure on the collar, and take him in your arms and talk to him and pet him. If you do this two or three times, he'll quickly find you mean to do him no damage with the collar—and you'll avoid a knock-down drag-out argument.

In one lesson he should get to walking along beside you, on the leash, without pressure on the leash. But if he's a little stubborn about it, apply pressure only in quick tugs, pulling him up beside you, then releasing the pressure on the collar immediately. Keep using the command "come," which he already knows, until he is going along cheerfully beside you on a slack leash.

Then it is time to start saying "heel" as he walks in correct position. Keep repeating this constantly, in a cheery tone when he's right, sternly when he lags or forges ahead. Pull him into position with a short jerk on the leash.

Sometimes with an eager lunatic like Muscles, for instance, who insists on forging ahead, you need to jerk him back until your arm is tired, and your patience begins to wear thin. A simple cure for this is to hold a stick in front of his nose. If he tries to push ahead of it, rap him on the nose with it, lightly. This will soon convince him that when you say "heel," you don't mean "lead the parade."

As soon as he is responding to the "heel" command on leash, take it off. Step along briskly, patting your leg and repeating the command constantly. Use the stick if necessary to keep him from getting ahead.

A dog should learn to heel in one lesson, so you can even dispense with the stick in front of his nose. The four pictures (Illustrations 46–49) are actual photographs of the first ten-minute session I had with Muscles on this command. I'll admit I've had to give him a few reminders with the stick since, but he was doing pretty well at the end of that first lesson. Any *normal* dog should do much better.

Thereafter, every time you take him out, give him some walking at heel, and insist that he do it perfectly—just as you do with each of the other commands.

5. THE COMMAND: HIE ON
(See Illustration 51)

You need devote no particular lesson time to this. Eventually it will come to mean to the dog, "Never mind walking at heel. *At ease.* Run on ahead. Beat it. Go hunting. Use your nose. Or, do your business."

Whenever you have the dog where it is safe for him to run a bit, without getting on a street or highway, send him on with this command. First have him walk at heel, then wave him ahead with a sweeping arm motion, and say, "Hie on!" You should begin this before he gets too good at the heeling. If you wait too long before he begins to understand this one, he may be reluctant to leave your side.

Then you might have to run ahead, get him running, and stop suddenly, to convince him it's actually okay for him to get out in front of you.

It is good for a pup or young dog to take him for a walk in open country and give him a chance to run, whenever it is convenient for you. If you live in a crowded city, you can still give him a run occasionally in a big vacant lot, in a park or a golf course, or on a beach.

But when you do this, don't let him get too far away from you. If you prevent him from ranging too far out, right from the start, you won't have to break this bad habit later when you begin using him to hunt ahead of you, and want him to flush birds within easy gun range.

When you tell him to hie on, call him back whenever he gets more than twenty-five yards away from you. A fast youngster who is eager to run will sometimes discover the only way he can do so, without being called in all the time, is to dash back and forth in front of you, like a windshield wiper. Thus, he'll be teaching himself to quarter ahead of the gun, while he's just out for a romp. Some dogs will do this—some won't. Don't worry about it if yours doesn't. It's simple enough to teach him to quarter correctly, after he's learned in college to take directions from hand signals.

For now, just don't allow him to get more than twenty-five yards from you, after the command "hie on." The only time a retriever should be permitted to go farther afield is when he is sent to retrieve. And for that, of course, the command "hie on" will never be used.

6. THE COMMAND: NO

This is a very useful and important command, but here again no formal lesson time need be wasted on it. Whenever the dog does a wrong thing, and you wish him to stop it, simply restrain him or stop him, using whatever physical force is necessary—at the same time saying "no!" Say it as sternly as you can. Shout it if necessary.

He will understand what it means very quickly. Then you must insist on instant obedience, even if you have to resort to severe punishment to convince him you mean it. For this command—in addition to making him a decent citizen—will quite likely save his life, sooner or later. It will save him from a truck, or a mowing machine, or a rattlesnake, or quicksand, or some other form of sudden death. It is one command on which I will not compromise with any dog.

7. THE COMMAND: DOWN
(See Illustrations 52 and 53)

No dog should be permitted to jump up on people. And for a gun dog, it must be absolutely forbidden. It is exceedingly dangerous to both man and beast for a big retriever suddenly to leap up on you when you have a loaded shotgun in your hands.

Probably the most commonly recommended cure is to step on the dog's hind toes when he jumps up on you. I've never had much luck with this. Maybe I'm not fast enough on my feet. Either I miss those hind toes entirely, or in lunging for them, throw myself off balance. About that time I'm hit on the chest by those big forepaws—with eighty pounds or so of projectile behind them, and I land flat on my back.

I've found it much easier and more effective simply to grab those *forepaws* as they come up, and squeeze them—at the same time saying "no!"—immediately followed by "down!" Each time the dog jumps up, squeeze the paws a little harder. They are quite sensitive, and you'll be surprised how few times it will be necessary to squeeze them before "down" is thoroughly understood.

Each time, as you squeeze his toes and push him down, scold him a little, and repeat the command a few times. Tell him he's a bad dog. He'll get it.

This same command should also be used for keeping any dog down off the furniture. Whenever he gets up on something, throw him off, at the same time saying "down!" Bothering to do this is cheap insurance for a continuing happy marriage.

8. THE COMMAND: CHARGE
(See Illustrations 34-37)

This command means "lie down," but don't ask me why. It is used by most of the obedience trainers, and is part of the customary jargon in the obedience classes in bench shows. Use it if you like, or if you feel too silly saying it, it's perfectly all right just to say "lie down" instead.

The professional retriever trainers don't usually bother to teach this command. There is little practical reason for it in retriever work, if the dog is kept confined in a kennel most of the time. I've heard people say it is useful at times to have a retriever lie down beside you in cover, to hide him from ducks.

I claim any cover that will hide me from a duck will hide a dog sitting up. I also claim ducks pay no attention to a sitting dog, even right out in the open. And I like to have my dog sitting up, so he can mark falls. I can't recall a single time in my own hunting experience when it would have been of any value to have a dog respond instantly to the command "charge."

If you have your dog in the house a lot, you may want to teach him this command. Of course if you just have him sit, he'll lie down anyway, when he sees nothing exciting is going to happen, after a few minutes. But if you enjoy showing your friends how he will instantly flatten out like a rug before the fire, there's no harm in it, and it will take only a few minutes to teach this one.

First have him sit. Then pull his front paws out from under him, toward you—and he's lying down. At the same time say "charge!" Repeat it two or three times, and he has it. That's all there is to it.

REPETITION OF OBEDIENCE COMMANDS

Your dog now knows what you mean by these commands. To keep improving his response to them, all you need is a little repetition every time you take him out.

This will require no special effort on your part, for you'll automatically give him all the reminding he needs if you simply keep him under control, as you should anyway if you want a decent hunting dog.

When he's out with you he should either be walking at *heel*, *sitting*, *lying down*, ranging just ahead of you after the command *hie on*, or *coming* to your command or to your whistle.

Never just let him wander around aimlessly, either inside or outside the house, on his own. Even when you have him out for a walk, and have told him to "hie on," leave him out in front only as long as he runs around and hunts happily and aggressively. The minute he gets listless and appears indifferent, bring him right in and finish the walk with him at heel.

Likely you won't see the importance of this at first—but take my word for it. If you want a really keen performer in the field— a dog you can be proud of—then form this habit right now. Keep him under control every minute he's out of his kennel.

Order him "down" every time he jumps on you, a guest, or the living-room couch.

Say "no" whenever he does any undesirable thing, and make it stick.

Say "kennel" whenever you put him away, or want him to get in the car.

All this will seem a bit stuffy right at first, but if you stay with it you'll be surprised how fast you're doing it unconsciously, like shifting gears in a car. Then, with no particular effort on your part, you'll be improving your dog every time you're with him.

Chapter 13

JUNIOR HIGH—SINGLE MARKED RETRIEVES

FOR MANY GENERATIONS retrievers have been bred and selected for the powerful instinct to do one special job—to go out and retrieve anything that falls. It should never be necessary to "force break" one of these dogs to perform this function.

Pointers and setters, whose main purpose is finding and pointing live birds, often lack interest in retrieving, and must be force trained. I have shot quail over many such dogs whose work was a joy to see—until dead birds were down—but who then were indifferent and even downright sulky about bringing them to bag. You could make these dogs do it, but you couldn't make them like it.

There is some excuse for putting up with slovenly retrieving work from a good pointing dog. But I certainly wouldn't give a nickel for a *retriever* who must be forced to go out and do the thing he was born to do. I wouldn't waste time on such a dog, and I wouldn't recommend that you do, either.

Force training such a dog is really a job for a top-notch professional trainer. But if you insist on trying it yourself, there are many good books on bird-dog training that will tell you how. One of the best is *Elias Vail Trains Gun Dogs*, by Ella B. Moffett.

So I won't waste space here on detailed methods of force training. They are all fundamentally the same. One way or another you force the dog to go out to the dummy—either by dragging him out there yourself, or by having a helper haul him out on a rope. Then you put the dummy in his mouth, and make him hold it. Then you haul him back to where you were in the first place.

This can be a long-drawn-out process that *really* requires a lot of time and patience. And even when you get through, you'll probably have at best a slow, sloppy, indifferent performer. It's no fun to hunt with a dog like that.

I would hang him in the smokehouse, and get a dog who is downright delighted to be given the opportunity to retrieve.

STARTING A DOG TO RETRIEVE
(See Illustrations 54–57)

If your dog is a year old or more, and has had his two-week course in obedience, he's ready to start retrieving. Even at eight or nine months, if he's really keen for it, it won't hurt a pup to give him two or three simple retrieves a day—but no more than that, *please*.

Never throw a stick or a ball for him, or anything else but his regular training dummy. Never send him to fetch a bottle of beer, or your bedroom slippers. Such parlor tricks are amusing to your friends, but are confusing to the dog. In the field you don't want him bringing you a stick or an empty bottle when you've sent him to trail a crippled pheasant.

Let him know right from the start that the training dummy means business. When you send him after it, he's to hunt until he finds it—and nothing else.

The land dummy, made of an old gunny sack, should be rolled quite tightly into a cylinder about a foot long and two inches in diameter. Bind it together securely with strong cord, so there are no loose edges by which the dog can pick it up. You want him to start right out taking a proper "body hold" on it.

For the first lesson in retrieving, be sure to be alone with the dog, in an enclosed place. A two-car garage, with doors closed, is big enough. Or a well-fenced yard, containing no cats to chase, or other distractions.

Hold the dummy in your hand, and tease the dog with it. Wave it around, and try to get him jumping and grabbing at it. Don't frighten him by shaking it too close to his nose. You don't want him to get the notion you're going to hit him with it. Some youngsters take a little more time than others to get the idea that this is a new and exciting game.

It often helps to jump around yourself as you wave the dummy, and occasionally feint at throwing it. Keep up a running fire of excited conversation. Such as, "Oh, boy! What's this? Some fun, hey keed?" It doesn't matter what you say. Your tone of voice will help to fire the dog with excitement, and to awaken his fierce instinct to retrieve. Keep up this teasing until he is fairly frantic to get the dummy.

Then maneuver yourself to the middle of the room or yard, so you will have plenty of room to run *away* from the dog the instant he picks up the dummy. Throw it a short distance, only ten or twelve feet the first time. If you have teased him enough, the dog will leap after it, very aggressively.

Pop your whistle in your mouth, and start blowing one sharp blast after another as soon as he grabs the dummy. Run away from him, keep running until he catches up to you, and lean down suddenly and snatch the dummy out of his mouth as he passes.

The only difficult part of this routine seems to be running away from the dog until he *completely* catches up and is about to pass you. A new trainer invariably stops too soon, turns around and lunges *at* the dog. This causes him to slow up, or even stop, and quite likely to drop the dummy before you can get your hand on it.

So force yourself to keep moving away—until you can scoop the dummy from his mouth as he passes you at full speed. If you do this, you can have your dog doing fast, stylish retrieves, and coming back fast, and *delivering to hand*—within a ten-minute lesson.

You may wonder why this running away business is necessary, when the dog has already been trained to come to your whistle. The main reason is literally to give him no chance even to *think* of dropping the dummy, after he has picked it up. If the first few times he retrieves, he delivers to your hand, this good habit will be established. Also, he will become accustomed to returning with the dummy just as fast as he goes out after it.

These habits can be well started in the first retrieving lesson. And by stirring your stumps a bit, you will have saved yourself a lot of later work, such as force training the dog to deliver to hand—and giving him exercises to speed up his return.

However, if you aren't a very classy fielder, and fumble the dummy, and the dog gets to dropping it somewhere near you, don't worry about it too much at this stage of the game. Don't try to make him pick it up again, or to force him to hold it in his mouth.

It is much more important for the present to develop fully his enthusiasm for retrieving, before you attempt any fussing or arguing about delivering to hand. You want no unpleasant association with that training dummy until he has reached the point where he would rather sail out to fetch it than go to heaven.

That's the easy, happy way to train a retriever. If he sizzles out when you throw the dummy, and brings it even part way back before dropping it—you're doing fine. Just pick it up. Pet and praise him, and assure him he's an elegant dog.

Then tease him with the dummy, and throw it again, and this time try to improve your own footwork, as well as your fielding. You're almost sure to have him retrieving to hand very soon.

The first day, quit after four or five retrieves, no matter how eager the dog is for more. Let him think it over for twenty-four hours. The next day he'll be fairly busting to go.

It is unlikely, but if by the end of the second lesson he is still dropping the dummy before you can grab it, then try using a much smaller one—say about an inch in diameter. After he gets to delivering this, you can then switch him back to the larger dummy. Of all the Labradors I've trained, I had to resort to this with only one—a young bitch with a very small mouth.

THE COMMAND FOR RETRIEVING

There is only one proper command for sending a retriever to make a retrieve. That is to speak his name. Whether you see any sense in it now or not, you'll be happy later if you train your dog this way.

Bird-dog trainers commonly use "fetch," or "go fetch," or "dead bird!" Obviously the big drawback to any of these is that when the command is spoken, every dog within earshot will go for the bird. Results: a spectacular dog fight, and a torn-up bird. For any kind of hunting, when there is more than one dog in the party, it's best if they're trained to go only on their names. And this is a must if you think you might ever wish to run your dog in a field trial.

No matter what sort of a long-winded and fancy registered name he has, select a short training name for him—a word of one or two syllables that is easy to say and to understand. Avoid a name starting with "s." Reason: you'll want to hiss at him to keep him steady. If his name is Sam, and you use that to send him, he's likely to end up with a nervous breakdown—trying to decide whether you mean *sit* or *Sam*.

After the first lesson in retrieving, begin speaking his name every time you throw the dummy. Say it with excitement and enthusiasm in your voice. Thus he will begin immediately to associate the name command with your permission to go and retrieve.

PLAYING WITH THE TRAINING DUMMY
(See Illustrations 58–61)

Sometimes an aggressive pup or young dog will have a tendency to shake the dummy like a rat, play with it, or even run away into a corner and lie down and chew on it. This must be corrected at once.

The easiest cure is simply to redouble your own exertions, which have already been described. Don't give him a chance to play with the dummy. Start blowing that whistle a split second *before* he reaches the dummy. Yell and clap your hands and run away like the devil himself was after you. Make so much racket that it's more exciting for the rascal to chase you than to play with the dummy.

This will almost always work. When the dog has thus been kidded and coaxed into delivering to hand just a few times, he discovers that if he doesn't waste time playing with the dummy, you'll throw it again for him just that much sooner. And that, after all, is the big treat. It's much more fun chasing the dummy than chewing it.

However, I'll admit this method involves a few minutes of strenuous exercise for you. If you run out of wind, perhaps you'd better have a small argument with the dog, and get it over with.

Tease him with the dummy, but hold your hand around it in such a way that he can't clamp down on it without biting you. When he tries to snap at it, scold him severely. Say "no" each time he tries to handle it too roughly. This is a good time also to start using that warning command "ah, ah, ah." (Like the "a" in cat.)

He will soon understand he must not bite that dummy, any more than he would bite your hand. But don't do more than two or three minutes of this exercise at one time, unless you have a very tough and aggressive dog who is really rough on the dummy. The danger, with an average young retriever, is that too much of this might make him dummy shy, and reluctant even to pick it up.

THE COMMAND: LEAVE IT

On training dummies, and later on birds, a retriever should take a sufficiently firm hold so that he won't drop even the heaviest cock pheasant. According to Martin Hogan's definition, a retriever is not "hard mouthed" if the birds he brings in are not crushed, and are fit for the table. However, he should give up a bird readily when you take it from him.

This is no problem with most Goldens or with at least half the Labradors, which are apt to be tender mouthed almost to a fault. But if your dog shows any tendency to hang onto the dummy when you try to take it, you should teach the command "leave it," starting early in the game.

Take hold of the dummy with one hand. Say "leave it," very firmly. At the same time grasp the dog's lower jaw with your other hand, and force his mouth open. If he needs more pressure than this to give up the dummy readily, then wrap your hand around his *upper* jaw, and press his upper lips against his teeth. Usually a very little of this will have him gently depositing the dummy in your hand when you say "leave it."

Later on, when you introduce him to real birds, you may need to give him a brief refresher course on this, using the same technique exactly.

TAKING A LINE

For the first three or four retrieving lessons, just keep tossing the dummy, gradually increasing the distance until you are throwing it as far as you can. Keep at this until the dog is retrieving it perfectly, going out *and* coming back with it as fast as he can run. With a really keen dog, you should be able to stop violently running away from him after the first or second lesson, without slowing his return. But please continue to *move backward* a step or two, just as he is approaching you, and snatch the dummy from his mouth *as you are moving away*.

If you begin standing still too soon, or lunging a step or two *toward* the dog to grab the dummy—you're just building up unnecessary trouble. This will cause almost any youngster to slow the last few yards of his return, and may start him dropping the dummy in front of you. If this fault is allowed to start, it can become progressively serious. At last, like old Nell, your dog will be spitting out the duck at the edge of the water, and telling you if you want it you can damn well walk over there and get it.

It can make you mighty mad if, just when you emerge from the blind to finish a retrieve for your dog, you frighten off a new flight of ducks. Also, it's a nuisance if you have to wade deep mud to get the abandoned bird.

For many practical reasons a retriever should always deliver right to hand. The easy way to accomplish this is to kid him into always doing so, right from the start.

The next step in his training is to start him taking a line, at the same time giving him longer retrieves. For this you'll need a bit larger area to work in, and a part-time helper to throw the dummy for you.

"Taking a line" means training the dog to follow the exact direction of a gesture you make with your hand, and to stay right on that line all the way to the fall. The simple way to teach this is to begin early giving him this line with your hand, just as you send him for every marked retrieve he makes. Later, when you come to blind retrieves, he will have become so accustomed to finding something right where the boss said it was—and where he knew it was anyway—that he will take your word for it even when he has seen nothing fall.

This is also exceedingly useful for assisting the dog's memory on double and triple retrieves.

If you work your dog from the left side, give the line with your left hand. Reach across and hold him lightly by the collar with your *right* hand. Don't make him sit—yet.

Have your helper walk out about as far as you've been throwing the dummy yourself. If your pitching wing is as old and tired as mine, this will be about twenty or twenty-five paces.

He should wave the dummy, and shout if necessary to get the dog's attention. But *don't* let him yell the dog's name. He can shout "boo," or make a noise like a gun—anything except any word that you use as a command.

When the dog is looking, the helper should toss the dummy high in the air, so it will land a few feet in front of him. Then he should stand absolutely still, make no motion or sound, while the dog is retrieving.

Let the dog go at once, while the dummy is still in the air. At the same time, speak his name enthusiastically—and give him a line straight toward the spot where the dummy will fall. Do this by letting your left hand hang beside his nose, and jerking it sharply forward, in the proper direction, as you send him.

You must time this gesture to keep your hand moving just ahead of his nose as he leaves, so he can see it from the corner of his vision as he takes off on the correct line. Obviously it is useless if you miss the bus, and merely wave good-by at his tail.

Now don't make this a full-armed sweep—a great exaggerated motion—like a desperate bowler trying for a strike. This isn't necessary, and it looks poor in a field trial. Also, you don't want to be pitching yourself out of a duck boat every time you give your dog a line.

Just snap your hand forward, breaking only your elbow and wrist—not the shoulder. Your hand shouldn't move more than two feet. It's better in a trial if it moves less, when you're trying unobtrusively to help your dog remember a fall he's supposed to have marked.

Frank Hogan used to give his dogs a line by moving one finger about three inches. It was spectacular to see his dogs sail out on a perfect line to the most difficult blind retrieves, as a result of that slight gesture of his finger.

But at the start, you'd better give your dog a bit more hand movement than that. As you go along, you can gradually cut it down, if you want to be very fancy in your handling.

Always, from now on, when you send your dog for a retrieve, give him the line with your hand.

The first time a helper throws the dummy, your dog might want to return it to him. After all, he's been accustomed until now to return it to the guy who threw it. So be ready with your whistle, and if necessary take to your heels once more. Run away. Call him in to you. He'll quickly understand that, no matter who throws the dummy, he's to bring it only to the boss.

Which brings up another point. Later, when yours is the only dog in a hunting party, never allow even your best friend to take a bird from him. Even if this means you have to lug forty pounds of other people's pheasants in your coat, while you finish walking a mile-long corn field—insist that *your* dog retrieve only to *you*. Conversely, of course, never accept a bird from another man's dog. A retriever that gets to wandering around, trying to deliver to everybody, won't do a decent job for anybody. He'll end up as a no-good tramp.

You'll need a helper for only a few retrieving lessons, until it's safe to require the dog to be steady. After that you can have him sit while you walk forward and throw the dummy yourself.

For these first few lessons it's best to stick with sight retrieving. Use a big lawn, a golf course, a sand beach—any place where the dummy will always fall in plain sight. Have the helper gradually move out farther, just two or three paces each time, until you have the dog doing retrieves up to 100 yards. Then start mixing them up, long ones and short ones. Don't give him the chance to form the habit of just going out a certain distance, and then stopping and hunting short. Let him learn to keep going out on the line of the fall until he sees or smells the dummy. Most dogs have poor close vision, and even on bare ground they often won't see a dummy or a bird until very close to it.

In each of these lessons, quit after four or five retrieves. Quit while he's still frantic for more. Spend the rest of the ten minutes brushing him up on the obedience commands.

CURING INDIFFERENCE

If, after you have thoroughly teased your dog with the dummy, he won't go after it when you throw it or if he goes after it half-heartedly—call the whole thing off right then and there. Put him back in his kennel, and let him think things over for at least a week. Don't take him out for *anything*.

You'll probably be surprised at how he wakes up, after a week of solitary. (This is also good medicine for any dog at any age, who goes stale, slow, or sulky.) But if this still doesn't do the trick, try to find someone in your vicinity who will let your pup watch him work his trained retriever. Sometimes this will make a youngster jealous, and arouse his instinct to retrieve.

If this doesn't wake him up, you can resort to force training if you like. I wouldn't. For the dog will never make a happy worker.

WHEN TO REQUIRE STEADINESS
(See Illustrations 62–64)

As soon as you feel your dog is a retrieving fiend—when he is sailing out and sailing in with every dummy tossed for him at any distance up to 100 yards—that is the proper time to begin requiring steadiness. When in doubt, wait a little longer. Don't risk spoiling his enthusiasm, or slowing him up.

Have the dog sit, beside you. Hold his collar with your left hand. Toss the dummy with your right. Or if you have a helper handy, he can toss it. But make it a short retrieve.

Make the dog sit after the dummy is on the ground, only until you count five. Then send him, with all the enthusiasm you can. Fairly shout his name as you let go of his collar, and swing that hand out fast, giving him the line.

The first day of this, don't give him any retrieves longer than thirty yards, no matter how well he's doing. Remember, until now he's been charging out while the dummy was in the air, and was halfway to it before it hit the ground.

If he shows any confusion or hesitation about going out, don't make him wait so long. If necessary, send him a few times while the dummy is still in the air. Or make the retrieves still shorter. Or both. During this first period of making him steady, don't allow him to lose any of his steam. Actually, this is the most crucial moment in his training, and about the only one that may need a little special care on your part.

But a keen young dog should sit there quivering, straining to go, his eyes glued on the spot where the dummy fell. He should go like an exploding rocket when you send him, straight to the fall. If he doesn't, it means you're pushing him too fast, and then you should simply put him back a grade in school.

If all goes well the first day, you can then make him stay steady without your hand on his collar. Stand out in front of him when you throw the dummy. Keep saying "sit!" as you throw it. Be ready to grab him as he goes by, if he tries to break. If necessary, do a flying tackle. But stop him if you possibly can before he gets to the dummy. Scold him, put him back on the exact spot he left and make him *sit* there, but don't be more severe than that for now. You don't want to give him the idea that *retrieving* is a bad thing.

Pick the dummy up and throw it again. Keep at this until he doesn't offer to break. Then gradually move back, until you're standing beside his head. Even from this position you can grab him if he starts to leave, if you're quick about it.

It's much easier never to let him break than to fight it out with him after he's once gotten away with it. And remember this: If he *should* get away from you, and run clear out and retrieve the dummy, *you cannot whip him or even scold him then*. That is the surest way to confuse him, and spoil his enthusiasm for getting the dummy.

From now on, always require him to be steady. Wait at least a couple of seconds before sending him to make every retrieve.

SITTING TO DELIVER
(See Illustration 65)

Some trainers require their dogs to *sit* to deliver the bird. I never saw any practical use for this. With some dogs I believe it is even harmful, causing them to slow down the last few yards of their return.

The AKC Standard Procedure For Retriever Trials says that a dog sitting to deliver should not outscore a dog that delivers cleanly to hand without sitting. My advice is not to bother with it.

HUNTING WITH NOSE

After a dog is doing faultless retrieves up to 100 yards on bare ground—is marking the falls perfectly—it is time to start switching him from sight retrieving to using his nose. By now there will be plenty of your hand scent on the training dummy so he can smell it easily from amazing distances.

Start throwing it in fairly light cover at first, just enough to hide the dummy. The first retrieves should be very short, not more than fifteen or twenty yards, and *straight into the wind*. If your dog has a nose, he'll discover what it's for very quickly. Keep gradually increasing the length of the retrieves, into the wind, until he is going out 100 yards.

Then you can move around and give him a cross wind, but be sure to start this again with much shorter falls. He may have a little trouble with these, either hunting short, or passing the falls on the upwind side. But he should soon learn from experience to use the wind by swinging a little to the downwind side of the line as he goes out, and keeping on until his nose stops him.

Until he is doing these perfectly, don't give him any work straight downwind. This, of course, is the most difficult retrieve of all. For the dog must not only get clear out beyond the fall, but also must be right on the line of fall in order to smell the dummy.

HUNTING SHORT

Hunting short, particularly in fairly high cover, is a common puppy tendency. To understand why, squat down beside your dog so your eyes are on the same level as his, and have your helper throw the dummy far out in the field. It will appear to fall much closer than it actually does, because you get no perspective on it, when your eyes are so close to the top of the cover.

To compensate for this, a dog must learn to keep going out on the line until his nose stops him. This can be taught with a simple exercise. For this you will need three training dummies, and a helper. Let's use the imaginary baseball diamond to describe it.

The dog sits beside you, at home plate. A cross wind is blowing, from third base toward first. The helper walks out to the pitcher's mound. He stands facing third. Then he throws one of the dummies straight up in the air, to land right at his feet. Send the dog at once, while the dummy is still in the air. At the same time the helper should step backward five paces, toward first base. The dog will have a tendency to swing slightly toward him, which will pull him to the downwind side of the fall. By simply running out to the helper, he will be where he must wind the dummy, spin around, and retrieve it fast.

The helper then moves back to the pitcher's mound, and out five steps toward second base, and throws another dummy. He moves backward, straight downwind, the same as the first time.

Each time the dog goes out and makes a perfect retrieve, without hunting short, move the next one out another five yards—on exactly the same line. Thus you can soon have the dog sailing out

100 yards or more—swerving slightly to use the wind—and going at a sizzling run until his nose stops him.

But don't overdo this exercise at any one time. And don't get him swinging too far off the actual line, for this might give him trouble later, when he gets to doing straight downwind retrieves. You can regulate this by the distance the helper moves back from the fall.

This is good corrective medicine for any dog of any age who falls into the habit of hunting short. At the same time it improves his marking ability, and gives him good practice at taking a line from your hand signal.

INTRODUCING TO THE GUN

Retrievers are not likely to be gun shy, no matter how rudely they are first introduced to the gun. But it is so little trouble to do it right, there is no sense in taking chances on ruining a particularly sensitive individual.

Have your helper fire the first few shots at a considerable distance from the dog—at least 100 yards. And have them associated with something pleasant, either retrieving or eating. Use a .22 pistol or rifle. If the dog pays no attention to this, keep increasing the noise, until at last the helper can fire a 12-gauge shotgun just as he is throwing a dummy to be retrieved. The whole job shouldn't take more than five minutes.

INTRODUCING TO WATER
(See Illustrations 66–69)

Young Goldens are sometimes hesitant about going in water. Chesapeakes and Labradors are more likely to plunge right in and start swimming, the first time they get near a pond.

But with any of them, it is well worth while to start them correctly, so they will love the water and go in enthusiastically, instead of grudgingly. It is best, if possible, to use a fresh-water pond for the introduction of a young dog to this element. Try to avoid salt water, as he is likely to drink some of it, become sick, and form an aversion to all water. And by all means, avoid putting him through surf until he is a seasoned swimmer. At the outset, don't use a pond with deep mud at the edges, as this might slow up and even frighten a potentially fine water dog.

Pick a spot where the dog can wade out some distance on a fairly hard bottom, and play around in shallow water, before he must start swimming.

Don't start by throwing something for him to retrieve. There's no reason to risk his refusing. And don't *ever* throw the *dog* in the water.

Just put on your waders or swimming trunks and wade out in the water *yourself,* while the dog sits on shore. Have him wait until he is busting to follow you. Then call him, with great enthusiasm. Blow hell out of your whistle. He'll come in. Even a very shy pup will soon be over any fear of the water, plunging around, romping and playing in it. Before he knows it he'll venture out over his head, and be swimming.

SINGLE RETRIEVES FROM WATER
(See Illustration 69)

Only after the dog is thoroughly at home in the water, and follows you in with no hesitation, should you give him his first water retrieve. For this, use the smaller water dummy.

Toss it from shore, only a short distance, to land in shallow water where the dog will not have to swim. Send him at once. Don't give him time to hesitate. Call his name while the dummy is still in the air.

Thus he will form the habit of hitting that water with a spectacular splash every time he goes in to retrieve. Throw the dummy a bit farther each time, until it is landing well out in swimming water. When he is retrieving it as far as you can throw it, have your helper throw it from a boat. Keep moving it out just a little farther each time, always on the same line, until at last he is doing 100-yard retrieves from water.

Probably your dog will have a tendency to drop the dummy just as he comes out of the water, stop there, and shake. You can kid him out of this by standing right on shore yourself while he is retrieving. As he returns, when he reaches the shallow water, start blowing your whistle vigorously. Then move away, calling him, and try to get him to run after you, so you can grab the dummy out of his mouth before he drops it.

This is all that is needed to get most dogs delivering to hand, even from the water. But if your dog persists in dropping the dummy at the shore, don't worry about it at this stage. You can easily force train him to hold it, a little later. The important thing now is to develop his enthusiasm for water retrieves.

Gradually increase the time you make him sit before sending him, until you are counting five *after* the dummy is down on the water. But do this only as long as he is hitting the water enthusiastically, and marking the falls perfectly. If he begins slowing up, or marking short, start sending him again while the dummy is in the air. And don't give him more than five retrieves in one session.

Never allow your dog at any age to become lackadaisical, to hesitate, or to tiptoe slowly into the water. If he starts this, give him the solitary treatment. Lock him up for a week. Then start over. Have him sit on shore. You wade out, or go out in a boat. Make him wait until he is dying of suspense. Then call him. If this doesn't get him hitting the water with a splendid splash, he just wasn't meant to be a water dog.

USING A YOUNG DOG AT STUD

Along about now, some local yokel will want to use your dog at stud. The candidate is almost sure to be an unworthy bitch, for an experienced breeder wouldn't use an unproven stud, no matter how good his pedigree.

But you're nutty about your dog, and the temptation will be strong to carry on his line. Don't do it, friend. Not yet. Don't breed him until he's at least two years old. If you have field-trial ambitions for him, don't do it until after he's made his field-trial championship.

Love is a mighty potent thing. It will distract a youngster from his school work, if he gets interested in the girls too soon. Wait until he's thoroughly trained, and doing his main job well, before you risk dividing his interest.

While he's still in junior high, you don't want him walking with a swagger, smoking big black cigars, and whistling at every girl who goes by the drugstore.

Chapter 14

HIGH SCHOOL—DOUBLE MARKED RETRIEVES

AFTER YOUR DOG has learned to do a perfect job of marking and remembering single falls, that is the proper time to start him on doubles. If you rush this, there is danger of causing indecision, having him run out between the falls, and not really mark either of them. This can develop into a nasty fault. The cure is to put him back on singles for a while.

DOUBLE MARKED RETRIEVES

No matter how well he's been doing with the singles in cover, start the doubles on bare ground, where both dummies will land in plain sight.

Again using the imaginary baseball diamond, stand beside the dog at home plate. Toss one dummy toward third base, not more than fifteen feet. Then turn and toss the other toward first, the same distance. Be sure the dog sees you toss the second one. Then send him for it at once, giving him the line with your hand.

When he returns, take the dummy from him, and hold it out of sight, behind your back. Turn the dog around and have him sit so he directly faces the first dummy. Let him sit until he sees it lying there. Then send him, with great enthusiasm. Repeat this a few times, until he begins to get the idea of going back for a second dummy.

From now on it is simply a matter of gradually lengthening the falls, just as you did with the singles, until at last he is doing doubles, widely separated, each at least 100 yards out. Normally, the *last* fall, being freshest in the dog's memory, will be the *first* retrieve. So the first fall is the difficult one. If at any stage the dog has difficulty remembering it, shorten up on that first fall for a while.

Until he is doing a perfect job on long doubles, keep the falls widely separated, so there will be no temptation to him to switch dummies, or to attempt to bring in both at once. To avoid this further, arrange the falls so he can't possibly wind the first while bringing in the second dummy.

For example, the cross wind is blowing from left to right. Throw the first dummy toward first base—the other toward third (which he will retrieve first). Thus, as he is coming in with that one, he can't possibly smell the other, being upwind of it.

DOUBLES IN LINE

After he is doing nicely on wide-angle doubles, try a long and a short, exactly on the same line. Have your helper throw one out about thirty yards, run out and throw the other thirty yards farther, and then stand perfectly still. The dog will sail out toward the far fall, but likely spin on the short one when he runs over it, and retrieve that one first. Whistle him in with it.

Then send him back for the far one. He should remember it, particularly with the helper standing out there, to remind him how far out it is. But if he should start hunting short, have the helper pick up the far dummy at once and throw it up in the air again. Continue this, until you have him doing a faultless job on both dummies.

Then reverse the routine. Throw the far one first, then the short one. You may again have trouble getting him out far enough for the far fall. If so, have the helper walk out, pick it up, and toss it in the air again at the same spot. Keep at this until the dog is sailing out for that far one, even after the diversion of the short one. He should learn to keep going out on that line until his nose stops him.

This is excellent exercise for the dog's memory—and also constitutes fine high-school work on taking a line. But don't overdo it at any one time. Occasionally mix it up, throwing in a widespread double, to keep reminding him of those, so he doesn't expect *always* to find the second bird on the same line as the one he has just retrieved.

After he is sharp at both types of double retrieves, the next step is to start doing them in cover. Again starting with short falls, keep at this practice until he can do them up to 100 yards. Always give him the line with your hand, to both falls. If, as young dogs often do, he has a tendency to forget the second fall, and swing back toward the one he has already retrieved—take him right back to bare ground for a while. Shorten the retrieves. Lengthen them again only as fast as he will go directly to the second fall, without swinging off the line.

If he has a reasonably good memory, he will learn to use it very fast. At the same time, he'll be learning to rely on the line you give him. That will be very important a bit later, when you get ready for blind retrieves. So never fool him. Be sure he *always* finds a dummy when he takes the line you give him.

DOUBLES ON WATER

Don't give him doubles in water until he is doing them perfectly on land. Then start all over, with very short retrieves, with plenty of spread between the falls. If necessary it is worth one trip to a large enough body of water so that you can get up to fifty yards between falls. If he starts switching dummies in the water, it's hard to stop him. Personally, I'm poor at walking on water.

Stand at the edge of the water, and toss a dummy toward third base, another toward first. Then the routine is pretty much the same as when you started the doubles on land. Allow the dog to shake the water from his coat after the first retrieve. Then have him sit, facing the other fall. This should be close enough so he can easily see it. Wait until he does. Then send him with violent enthusiasm. This way you will give him no chance to start hesitating about entering water for a second fall. Lengthen the retrieves *very* gradually. After you are throwing them as far as you can from shore, call in that patient helper again.

Have him throw the dummies from a boat, or from the far shore of the pond, if that can be done without making the retrieves too long. A long narrow pond from 75 to 100 yards wide is ideal. You can work across it, and there is no temptation for the dog to return by land. In a small round pond, when widespread falls are near the side shores, any sensible dog is likely to go ashore after each retrieve, and run back by land. A dog who is started in such a pond, and has most of his practice there, is likely to form this habit.

Then, when you get him suddenly into big water—whether duck hunting or in a field trial—he is likely to make enormous detours, trying to find a way back to you by land. This can become a bad fault, and it's best to avoid letting it get started.

One word of caution. Don't start your double retrieves in a river with a swift current. Obviously, if the dummies drift far from where the dog sees them fall, he'll be badly confused. No retriever should be sent for doubles in a swift current until he's finished college. Then you can correct him with hand signals, and help him to learn about current drift.

Do not give him doubles in line, in the water, until later—after he has been thoroughly broken of any notion of switching dummies. For the present keep the falls well separated, at a wide angle.

RETRIEVING TO HAND: "FETCH"
(See Illustrations 74–77)

Until now you've done nothing to *force* the dog to hold the dummy firmly in his mouth until you take it from him. If your footwork has been good, you probably have kidded him into chasing after you and doing a pretty fair job of delivering to hand, on land at least.

By moving away from him briskly as he comes out of the water, and calling him, you may even have him waiting to shake himself until after delivering. But it's a big temptation to any dog, when coming out of cold water, to drop the dummy as soon as he gets out into the air, in order to shake.

Even though he isn't doing it now, he may slide into this nasty habit later, if he is not taught the command "fetch." In retriever language, this means, "Don't drop it. Hold it. Put it right in my hand."

It sounds much better in a field trial, or to your admiring hunting companions, if when your dog emerges from the water you quietly say, "*Fetch* it here, old boy," than if you bellow, "Don't drop that duck, you such-and-such of a so-and-so!"

You should teach the command "fetch" only after the dog is a confirmed retriever, hurling himself out enthusiastically after double falls, on land and water. By then, there's no danger of slowing him, or spoiling his enthusiasm for his main job.

Strangely, I personally have never had a serious argument over "fetch" with a male dog, but have had to fight it out with several bitches. For some reason, they often hate it. Like women, they resent being forced to do anything.

Have the dog sit. Force open his mouth and quickly pop the smaller training dummy in it. When he tries to spit it out, support his lower jaw, firmly at first. Hold both jaws together if necessary, so he can't spit out the dummy. Meanwhile keep saying "fetch!"

The first time, make him hold the dummy only while you count five. Then say, "Leave it," very cheerily, and take it from him. Pet him a moment. Tell him he's a fine dog.

Then repeat the process. Each time should require less physical force on your part. The third time, you can probably get him to hold the dummy by very light pressure with a finger under his chin. Keep repeating the command, and then try taking your finger away entirely.

An eager-to-please dog will learn this command in eight minutes. To prove this, at the risk of slowing up a promising pup, I used Freehaven Rook, age ten months, for the demonstration shown in Illustrations 74–77. With an older dog, already accustomed to delivering naturally to hand, it can be done even faster.

Don't overdo this exercise at any one session. But give him a minute or two of practice at it every time you take him out from now on, until he is perfect. At last, you should be able to put the dummy in his mouth, say "fetch," and walk away. He should hold it for several minutes, until you return and take it from him.

Then it is time to start using the larger and heavier dummies, to prepare him for handling big ducks and pheasants without dropping them.

SWITCHING BIRDS

Every retriever should be taught at this point that he must never switch birds. He should go for the bird he's sent for, and return with it, even if he stumbles over another on the way in.

Some old hunters will debate this. "I want my dog to leave a dead bird and go after a cripple," they say. "That shows good sense."

Well, in the first place, a dog has no sense. He does what he's in the habit of doing. True, there is a rare situation when it might be best for him to drop a dead bird and get a fast start after a runner. But there are many more times when he'll be dropping *your* bird to go after another man's cripple. And if the other man has sent his own dog for it, yours may return minus his ears. Most retrievers won't go out of their way to pick a fight, but they won't back away from one, either.

A dog should never be permitted to try to bring in two birds at once. This is a sure way to start hard mouth. No dog has a big enough mouth to hold two mallards or cock pheasants without damaging them.

Another thing. A dog who once starts switching usually develops indecision. On a double retrieve, he will start out between the falls, and swim around all day trying to make up his mind which to get first.

If these arguments aren't enough to convince the wise characters, here's the topper. Virtually all judges in retriever trials penalize severely for switching birds. Sometimes they even disqualify for it. They must have reasons. They are the men who have the most experience at actually hunting over good retrievers.

To teach your dog about this, throw two dummies just fifteen feet from you, to fall about ten feet apart. Send your dog for the *last* one thrown. If at any time, going out or coming in, he moves even one step toward the other dummy—run out there at him, roaring "no!"

Drag him back to the exact spot where he picked up the correct dummy. Put it in his mouth. Tell him to "fetch." Have him sit right there, holding it. Walk back to your original position. Then whistle him in with it. Then take it, and send him for the other.

Keep at this exercise until he will do it perfectly, coming straight in with the one dummy without even looking at the other.

Then it is time to increase the temptation. Throw one dummy as far as you can. Send the dog for it. As he is returning, toss the other to fall just five feet in front of him. Be ready to roar "no!" if he tries to switch. If he persists, and actually switches, rush out there, take the second dummy away from him, and put it back on the exact spot where it fell. Drag him back out to where he picked up the first one, put it in his mouth, and make him sit there. Go back to your original position, and whistle him in. Keep at this until you have him coming in, running right over the other dummy, without offering to switch.

You can accomplish this lesson in less time than it has taken me to tell you how, and it is well worth doing.

RETRIEVING DECOYS: "LEAVE IT"
(See Illustrations 70–73)

Unless you like to get your feet wet, the simple way to teach a dog about decoys is to set out a few on *land*.

Put your dog on leash, and walk him through the decoys. When he offers to grab one, jerk him back sharply, and say, "No! Leave it!" Keep doing this, back and forth, until he will walk through without even offering to look at one of the blocks. The light will dawn for him suddenly.

Then he'll look up at you as if to say, "I get it, boss. You don't want these *wooden* ducks!"

After that, toss a dummy across the decoys, and send him for it, straight through them. Keep at it until he will go and return without paying the slightest attention to the decoys. Then place them in shallow water, and repeat the routine. You may occasionally have to remind him by shouting, "Leave it," but you should be able to keep your feet dry.

WORKING FROM A BLIND
(See Illustrations 86–89)

In the retriever trials, dogs are required to work from a portable "blind," which bears little resemblance to any real duck blind you ever saw. This is made of plywood, standing as high as a man's chest. It has wings on either side. There is a hole in the front section, large enough for a dog to jump through. If your dog will work from one of these—he'll have no shyness about going into any blind you can imagine under hunting conditions.

It is hardly worth while to make one of these just to train one dog, for you can teach him to work from the blind in one brief lesson. The first time you go to an informal field trial, you can borrow the blind they have there, while it is not in use.

Set it well back from the edge of the water. Lead your dog in on leash. He may be a little shy about going in this strange contraption. Say "kennel," and pull him clear up front, and have him sit squarely in front of the hole. Pet him for a moment, and let him relax.

Then toss a dummy *through the hole*, to land on the ground just three or four feet in front of the blind. Send the dog immediately. He'll jump through the hole to retrieve it.

Don't try to make him return through the hole. Let him come around the side. But you stay in the blind to receive the dummy from him.

Repeat this two or three times. Then throw the dummy clear

out in the water. The dog will leap through the hole like a veteran, and from then on, you'll find he'll march right into the blind at heel, and take his position before the hole, with no trouble.

WORKING FROM A BOAT

Retrievers are not asked to work from a boat at the trials, but this is often necessary when you're duck hunting. It's a good idea to get your dog used to it before the opening day. If you don't own a boat, you can borrow one of these when you go to a trial.

Pull it well up on shore. Say "kennel," and make the dog jump in it. Get in and stand beside him, and have him sit. Toss a floating dummy in the shallow water. Send him for it. He will readily leap out after it, with the boat stationary on shore. When he returns, don't let him jump in the boat with it. Reach out and take the dummy, saying "leave it," just as he reaches the side of the boat. Then call him on in, and have him sit. Repeat this two or three times.

Now move the boat out into about six inches of water. Go through the same routine there. It won't bother him to jump directly into the shallow water. Gradually move out farther, until finally you have him taking off into deep water, with no hesitation. When he swims back to the side of the boat with the dummy, reach out to take it from him. Then grab him by the scruff and help him in. Just pull him up until he can hook his front legs over the side of the boat. Then push down on the top of his head, to give him leverage. He'll do the rest. This is much easier than trying to lift eighty pounds of dog plus many pounds of water clear into the boat.

Never try to get him clear in the boat with a duck in his mouth. He can't help clamping down on it as he struggles into the boat, and this might make him hard mouthed.

INTRODUCTION TO FEATHERS
(See Illustrations 78–81)

Before you send your dog to pick up his first shot bird, spend a couple of minutes properly introducing him to feathers. This is the cheapest possible insurance against hard mouth.

Use a freshly killed pigeon. If you live in the city, and a pigeon is a hard prop to come by—go to an informal field trial, once more. The field-trial chairman will gladly loan you a slightly used one.

Go out behind a hill where you won't bother anyone. Wrap a piece of string around the dead pigeon, so the wings won't flop around when you throw it. Bind it up tight, so it's pretty much like a training dummy—only with feathers on it.

Tease the dog with it. Get him interested. He probably will grab at it. Hold your hand around it so he can't bite it without biting you—just as you did to keep him from roughing the training dummy. Say "no!" whenever he tries to bite it. Tell him to be careful.

After he has calmed down, have him sit. Place the pigeon in his mouth. Say "fetch." Watch him carefully, and if he starts to bite it, be ready to pinch his lip against his teeth, and say "no!" very sternly. He'll quickly get the idea that the pigeon is for fetch—not for food.

As soon as he sits quietly, holding it gently in his mouth, back away from him a few steps. Then call him to you, and take the pigeon from him. If he is at all reluctant to let go, pinch his lip against his teeth and say "leave it!"

Now throw it for him, just a few feet away. Have him retrieve it. If he offers to treat it roughly when he picks it up, scold him severely, and take the bird away from him. Have him sit, put the bird in his mouth, and make him hold it gently for several minutes. As soon as you make him understand the pigeon is to be considered just as a training dummy, he'll handle it gently. With a good dog, this should take only a few minutes.

Gradually increase the length of the retrieves, until you're throwing it as far as you can. At last, take the string off the pigeon. Throw it, flopping wings and all. By now the dog is accustomed to this new taste and smell, and the feel of the feathers in his mouth. He'll retrieve it like a veteran. And now, you have a bird retriever. He should never offer to damage your game.

Live pigeons can be shot for him to retrieve any time you have the opportunity, from now on.

INTRODUCTION TO SHACKLED DUCKS
(See Illustrations 82–85)

After your dog is handling dead pigeons, it is time to introduce him to live shackled ducks. If it is too much trouble for you to keep a couple of these on hand, you can also borrow a live duck for the purpose at an informal trial.

At most of the Eastern trials, full-flying ducks are shot for the dogs to retrieve on water. But in many of the trials throughout the country, shackled ducks are used. These of course are birds legally raised on game farms, and purchased for this purpose.

But whether or not you have field-trial ambitions, your dog should be taught to handle a shackled duck before you take him shooting. Again, this is cheap insurance against hard mouth. If you neglect it, and you have a fairly tough aggressive dog, he's likely to flatten the first crippled duck you send him for. Once he starts killing cripples, he may be too rough on dead birds as well.

On the other hand, a sensitive youngster may become cripple shy, if his first experience with live birds is rudely thrust upon him when you take him hunting. A big old greenhead with nothing wrong but a broken wing can put up quite a bluff.

Before you introduce your dog to a big duck, you should have him easily handling the big and heavy training dummies, without dropping them.

Then the routine is exactly the same as with the pigeon, except that the duck is very much alive. The wings are tied securely, at the base. The legs are tied together, near the feet.

Tease the dog with the duck. Get him interested. But don't let him grab it. Protect it with your hand. Make him understand this strange live critter is in exactly the same category as the training dummy and the dead pigeon.

Then force his mouth open, very wide, and stuff in the duck. Be sure he has a good full body hold on it. Tell him to "fetch." Don't make him hold it more than a couple of seconds at first. Repeat two or three times, each time having him hold it a bit longer. He'll get used to it quickly, and get the knack of getting a firm but gentle hold on this big bird. Then you can toss it in the water for a short retrieve, and from then on, he's a cripple retriever. If he picks up the duck by the neck, the feet, or by a wing tip, always correct his hold. Put the body of the bird squarely in his mouth. Tell him to "fetch." Make him hold it correctly for a moment, before you take it from him again.

TAKE HIM HUNTING

Now you can take your dog hunting any time. He is ready for everything but blind retrieves, and he should be a real help to you in the field or in the blind. Don't hesitate to send him for anything on land or water, *provided you're sure he saw it fall.*

But don't, please, expect him at this stage to do blind retrieves. If you're shooting over decoys, take a little trouble to get the dog placed so he can see where the ducks are likely to fall. If you're in a shore blind, or even a boat blind, make a hole in it big enough for the dog to see through, and to jump through when he goes out to retrieve.

If you're in a sunken barrel, try to find a dry spot nearby where the dog can sit and mark the falls. Even if he's right out in the open, the ducks won't pay any attention to him. If you're out in a marsh, the top of a muskrat house is a good place for the dog. However, if you set him out at some distance from you, he has to be mighty steady.

Don't let him start breaking shot. Many hunters make this mistake. Some even encourage their dogs to do it. If you do, you'll regret it. Once started, it's a tough fault to cure.

The first time you take a green dog hunting, pay more attention to him than you do to your shooting, even if you thereby miss some shots. This is hard to do, I know, but it's the best investment you can make in the future of your dog. You won't have to do this many times. He'll quickly understand hunting is just like the practice at home, and that the boss will stand no nonsense.

Once you get that across, you can forget you have him with you except when you need him. You can go ahead and tend to your shooting, confident that the dog is walking smartly at heel, or sitting right where you put him, and that he isn't going any place until you send him.

Chapter 15

COLLEGE STUFF—BLIND RETRIEVES

THE OLD DUCK HUNTER, in his beaten-up shooting coat, had the air of a man who was slumming. He was about to witness his first and last retriever field trial, and he didn't care who knew it.

Before the first stake got under way, I heard this old character talking loudly to a crony in the gallery. He sneered, "If this is like the bird-dog trials, it's nothing but a lot of fluff and guff. These fancy trial dogs are no good for bringing home the meat."

Late the following afternoon, when the trial was nearly over, I saw him again. He was watching the final series of the open all-age stake, a difficult handling test. On the far side of the lake, a good 300 yards away, a dead duck was being planted for each dog to retrieve. It was placed well up on the land, in heavy cover, some fifty yards beyond the far shore.

The competing dogs were held behind the gallery, and called up one at a time, as their turns came. They heard no shots, saw nothing fall. This was a blind retrieve to end all blind retrieves.

The old duck hunter watched intently as a black dog sat beside his handler, waiting. One of the judges spoke his number. Then the handler quietly said the dog's name, and gave him the line with a very slight hand gesture. The dog sprang forward, hit the water with a mighty splash, and started straight across the lake. He swam powerfully, and never deviated from that line.

The old duck hunter moaned softly. There was a dazed look about his eye.

"Well," I said, "how do you like these 'fancy trial dogs' by now?"

He didn't even turn his head. He was watching a dog. A duck dog.

"Lord," he muttered, "what I'd give for a dog like that."

Soon the dog climbed up the bank on that far shore. He was just a black speck in the distance. He began hunting up the shore, to the left. The handler blasted sharply, once, on his whistle. The black speck stopped instantly, and stayed motionless. The man made a hand signal to the right. The black speck scuttled fast to the right, down the shore. Then the whistle blasted once more. The black speck stopped, exactly on the line of the fall.

Now this retrieve was straight downwind, the toughest kind there is. The handler waved his arm in the "get back" signal. The dog turned and went straight back on the land, hell bent. But the heavy cover threw him slightly off the line, and he swerved a bit to the left. When he was just beyond the hidden duck the handler hit him with one more whistle blast, and gave him a hand signal to the right. The dog spun into the wind, nailed the bird not five yards away, scooped it up, and started back with it at a dead run.

The old duck hunter was breathing hard, through his mouth.

"How do you like that?" he croaked. "Why, it's like retrieving your ducks with a guided missile!"

One of his cronies was still unconvinced. He said, "Yeah, but what for? *My* ducks fall right in the decoys."

The old duck hunter turned on him scornfully. "Don't give me that," he snorted. "I've seen some of your cripples fall a lot farther than that there duck."

It is a thrilling and spectacular sight to see a finished retriever respond perfectly, at great distances, to hand and whistle signals. But more than this, it is very useful to own a dog that can do it.

Whether you want a field-trial prospect or just a meat dog, you should teach him to handle on blind retrieves. Then you can place him just downwind of any fall that he hasn't seen, as much as a quarter of a mile away. This looks like black magic, when you first see a retriever obeying quiet hand signals from a fabulous distance.

Actually, it's a cinch for the greenest amateur to teach a good dog to "handle" perfectly on blind retrieves—and to do it furthermore with no arguments, no sulks, no lost tempers, no hauling the dog around by a rope, no army of assistant trainers—and with everybody happy.

The main danger is in teaching this too soon. Try to resist this temptation. Wait until the dog is two years old, or until he has had a full season of hunting experience, before you give him hand signals. First let him fully develop his powerful instinct to hunt on his own, and to mark and remember falls. Then there will be little danger of his becoming too dependent on your help, getting sloppy about his marking, and asking you for directions to falls he should damn well remember for himself. The ideal retriever is a dog who finds every bird he has seen fall, without help from his handler, yet will handle perfectly to falls he had no opportunity to see.

My method of teaching hand signals is like a jigsaw puzzle—simple when you see it all assembled. But it took me several years to put it together, out of pieces "borrowed" from Frank Hogan, Jim Hogan, and other good trainers—plus a few I whittled out for myself. The routine is easy to demonstrate, but I always had difficulty *describing* it to people, until finally I hit upon this baseball gag.

Now I call it The Baseball Diamond Method of Teaching Hand Signals. If you've ever seen a ball field, you'll understand it. (See Illustrations 94-113.)

For your purpose, of course, the baseball diamond is purely imaginary. There is no need to put out any bases, or markers such as I have used in the photograph illustrations.

To begin, use a yard with no cover, so the dummy will always land in plain sight. Start at home plate. Walk out toward second base, with the dog at heel. As you cross the pitcher's mound, suddenly say "sit," and immediately blow *one* sharp blast on your whistle. The dog should sit instantly and stay on the pitch-er's mound, while you walk on a few steps toward second before you stop. Thus he will begin learning to stop and stay put on one whistle blast, no matter where you are or what you are doing. From now on, one whistle blast means stop and *sit*. (Two or more mean *come*.)

Now toss the dummy toward second base, to fall not more than 15 or 20 feet from the dog, where he can see it plainly. Leaving the dog on the pitcher's mound, you return to home plate. As you do, keep looking back and commanding "sit," followed by one whistle blast, if the dog shows any inclination to move.

Stand at the plate a moment while the dog watches you, won-dering what in the world the boss is up to *now*. Then suddenly make an overhead arm signal, like a *girl* throwing a ball toward second base. At the same time shout the dog's name, followed immediately by the command "get back!" The dog may hesitate a moment, slightly confused by these strange doings. But then he will remember the dummy, then look around and see it, and *get back* to retrieve it. The instant he picks it up, encourage him with *several* quick whistle blasts to come in with it fast, all the way to you at home plate.

For the first lesson, concentrate on this one direction. Each time the dog performs perfectly, make the next retrieve a bit longer, until at last he is *getting back* smartly, clear out into center field. Before this session is over, you should be able to stop calling his name to send him. The overhead arm signal, plus the command "get back," will be all the permission he needs, very quickly.

The next day you can teach him the arm signal to the right. Start at home plate. Walk out and again have him *sit* on one whistle blast, at the pitcher's mound. Toss the dummy toward *first base*. Return to home plate, again leaving the dog out there on the mound, of course.

Then call his name, and throw your arm straight to the right, from the shoulder. At the same time, sway your whole body to the right. Keep at this until the dog will go straight right to the dummy, just on the arm signal, and you can stop calling his name. And, of course, gradually increase the length of the falls, until they are far out in right field.

To teach the arm signal to the left, simply reverse this process, tossing the dummy toward *third* base instead of first. After you have devoted one lesson to each of the three directions, spend a session at mixing them up. First give him a "get back," than a signal to the right, then one to the left. If this confuses him at all, shorten the retrieves, so he can look around and easily spot the dummy. But by now he should be well on his way to associating these arm signals with the exact direction of each fall.

Next, move to a field with sufficient cover to hide the dummy. Thus you are removing the sight aid, and the dog will have only his memory and marking ability to help him respond to the hand signals. Start all over, with very short retrieves. Give him rights, lefts, and "get backs." Mix them up as long as the dog is doing them perfectly. But if he gets confused, concentrate on one at a time for a while. Continue this practice until he is hitting them all right on the button, in cover, at distances up to 100 yards.

Now, in these exercises, keep your imaginary baseball diamond in exactly the same spot. If the dog beats paths in the cover from the pitcher's mound to first, second, and third—so much the better. Let the routes to the falls become thoroughly familiar to him. Then comes the big moment when you remove the *marking* aid.

Take the dog behind a bush, or stand in front of him so he can't see what's going on. Have your helper sneak out and drop the dummy on the line between pitcher's mound and second base.

Then walk the dog out and have him sit as usual (with the customary single whistle blast, of course) at the pitcher's mound. Return to home plate. Then give him the overhead arm signal, and yell "get back" with great enthusiasm.

The dog will probably make a take, and wonder whether you have suddenly gone nuts. But if your preliminary work has been well done, he should suddenly remember about that arm signal and that command. He should spin and tear out along the familiar route to second base, and hit the dummy right on the nose. If he doesn't, it simply means you are rushing things too fast, and you should give him another session or two with the marking aid.

But the minute he obeys a hand signal, without seeing anything fall, the job is 90 per cent done. From then on, you simply give him occasional practice at blind retrieves. Mix them up, on both length and direction. As soon as he is doing them faultlessly on the old familiar baseball diamond, move to fresh ground, and eventually to heavier cover. And then, finally, to water.

As you go along, you can gradually cut down on the exaggerated motions of your arm to the right and left. Finally, you can keep your elbow tight against your side, and just flip your hand slightly to the right, and the dog will respond perfectly. Always use the right hand to send him right, of course, and the left to send him left. Sometimes you see handlers using the right hand for both directions. This looks awkward, and is confusing to the dog.

As you practice the blind retrieves, keep increasing the distance between you and the dog, until you have as much as 100 yards between home plate and the pitcher's mound. The ultimate objective is to have him stop instantly on the whistle, as far away as he can hear it—and to take a hand signal from you from just as far as he can see you.

Then it's time for the final step—to teach him to take a line to a fall he hasn't seen, *starting from your side*. This should now be very easy. In his preliminary training, you've been giving him a line to every marked retrieve. He is already well on his way to understanding what this gesture means.

Have your helper plant the dummy between the pitcher's mound and second base. Walk the dog out to the mound and have him sit. This time you stay there beside him, on the mound. Speak his name, and give him the line with your hand. If he hesitates, say "get back," and give him the overhand signal. He knows by now what these mean.

He should romp straight out on the now familiar path, straight to the dummy. Keep at this until you can send him just by speaking his name, and giving him the line with a slight underhand gesture of your hand. Send him out from the mound in all directions. Keep increasing the length of the falls. If he gets off the line, stop him with the whistle, and direct him with hand signals to a spot just downwind of the fall.

In all of your practice, make sure he finds the dummy exactly where you told him it was. Then he'll quickly learn to trust and rely on your directions. Never let him quit before he finds it. If necessary, walk all the way out and show it to him. Have him sit. Put the dummy in his mouth and let him sit there holding it while you walk back to the spot from which you sent him. Then call him in with it. He'll learn to believe what pappy tells him, very fast.

You'll find it's a lot of fun to stand in one spot and direct a guided missile. But don't get so fascinated with this game that you play it all the time. Mix up the blind retrieves with plenty of practice on marked falls. Don't give your dog a chance to get lazy, and start asking for help he doesn't need. If he ever should stop and turn, and ask for a hand signal, on a fall he has seen, just turn your back on him. Wait him out. Make the rascal go on out and find it for himself.

⌐ㄴㄴㄴㄴㄴㄴㄴㄴㄴㄴㄴㄴㄴㄴㄴㄴㄴㄴㄴㄴㄴㄴㄴㄴㄴㄱ

Chapter 16

FINISHING TOUCHES AND MINIMUM MAINTENANCE

NEARLY ANY GOOD retriever will take naturally to working like a spaniel, quartering ahead of the gun, and flushing upland birds. In fact, many retriever-happy people claim these dogs are far superior to the spaniels at their own specialty.

I won't go quite that far. But for heavy work, the big rugged retrievers are hard to beat. They have the stamina to keep going all day, routing pheasants out of the heaviest marsh cover—in the kind of going that wears out a spaniel in two or three hours.

However, before using your dog for this work, it is best to give him one full season of hunting strictly as a retriever, keeping him at heel except when you send him for a shot bird. It is a great temptation to get him out in front too soon. But you'll do the youngster a favor if you resist this. He must be absolutely steady to flush and shot before you start him quartering, and any keen young dog is likely to forget this if, when a bird goes up and guns go off, you are not right beside him to remind him to sit.

And of course if you have field-trial ambitions, you'd better postpone using your dog for flushing birds until after you have retired him from serious competition. There is no question but that this takes the sharp edge off a dog's retrieving performance. Often in a trial you see a dog quartering all the way out to a long fall, instead of sizzling straight out on the line. This invariably proves to be a youngster who was used *too soon* for flushing pheasants.

If you give your dog time to develop fully the *habit* of taking a line direct to a shot bird, then he is not likely to become confused if you begin also using him for quartering and seeking *live* game. Let him learn his main job thoroughly before you teach him what is essentially an entirely different trade.

Give him at least one full season of working only as a retriever. Get him absolutely steady to flush and shot. Then teach him the hand signals. After that, it will be easy to develop his natural instinct to hunt ahead of you, and flush live birds—and without hurting him very much in the retrieving department.

You can introduce him to this new job before the season opens, if you can procure two or three live pigeons, and get a good man with a scatter-gun to shoot them for you. For this exercise you will need to find a fairly good-sized field, with sufficient cover to hide a pigeon.

Tie the dog where he can't see you while you go out to plant the pigeon, at least 150 yards out in the field. Hold the pigeon in both hands, and as you walk out dizzy it by swinging it continuously in a tight circle. Its head will weave drunkenly, and flop over on its chest when it is ready to plant. Drop it quickly in a good patch of cover and keep right on walking away, fast. If you do this, the pigeon won't fly, and will stay put until the dog flushes it.

Now go back to your dog, and smoke a cigarette while the pigeon regains its equilibrium. Then start working slowly across the field, directly toward the pigeon. Have your friend walk beside you, with his gun ready.

Tell the dog to *hie on*. If he runs straight ahead, stop him with the whistle when he gets out about twenty yards. Give him a hand signal to the right. Stop him again with the whistle while he is still well within easy gun range. Give him the hand signal to the left. Continue this, working him back and forth in front of you, just like a windshield wiper, as you walk forward slowly, on the line of the hidden bird.

As the dog gets close to it, have your whistle ready. The instant the pigeon flies, yell "sit!" and blast once on your whistle. If the dog starts to break, keep yelling "sit!" and get to him as fast as you can. Put him back on the exact spot he occupied when he flushed the bird. The gunner should hold his fire until he sees the dog is steady. If the dog sits immediately when you yell, the pigeon should be shot, and you should go to your dog, keep him steady for just two or three seconds, and then send him to make the retrieve.

But don't worry if you have to let the first pigeon fly away. The main thing is *not to shoot it* if the dog breaks and gives chase. Thus he will learn he can't catch a flying bird. If this happens, you should go after him, catch him, and reprimand him severely. Drag him back to the exact spot from which he broke, and make him sit there for a good long time, thinking it over. If he breaks a second time, you may as well give him a good walloping, and get it over. For he will be utterly useless as a gun dog if he runs wild, flushing other birds in cover far ahead of you, and chasing them over the horizon.

To cure a chronic breaker, have the dog drag a fifty-foot line. When he gets close to the pigeon, sneak up and get the line in your hand. Give the dog enough slack so he can start running when the bird gets up. Then give him the surprise of his life, by jerking him end over end.

But this will be unnecessary if your dog is steady and under control, as he should be, before you start him quartering. If you're on your toes you can, with whistle and voice, make him sit and stay the instant he flushes his first bird. The bird can then be shot. And after the first few times, you can stay right where you were, and send the dog to make the retrieve from there, by quietly speaking his name and waving him toward the fall.

You'll be amazed how quickly he will catch on to this exciting new game. After he has quartered correctly across a field only two or three times—each time thereby finding and flushing a live bird, which is then shot for him to retrieve—he will suddenly look up at you as if to say, "Hot damn! How long has *this* been going on?"

If it's too inconvenient to give your dog this preliminary practice, you can do it just as well on wild birds, during the first hour of the opening day of hunting season. But you'll want to pick your hunting partner pretty carefully. Get someone who won't think he's killed if he has to pass up a few shots for the sake of a good dog. It's no job for a game hog. Don't try to shoot these first two or three birds yourself. You may be plenty busy with the dog, without being encumbered with a gun. And don't attempt to start the dog on his quartering career with a large party of hunters. Someone is sure to make you feel uncomfortable about holding up the hunt, and you will hurry and fail to start the dog properly.

If you just take your time that first day, it is so easy to have the dog steady as a rock, to flush and shot. Once he gets this idea, you can begin forgetting him, and tending to your own shooting. And, brother, that is worth while. From then on, he'll kick up birds for you that would sit tight while an army of dogless hunters marched right over them.

From then on, you and the dog will both learn from experience, hunting together. If he responds to hand and whistle signals at *any* distance, and if you keep him absolutely steady—never allow him to break under any circumstances—you'll find yourself improvising all sorts of tricky teamwork for bringing game to bag.

Old Freehaven Jay has become fantastically wise about driving pheasants *to me*. One day years ago, in North Dakota, birds were running ahead of us, down the bottom of a big ditch, just beyond gun range. Jay, quartering close ahead of me, was becoming fully as annoyed and frustrated as I was. I decided to try an experiment. Stopping Jay with a quick beep of the whistle, I hand-signaled him to the right, up out of the ditch, at the same time climbing out myself. He looked at me in amazement, but then reluctantly obeyed. Then I waved him back, down the deserted section-line road that paralleled the ditch. He went, but of course kept trying to swing back down into the ditch, where he knew the pheasants were. Each time I stopped him with the whistle, and signaled him back onto the road.

When he was 150 yards away, I stopped him, and hand-signaled him back down into the ditch. I went back into it myself, crouched down low in the cover, and softly whistled the dog toward me. He intercepted those running pheasants, busted right into them, and put three beautiful cocks right over me. I shut my eyes, shot, and got two of them. You never saw a more delighted dog. And from then on, we had a new way to work ditches.

Today, with running birds ahead, we need no whistle signals. Jay will look back, and I swear he lifts an eyebrow, as if to say, "We've got a track man here, boss. Shall I head him off?" All I do is give him a slight hand signal to right or left, and he does the rest—circling well ahead of the runner, and flushing him back in my direction.

This stunt is very useful on pheasants, but I have since found it comes in even handier on these California quail, which *really* love to run. If Jay and I can get a big covey going up and down the bottom of a canyon, we really confuse them. That's all we need to fill our limit—one big running covey—provided I can hit them.

As you hunt with your dog, you and he will develop a means of communication all your own. When he first starts quartering ahead, you should watch him closely all the time. Be sure you aren't asleep when he flushes a bird for you. Nothing is more discouraging to him than to put up a fine cock, big as a bucket, and have you finally fire two parting salutes as it disappears over the skyline.

But before long you'll be able to tell, just by looking at the dog, at his tail action and his whole attitude, just what is going on. He'll tell you as clearly as if he could talk whether he's just hunting hopefully, or on a hot trail, and at last whether the bird is sitting tight or running ahead. I can't describe exactly how he'll tell you these things, for different individual dogs do it differently. I can positively assure you that if you watch him closely, you'll soon understand what he's saying. And then you'll know when it's safe to be lighting a cigarette, and when it isn't, and when it's time to throw it away and get your thumb on the safety of your gun. After that you can relax, and let your dog take you hunting.

MINIMUM MAINTENANCE

Whether you have bought a trained dog, or trained him entirely yourself, you now own a valuable property. He can stand a lot of neglect without depreciating in value, but not total neglect.

In between hunting seasons, spend a few minutes at least once a week giving the dog a little practice. Don't allow him to forget anything he has learned. Don't let him get sloppy about the obedience commands.

Keep him up to snuff on his marking by giving him a few double marked retrieves. Vary the lengths of the falls, so he doesn't get used to finding them at any certain distance. Then give him a good tough blind retrieve, so he doesn't get rusty on the hand and whistle signals. You can use training dummies for all this. Once the dog has had a season or two of hunting, he'll never forget about the real birds.

But don't fall into the lazy habit of giving him all his practice in the same small yard, where there is no opportunity for variety. A dog can quickly form the habit of going off the porch, around the rose bush, down the garden path, and finding the dummy at the same old corner of the tool house. In any vicinity you can find some strange vacant land not too far away, where you can take the dog occasionally.

Whenever you have the opportunity, put him in the water, to keep him keen, and to keep his swimming muscles in good shape.

If he should, through your neglect, develop some little fault, take a few minutes to pop him back in the proper grade at school, and correct it before it gets serious.

SLOW RETURN
(See Illustrations 90–91)

If he starts slowing up as he returns with a bird, give him a refresher course on coming fast to the whistle. It's easy to do this whenever you take him out for a walk. Have him sit. Walk on ahead, fifty yards or so. Stand and look at him, building up the suspense, until he is crazy to catch up to you. Then suddenly blow several blasts on your whistle, and just watch him come! Keep repeating this all through your walk, until you are leaving him behind as much as 100 yards before you call him. This will not only speed his response to your whistle, but is splendid exercise for him.

Also, when you give him practice retrieves, take to your heels once more. As he returns, the moment he slows up at all, run away from him. Keep running until he catches you, and you can take the dummy from him.

HITTING THE WATER
(See Illustrations 92–93)

Sometimes an unfortunate experience when duck hunting will make a young dog hesitant about hitting the water with that all-out splash—either an encounter with deep mud, or landing on a submerged stump, or just hitting really cold water for the first time. You can restore his confidence, and get him taking the water with proper enthusiasm again, with very little trouble. Get out in a boat, in a pond with a good hard bottom near shore, but with swimming water out in the middle. Have the dog sit on shore. Make him stay until he is dying of suspense. Then call him suddenly, with your whistle. He should, with a very little of this, get to hitting the water again. Let him swim around a bit, following you in the boat. This is fine for developing his swimming, and making him feel completely at home in the water.

If no boat is easily available, you can do much to get him hitting the water properly simply by standing on shore, tossing a dummy only ten or twelve feet, and sending the dog immediately, while the dummy is still in the air. Doing this a few times will often get amazing results. All you need do is to change his *habit* of entering the water, to get him hitting it again, with no unpleasant result.

SLOPPY HOLD

If your dog starts taking a sloppy hold on big ducks, correct this at once, for if neglected it can grow progressively worse, until at last he is *dragging* them in to you through the mud. Whenever he has the bird by the head, neck, wing tip, or feet, take it away from him. Open his mouth wide and jam the duck in, so that he has a full body hold on it. Tell him in a severe tone to "fetch." Make him hold it correctly for a minute or two. Then back away, call him to you, and receive the duck. It usually needs very little of this to convince a dog to take the right hold in the first place.

PIDDLING

A retriever is supposed to be so keen for his job that he will stop for *nothing* until he finds and retrieves the bird he's sent for. But sometimes a feisty young male will fall into the unnecessary habit of stopping to piddle on bushes as he goes out. This is a minor fault, which counts only slightly against a dog in a trial, and somewhat reduces your pleasure and pride in him as a hunting companion. But it's easy to correct, and you might as well do so, particularly if you think you might ever run him in a trial.

Always, before you work him, give him plenty of opportunity to run around and "be a good dog." Then, simply don't allow him to get away even once with stopping to do his business while on a retrieve—whether he's going out or even *returning* with the bird or the dummy.

The instant he stops to lift his leg, go roaring out at him, shouting "no!" Jerk him to a sitting position, and immediately send him on to the fall. If he tries to do it coming in, rush out the same way, drag him in with you to your original position, take the dummy from him there. *Then* tell him to "hie on," and "be a good dog." Thus make him understand he is to finish the job at hand before retiring to the gentlemen's restroom.

If some ignoramus sees you correcting this fault, he will probably think you are crazy or cruel, or both. He will sneer, "The poor dog. He's not even allowed to relieve himself."

Actually it takes a dog less than a minute to complete almost any retrieve if he's tending to business. If he can hold everything all through the night, to avoid fouling his bed, he can damn well hold it for one minute while he's doing his job. By now he knows what you mean by "no." If he persists in his leg lifting, it means he is defying you on that matter, and soon he'll be doing it on more important things. So I wouldn't waste too much time on this, before giving him a good licking and winning the argument once and for all.

WHINING AND YIPPING

We have already touched on the matter of whining, yipping, or giving tongue when on line or in the blind. Sometimes a three- or four-year-old dog will suddenly start this, for no apparent reason. Whenever it starts, crack down on it at once, as severely as necessary to put a stop to it. The dog already understands "stop that noise." All you must do is insist on obedience to this command. Scold him, pinch his lip, or give him a walloping as a last resort. For this can develop into a very serious fault.

HARD MOUTH

All through the book we've talked of little ways to avoid letting hard mouth get started. But even with these precautions, you will occasionally find a dog who has been tender mouthed for years, who suddenly begins flattening his birds, for no apparent reason. This is most unlikely, but if it should happen to you—you must crack down severely and at once. Show the crushed bird to the dog. Scold him severely. Put it in his mouth and make him hold it gently for a long, long time—meanwhile talking to him like a Dutch uncle. If it ever happens a second time—then it's time to get out the persuader. If you don't win this argument right now, you've lost a retriever. When the habit becomes confirmed, hard mouth is almost impossible to cure.

DEFYING THE WHISTLE

Sometimes a dog who stops instantly on the whistle when he is relatively close to you will develop a convenient deafness when he is out in the field or in the water 100 yards or more. Of course the hearing of individual dogs varies. But if you really give out on an Acme Thunderer, any young dog with clean ears can easily hear it at least a quarter of a mile—unless you are blowing directly into a very strong wind. So don't let your dog kid you. Be reasonably sure before you punish him that he can hear the whistle. If in doubt, send a helper out to see if *he* can hear it.

Then when you're sure, crack down hard, and win this argument. When he defies the whistle, go roaring out there as fast as you can. Catch him. Drag him back to the exact spot where he should have stopped. Blow a single blast. Say, "Do you hear that? *Sit!*" Repeat this several times. Meantime, give him a good licking, between these admonitions. I have found it easier on me and the dog, in the long run, to deal out a really good old-fashioned thrashing when this whistle deafness first appears. That usually ends it, and saves much nagging, yelling, and many lickings in the future.

BUT CHEER UP

We seem to be ending this chapter on a gloomy note, full of faults to correct, and dogs to be walloped. But these matters had to be included somewhere, just in case you might sometime run into one of them.

I could go on and on, describing many more specific stunts for meeting relatively minor problems that you might conceivably encounter with your dog. But this book is going to be thick enough without them, and by now you can easily figure them out for yourself, if the need arises. They are all based on *repetition* and *memory*.

When your dog does anything wrong, see that an unpleasant result occurs: Repeat it enough so it becomes associated in his memory with the improper action. He will quickly decide that petty crime doesn't pay.

Conversely, be sure that there is always a pleasant result when he does what he should. To him there is nothing finer than triumphantly to find the dummy or the bird, and then to receive a word of praise and a pat on the head from you.

Actually, if you started with a good dog in the first place, and then trained him the easy, happy way—and didn't overtrain him when he was too young—the chances are good that he'll never develop any serious faults for you to correct.

And the most painless way to keep him up to snuff for hunting is to run him in every retriever trial you can conveniently get to. Do it for practice, and fun, and experience for your dog. It is well worth the small entry fee, just to work your dog on ducks and shot birds occasionally, as a change from the training dummies.

But remember that out of all the dogs entered, most of them with more experience than yours, only four can win places in each stake. So don't expect to win. Be happily astonished if the lightning strikes, and you get a ribbon.

Even if you never win a place, you'll get plenty out of the trials. You'll be a better handler for this experience. Your dog will be a better meat retriever. And you'll both have more fun when you go hunting together.

PART III

RETRIEVER FIELD TRIALS

*How to find them, and what to expect and
how to act when you attend your first one.*

Chapter 17

HOW TO FIND A TRIAL

SCATTERED THROUGH THE East, the Middle West, some of the Mountain States, and up and down the Pacific Coast, there were twenty-seven clubs authorized by the American Kennel Club to put on *licensed* retriever field trials during 1948. These are the trials that count for championship points, and where you will see the largest entries and the best dogs competing.

Try to attend one of these if you can. Meet the officers, and the most active members of the field-trial committee. They are usually the more experienced people of the local retriever-happy clan, and they will answer your questions and help you in finding the pup or dog you want.

As we mentioned earlier, most of these clubs hold two *licensed* trials yearly—one in the spring and one in the fall. But many of them also have frequent practice trials, or "picnic" trials, in between times, to which new potential suckers for the sport are usually more than welcome.

Write to the secretary of the club closest to you, and he'll gladly give you the date and location of the next trial. But if by chance he doesn't answer reasonably soon, try writing one of the other officers.

ALPHABETICAL LIST OF CLUBS HOLDING LICENSED RETRIEVER TRIALS DURING 1948

AMERICAN CHESAPEAKE CLUB
General vicinity: National (Parent Breed Club)

President	*Vice President*	*Secretary*
Ferdinand A. Bunte	Anthony A. Bliss	Miss Oleva Groulx
3301 W. Franklin Boulevard	15 Broad Street	3301 W. Franklin Boulevard
Chicago 24, Illinois	New York 5, New York	Chicago 24, Illinois

DEL BAY FIELD TRIAL CLUB
General vicinity: Dover, Delaware

President	*Vice President*	*Secretary*
William B. Holden	Dr. Walter L. Parrott	H. C. Hancock
Dover, Delaware	Dover, Delaware	Roosevelt Avenue
		Dover, Delaware

DULUTH RETRIEVER CLUB
General vicinity: Duluth, Minnesota

President	*Vice President*	*Secretary*
Leonard Erickson	Art Massie	Arthur M. Clure
c/o National Iron Company	325 St. Paul Avenue	700 Torrey Building
Duluth 7, Minnesota	Duluth, Minnesota	Duluth, Minnesota

GOLDEN RETRIEVER CLUB OF AMERICA
General vicinity: National (Parent Breed Club)

President	*Vice President*	*Secretary-Treasurer*
George D. Alt	K. K. Williams	Carlton Grassle
Wayzata, Minnesota	2370 N. 32nd Street	P. O. Box 226
	Milwaukee, Wisconsin	Rochester, Minnesota

HELENA RETRIEVER CLUB
General vicinity: Helena, Montana

President	*Vice President*	*Secretary-Treasurer*
Carl W. Carlson	L. E. Barbeau	Joel V. Fiser
175 W. Lyndale	1919 Townsend Ave.	576 S. Rodney Street
Helena, Montana	Helena, Montana	Helena, Montana

ILLINOIS RIVER FIELD TRIAL ASSOCIATION
General vicinity: Chicago, Illinois

President	*Vice President*	*Secretary-Treasurer*
William T. Cline	James Simpson, Jr.	Mrs. Elizabeth P. Walker
175 W. Jackson Boulevard	8 South Michigan Avenue	Route 1, Box 18
Chicago 4, Illinois	Chicago 3, Illinois	Bartlett, Illinois

IRISH WATER SPANIEL CLUB OF AMERICA
General vicinity: National (Parent Breed Club)

President	*Vice President*	*Secretary*
Thomas C. Marshall	Ross Harrison	Mrs. Muriel Jarvis
1400 Unquowa Road	55 Morton Street	Box 8
Fairfield, Connecticut	New York, New York	Gillette, New Jersey

LABRADOR RETRIEVER CLUB, INC.
General vicinity: National (Parent Breed Club)

President	*Vice Presidents*	*Secretary-Treasurer*
Thomas W. Merritt	Daniel Pomeroy	Howes Burton
c/o Babson Bros.	47 Beech Road	Meadow Farm Road
2843 W. 19th Street	Englewood, New Jersey	East Islip, L. I.
Chicago 23, Illinois		New York
	J. Gould Remick	
	61 Broadway	
	New York 6, New York	

LONG ISLAND RETRIEVER FIELD TRIAL CLUB
General vicinity: Long Island, New York

President	*Vice President*	*Secretary-Treasurer*
Mrs. James M. Austin	E. Monroe Osborne	Lewis E. Pierson, Jr.
Old Westbury	Easthampton, L. I.	54 Franklin Street
New York	New York	New York, New York

MIDWEST FIELD TRIAL CLUB
General vicinity: Chicago, Illinois

President	*Vice President*	*Secretary-Treasurer*
Thomas W. Hellyer	Arthur Walcholz	L. F. McCue
177 Blooming Bank	9640 S. Hoyne Avenue	135 South LaSalle Street
Riverside, Illinois	Chicago 43, Illinois	Chicago 3, Illinois

MINNESOTA FIELD TRIAL ASSOCIATION, INC.
General vicinity: Minneapolis–St. Paul, Minnesota

President	*Vice President*	*Secretary-Treasurer*
Leonard W. Simonet	Howard Cless	W. Fiske Marshall
1620 Rand Tower	500 South 3rd Street	Box 133
Minneapolis, Minnesota	Minneapolis, Minnesota	Long Lake, Minnesota

MISSISSIPPI VALLEY KENNEL CLUB
General vicinity: St. Louis, Missouri

President	*Vice President*	*Secretary*
W. J. Kinsella, Jr.	Delbert L. Findley	Haworth F. Hoch
Kenmore Road	1335 Woodruff	20 Glen Oaks
St. Louis, Missouri	St. Louis, Missouri	Webster Groves, Missouri

Missouri Valley Hunt Club
General vicinity: Omaha, Nebraska

President	Vice Presidents	Secretary-Treasurer
F. M. Perrine	R. E. Hoye	H. F. Schoenman
2505 Read Street	655 South 41st Street	509 Brown Building
Omaha, Nebraska	Omaha, Nebraska	Omaha, Nebraska
	L. C. Coutts	
	2507 North 72nd Street	
	Omaha, Nebraska	

Montana Retriever Club
General vicinity: Billings, Montana

President	Vice President	Secretary-Treasurer
Robert E. McKenna	Harold Ruth	Norman A. Clark
1116 2nd Street W.	P. O. Box 13	P. O. Box 13
Billings, Montana	Billings, Montana	Billings, Montana

National Retriever Field Trial Club, Inc.
General vicinity: National (but National Championship Trial has been held frequently at Herrin, Illinois)

President	Vice President	Secretary-Treasurer
T. W. Merritt	Howes Burton	George W. Holmes
St. Charles, Illinois	Meadow Farm Road	c/o 1st Nat'l Bank of
	East Islip, L. I.	Lincoln
	New York	Lincoln, Nebraska

Nebraska Dog and Hunt Club
General vicinity: Lincoln, Nebraska

President	Vice President	Secretary-Treasurer
George W. Holmes	Marv Roberts	Fred Sehnert
c/o 1st Nat'l Bank of	Box 84	2216—O Street
Lincoln	Lincoln, Nebraska	Lincoln, Nebraska
Lincoln, Nebraska		

North Dakota Retriever Club
General vicinity: Fargo, North Dakota

President	Vice Presidents	Secretary-Treasurer
Maurice Jones	Dr. R. D. Weible	Earl Torgerson
1017—5th St. N.	1628 S. 9th Street	1625 5th Avenue S.
Fargo, North Dakota	Fargo, North Dakota	Fargo, North Dakota
	Max Taubert	
	Casselton, North Dakota	

Northeastern Wisconsin Kennel Club
General vicinity: Northeastern Wisconsin

President	Vice President	Secretary-Treasurer
E. G. Mauch	Robert Vedder	David Morgan
Mayville, Wisconsin	Oshkosh, Wisconsin	Fond du Lac, Wisconsin

NORTHERN CALIFORNIA RETRIEVER TRIAL CLUB, INC.
General vicinity: San Francisco, California

President	*Vice President*	*Secretary*
A. A. Jones	Herbert Fleishhacker, Jr.	Mervin F. Rosenbaum
955 West Santa Inez	130 Sansome Street	300 Montgomery Street
San Mateo, California	San Francisco, California	San Francisco, California

NORTHERN RETRIEVER FIELD TRIAL CLUB, INC.
General vicinity: Superior, Wisconsin

Secretary
Eugene C. Lee
Androy Hotel
Superior, Wisconsin

NORTHWEST RETRIEVER TRIAL CLUB, INC.
General vicinity: Seattle, Washington

President	*Vice President*	*Secretary*
A. W. Agnew	G. J. Short	L. J. Proby
314 Maritime Building	501 Jones Building	422 Smith Tower
Seattle 4, Washington	Seattle, Washington	Seattle 4, Washington

OREGON RETRIEVER TRIAL CLUB, INC.
General vicinity: Portland, Oregon

President	*Vice President*	*Secretary-Treasurer*
Al H. Schmidt	James A. Aaron	Wm. E. Dame
9038 N. Denver Avenue	6236 S. E. 40th Street	1435 N. E. Beech Street
Portland, Oregon	Portland, Oregon	Portland, Oregon

SHASTA-CASCADE RETRIEVER CLUB
General vicinity: Klamath Falls, Oregon

President	*Vice President*	*Secretary*
Dr. R. H. Engelcke	Hal Rotrock	Mrs. L. M. Watkins
929 Pacific Terrace	Oregon Vocational School	2036 LeRoy St. Apt. 8
Klamath Falls, Oregon	Klamath Falls, Oregon	Klamath Falls, Oregon

SOUTHERN CALIFORNIA RETRIEVER CLUB, INC.
General vicinity: Los Angeles, California

President	*Vice President*	*Secretary-Treasurer*
James L. Free	Robert E. Smith, Jr.	Paul Henry
	1460 Rubio Drive	2310 S. La Cienega Blvd.
	San Marino 9, California	Los Angeles 34, California

SWAMP DOG CLUB FOR TRAINING & TRIALS
General vicinity: Philadelphia, Pennsylvania

President	*Vice President*	*Secretary-Treasurer*
R. Ellison Thompson	Charles P. Davis	C. A. Griscom
Devon, Pennsylvania	Parks Run Lane	100 S. Broad Street
	Ithan, Pennsylvania	Philadelphia 10, Penn.

WISCONSIN AMATEUR FIELD TRIAL CLUB, INC.
General vicinity: Milwaukee, Wisconsin

President	Vice President	Secretary
Leonard Leader	Irving A. Puchner	Joe Ullrich
3531 N. 53rd Street	6910 N. Belmont Lane	3911 N. 23rd Street
Milwaukee, Wisconsin	Milwaukee, Wisconsin	Milwaukee, Wisconsin

WOMEN'S FIELD TRIAL CLUB
General vicinity: Long Island, New York

President	Vice Presidents	Secretary-Treasurer
Mrs. Edmund W. Poor	Mrs. Thomas W. Merritt	Mrs. Percy M. Cushing
St. Marks Lane	St. Charles, Illinois	Tahlulah Lane
Islip		West Islip, Long Island
Long Island, New York	Mrs. J. Gould Remick	New York
	Cedarhurst	
	Long Island, New York	

If you can't get to a trial put on by any of these older clubs, then your next best bet is to look for a new club in your vicinity. There were twenty-two younger clubs which put on one or more *sanctioned* trials during 1947, or 1948, or both. A *sanctioned* trial is run under AKC rules and supervision, with approved judges, but it counts no championship points. Each new club is required to have at least two of these, as sort of full dress rehearsals, before it can qualify to put on its first *licensed* trial.

ALPHABETICAL LIST OF NEWER CLUBS HOLDING SANCTIONED RETRIEVER TRIALS DURING 1947 OR 1948

AMERICAN AMATEUR RETRIEVER CLUB
General vicinity: Chicago, Illinois

President	Vice President	Secretary-Treasurer
Dr. G. H. Gardner	George H. Jenkins	F. C. Schwietert
720 N. Michigan Avenue	731 Monroe Avenue	1960 Balmoral
Chicago 11, Illinois	River Forest, Illinois	Chicago, Illinois

BEAVER DAM HUNTING DOG CLUB
General vicinity: Beaver Dam, Wisconsin

Secretary-Treasurer
Warren Clark
Park Avenue
Beaver Dam, Wisconsin

BLUFFS HUNTING DOG CLUB
General vicinity: Council Bluffs, Iowa

President	*Vice President*	*Secretary-Treasurer*
John E. Plank	Clifford E. Walters	Harold L. Stout
440 Fulle Avenue	616 23rd Avenue	634 South 1st Street
Council Bluffs, Iowa	Council Bluffs, Iowa	Council Bluffs, Iowa

BUTTE RETRIEVER & FIELD DOG CLUB
General vicinity: Butte, Montana

President	*Vice President*	*Secretary*
George Pera	Myles Newcomb	Robert D. Corette
1916 Thornton Avenue	1001 S. Main Street	422 Hennessy Building
Butte, Montana	Butte, Montana	Butte, Montana

CENTRAL MINNESOTA RETRIEVER CLUB
General vicinity: Central Minnesota

President	*Vice President*	*Secretary-Treasurer*
W. W. Holes	Matt Hamilton	William Campbell
343 3 Avenue S.	115 17 Avenue S.	325 5 Avenue S.
St. Cloud, Minnesota	St. Cloud, Minnesota	St. Cloud, Minnesota

COLONIAL RETRIEVER FIELD TRIAL CLUB
General vicinity: Boston, Massachusetts

President	*Vice President*	*Secretary-Treasurer*
Richard F. Piper	Sibley Smith	Charles B. Soper
Rice Road	Wakefield, R. I.	131 Clarendon Street
Sudbury, Massachusetts		Boston, Massachusetts

EUCLID ROD & GUN CLUB
General vicinity: Euclid, Ohio

Secretary-Treasurer
Walter Mapes
108 East 220th Street
Euclid, Ohio

GREAT FALLS RETRIEVER CLUB
General vicinity: Great Falls, Montana

President	*Secretary-Treasurer*
P. W. Callahan	John G. Nye
Donovan Park	710½ 2nd Avenue S.
Great Falls, Montana	Great Falls, Montana

GREEN BAY FIELD DOG CLUB
General vicinity: Green Bay, Wisconsin

Secretary-Treasurer
D. Delaporte
Route No. 1
Green Bay, Wisconsin

GREENE COUNTY CONSERVATION LEAGUE
General vicinity: Jefferson, Iowa

President
Bud Young
Grand Junction, Iowa

Secretary-Treasurer
Gene Try
Farlin, Iowa

HENNEPIN COUNTY AMATEUR RETRIEVER CLUB
General vicinity: Minneapolis, Minnesota

President
John Bird
8500 W. 35th Street
St. Louis Park, Minn.

Vice President
Vincent Petrowske
208 Page Street E.
St. Paul 7, Minn.

Secretary
Henry Johansen
4621—36 Avenue S.
Minneapolis, Minn.

KANSAS AMATEUR FIELD TRIAL CLUB
General vicinity: Wichita, Kansas

Secretary-Treasurer
Don G. Purcell
620 South Quentin Avenue
Wichita, Kansas

LINN COUNTY CHAPTER OF ISAAK WALTON LEAGUE OF AMERICA
General vicinity: Cedar Rapids, Iowa

President
Dr. A. N. Humiston
Higley Building, Room
409
Cedar Rapids, Iowa

Vice President
Earl North
309 Iowa Theatre
Building
Cedar Rapids, Iowa

Secretary-Treasurer
Mr. Frank K. Powers
2020 Park Avenue S.E.
Cedar Rapids, Iowa

THE MARYLAND RETRIEVER CLUB
General vicinity: Maryland

Secretary-Treasurer
Mrs. Allein W. Owens, Jr.
Greenridge Road
Towson 4, Maryland

MISSOULA RETRIEVER & FIELD DOG CLUB
General vicinity: Missoula, Montana

President
Lloyd E. Noel
301 North Avenue E.
Missoula, Montana

Vice President
Dr. R. C. Shaver
544 Blaine Street
Missoula, Montana

Secretary-Treasurer
Mrs. M. J. Sternhagen
421 Livingston Avenue
Missoula, Montana

NORTHWEST IOWA DOG CLUB
General vicinity: Northwest Iowa

President
Ed. H. Quinn
Storm Lake, Iowa

Vice President
Blaine Asher, Jr.
Spencer, Iowa

Secretary-Treasurer
George Wells
Wellzenheim Kennels
Storm Lake, Iowa

PINE VALLEY WILDLIFE CLUB
General vicinity: Eldora, Iowa

President	*Vice President*	*Secretary-Treasurer*
Paul G. Hodgson	James G. Bales	C. O. Rubow
Eldora, Iowa	Eldora, Iowa	Eldora, Iowa

RAVENNA FIELD TRIAL CLUB
General vicinity: Ravenna, Ohio

President	*Vice President*	*Secretary*
E. Nelson Robinson	Maxwell Riddle	J. T. Collins
732 S. Center Street	P. O. Box 286	869 W. Spruce Street
Mentor, Ohio	Ravenna, Ohio	Ravenna, Ohio

* SPOKANE RETRIEVER CLUB
General vicinity: Spokane, Washington

President	*Vice President*	*Secretary*
Charles Finucane	Cleon Carter	Kenneth Van Leuven
Davenport Hotel	Newport, Washington	1202 Old Nat. Bank Bldg.
Spokane, Washington		Spokane 8, Washington

    * Scheduled to have first licensed trial in spring of 1949.

SPORTSMAN'S CLUB
General vicinity: Halbur, Iowa

Secretary-Treasurer
William Rolfes
Halbur, Iowa

TRI-STATE HUNTING DOG ASSOCIATION
General vicinity: Winona, Minnesota

President	*Vice President*	*Secretary-Treasurer*
Ernest Butterfield	Hugh Puck	Bartlett W. Foster
606 E. 10th Street	408 E. Mark	Box 208
Winona, Minnesota	Winona, Minnesota	Winona, Minnesota

WEST ALLIS TRAINING KENNEL CLUB
General vicinity: West Allis, Wisconsin

President	*Vice President*	*Secretary-Treasurer*
Lester J. Krause	Ed Abraham	Mrs. Beth Rudell
Route 1, Box 186	2323 S. 27th Street	1135 S. 93rd Street
North View	Milwaukee, Wisconsin	West Allis 14, Wisconsin
Waukesha, Wisconsin		

If none of the above are close enough, then drop a line to The American Kennel Club, 221 Fourth Avenue, New York 3, New York, and ask for the name and address of the secretary of the nearest retriever club, on the chance a brand new one might have started in your vicinity.

Chapter 18

WHAT IT'S ALL ABOUT

A BALL GAME is pretty dull if you don't understand the rules. It's a lot more fun if you know a little something about the inside stuff—and what to watch. Similarly you'll get more enjoyment from your first retriever trial if you understand what's going on. It really isn't very complicated.

If you just read the following brief rules and suggestions, which have been laid down by the American Kennel Club, you'll be qualified to be a "field-trial lawyer" on your very first day in the gallery.

STANDARD PROCEDURE FOR NON-SLIP RETRIEVER TRIALS

(From pages 38, 39, 40, Rules Applying to Registration and Field Trials, Amended to October 1947, The American Kennel Club)

In order that trials may be conducted as uniformly as practicable, standardization of objectives is essential and therefore all judges, guns and officials who have a part in conducting or judging trials should be familiar with and be governed so far as possible by the following standard:

1. The purpose of a non-slip retriever trial is to determine the relative merits of retrievers in the field. Retriever field trials should therefore simulate as nearly as possible the conditions met in an ordinary day's shoot.

2. The function of a non-slip retriever is to seek and retrieve "fallen" game when ordered to do so. He should sit quietly in line or in the blind, walk at heel, or assume any station designated by his handler until sent to retrieve. When ordered, a dog should retrieve quickly and briskly without unduly disturbing too much ground, and should deliver tenderly to hand. He should then await further orders. Retrievers which bark, give tongue or whine in line, in the blind, on a drive or while retrieving should be penalized.

3. Accurate marking is of primary importance. A dog which marks the fall of a bird, uses the wind, follows a strong cripple, and will take direction from his handler is of great value. The judges must judge their dogs for sagacity, attention, control, steadiness, nose, delivery, courage, perseverance and style. Dogs should deliver directly to hand and not drop game on the ground, but distinction should be made between deliberately dropping a bird or readjusting a bad hold. No dog should be disqualified for hard mouth until injured game has been examined by two judges.

4. During water tests in all stakes, except puppy stakes and except during blind retrieves, dogs should be worked over wooden decoys anchored separately. A dog retrieving a decoy should be disqualified. When working on waterfowl a dog should remain in the blind until ordered to retrieve. The Handler shall then direct his dog from within the blind, or from any other position designated by the Judges.

5. In an All-Age Stake, if a dog makes a movement which, in the opinion of the Judges, indicates a deliberate intent to retrieve without having been ordered to do so, that dog shall be deemed to have broken and shall be eliminated. In any stake other than an All-Age Stake, if a dog makes a slight break and is brought immediately under control, the dog need not be eliminated, but shall be penalized for unsteadiness. In all stakes, after the judges have directed that a dog be ordered to retrieve, that dog is entitled to run in and retrieve and shall not be accused of, or penalized for breaking, even though the Judges did not see or hear the handler send the dog.

When the handler of a dog under judgment is ordered by the Judges for any reason to pick up his dog, he is still under judgment until he has left the line with his dog on leash and all provisions of Paragraph 5 of the Standard Procedure shall apply until that time.

6. A dog should not be eliminated on his first test on land nor on his first test in water on his failure to find behind another dog, but should be tested on a bird shot for him.

7. Tests which are not to be considered by the judges at the final summing up should not be held.

8. If, when a dog is ordered by the judge to retrieve a fall and another dog breaks for the same fall and interferes with the dog under judgment to the extent of causing him in any way to make a faulty performance, the dog interfered with should be considered as not having been tried and given a chance for another performance.

9. Dogs should work in the order in which they are drawn: *e.g.*, No. 2 should not be worked before No. 1 if in line together, insofar as practicable, but the judges should give consideration to the relative length of the fall in order not to give any dog too short a fall.

10. A dog sitting to deliver should not outscore a dog making a clean delivery without sitting to do so.

11. Nothing should be thrown to encourage a dog to enter the water or direct a dog to the fall.

12. Immediately birds are shot all guns in attendance should move as quickly as possible from the line of fall and out of the wind in order that handler and dog may have every advantage to work as nearly as possible under natural conditions.

13. A handler who is constantly nagging at his dog should be penalized. Any handler found holding, kicking or striking his dog to keep him steady when under judgment should be disqualified for the duration of the stake.

14. It is essential that all spectators attending a trial should be kept far enough from the line to enable the dog working to clearly discern his handler and nothing shall be done to distract the dog's attention from his work. A handler has the right to appeal to the judges if the gallery is interfering with his work in any way and the judges in their discretion may, if they believe the dog has been interfered with, give him another test.

15. Insofar as possible, game should be dropped on fresh territory for each dog and not on ground already fouled.

16. Field trial committees are requested to adjust the timing of stakes so that time shall be available for a fair test in each stake, especially the open all-age or limited all-age stakes.

17. Insofar as possible, an equal number of land and water tests shall be given and shall receive equal consideration.

18. The awarding of certificates of merit to dogs which have passed every required test in a stake and have shown themselves to be well trained and qualified retrievers should be encouraged.

19. Judges may, in their discretion, on application award a working certificate to a dog which has retrieved on land and water and in their opinion is qualified to be used in the field.

20. All field trial-giving clubs should clearly recognize that All-Age Stakes are of the first importance and that all other stakes are of relatively lesser importance.

21. Judges should call the number of the dog ordered to retrieve rather than the name of the handler or dog.

22. When an all-age stake carrying championship rating is included in a two-day retriever field trial, not more than two other stakes should also be included in the same field trial.

JUDGE'S AGREEMENT

American Kennel Club
221 Fourth Avenue
New York 3, N. Y.

Gentlemen:

I, the undersigned, having read the rules and standard for retriever field trials as adopted by The American Kennel Club, hereby apply for approval to judge and agree that any field trials at which I may officiate shall be judged by me in accordance with said rules and standard.

(Signed) _____

_____, 19__

Standard Procedure for Retriever Water Tests

1. The preceding rules and standard shall be adhered to wherever applicable in the water tests at retriever field trials.

2. Wooden decoys should be used for all stakes in the water tests at retriever field trials. Should the federal law be amended so as to permit the use of live decoys in water fowl shooting, the use of live decoys will then be optional with the field trial committee of a club holding a Retriever Field Trial, but live decoys should be used only if so stated in the premium list and/or entry form.

3. Dogs are expected to retrieve any type of game bird under all conditions, and the judges and the field trial committee have complete control over the mechanics and requirements of each trial. This lati-

tude is permitted in order to allow for the difference in conditions which may arise in trials given in widely separated parts of the United States which difference well may necessitate different methods of conducting water tests.

In addition to the above rules, if you absorb a few tips on field-trial etiquette you will be prepared for the role of sophisticated spectator, right from the start. Here are some suggestions that I wrote for distribution to new members and guests of the Southern California Retriever Club.

ETIQUETTE FOR THE SPECTATOR

1. *Spectator dogs.* At most trials, human spectators are more than welcome—but not spectator dogs. All field-trial committees have been plagued so many times by unruly pets that are not kept under control by their thoughtless owners, that no dogs whatever except those competing are wanted on the trial grounds. Obviously it is unfair to a competing dog if, just as a bird is shot for him, somebody's Pomeranian sets up a loud yapping and causes the retriever to turn his head and fail to mark his fall. I've even seen a Boxer, too trustfully allowed off his leash, suddenly run out and start a fight with a retriever who was in the field and under judgment.

2. *Loud talk in the gallery.* When a dog is sitting on the line or in the blind, it is just as bad form to risk distracting him with loud talk as it is to make a racket when a man is putting in a golf tournament.

3. *The proper time for applause.* (See Illustration 124.) By all means, don't hesitate to applaud a good performance heartily. But wait until the dog has completed his job. If it is a double or a triple retrieve, wait until he has delivered the final bird to his handler.

4. *Gallery crowding behind handlers.* The gallery should stay at least twenty yards behind the judges, to avoid distracting the dogs on a marking test. On a blind retrieve—or handling test—

the gallery is usually requested to split, and leave a wide empty space behind the handler. If a solid mass of people are standing directly behind a handler, it is very difficult for the dog to pick him out of the crowd from far out in the field. And it is well-nigh impossible for the dog to see his hand signals.

5. *Petting or touching dogs.* (See Illustration 125.) If you've already trained your own retriever, you know about this. You know why the handlers are more jealous about undue attentions to their dogs than to their wives. But most people quite naturally don't understand this. They are accustomed to petting and fondling any dog they see. Nobody wants to offend interested newcomers at the trials, and it is embarrassing to a handler to have to ask a well-meaning person to let his dog alone. So make yourself useful. If you see someone attempting to pet a competing dog, do the handler a favor. Step up and tactfully explain why it's best to let these dogs alone, when they are in competition. Tell the petter he has such a way with animals that the dog might fall in love with him, and try to watch him instead of his handler when his turn comes to be out in the field under judgment.

6. *Feeding tidbits to dogs.* Often there is a well-meaning female going around actually trying to *feed* the dogs. If you see one just tell her how heartbreaking it is to a man who has spent months getting a young dog ready for a trial—if the pup does a nice retrieve, and then refuses to bring the bird to his owner, but runs all through the gallery looking for that nice lady who slipped him the ham sandwich.

7. *Hysterical old maids, male and female.* At nearly every trial some Sunday driver drops in, attracted by the crowd, just to see what's going on. Such people know nothing of hunting, or dogs, or game conservation. Sometimes one of them becomes hysterical, and makes a scene over "cruelty" to pigeons, pheasants, or shackled ducks. Strangely enough a man who gets this obsession is likely to make more noise and be less reasonable than a woman.

The most annoying of these I ever encountered was a strictly minor-league celebrity with major-league hallucinations. He showed up at a trial, and he wasn't getting much attention. The people there were more interested in first-rate dogs than second-rate hams. Suddenly this character became greatly excited over how "cruel" and "unsporting" it was to have *two* men shooting those poor defenseless pigeons with *shotguns*. He gathered a crowd, all right, but he never did make it quite clear just what he wanted—whether we should arm the pigeons to defend themselves, or have our gunners use deer rifles. At last, to everybody's relief, he stormed off, loudly threatening to call the cops.

But most of the people who become concerned about the killing of the feathered livestock are perfectly sincere, nice folks. They usually calm down at once if someone bothers to explain that the relatively few pigeons and pheasants shot at the trials are martyrs to the cause of conservation. That they are killed much more quickly and cleanly by expert gunners, for instance, than squawking and terrorized barnyard chickens that are beheaded by an ax. That for every barnyard pigeon or game-farm pheasant we kill, at least ten wild birds are saved, by retrievers, through finding and bringing to bag thousands of dead and crippled birds that otherwise would rot or die lingering deaths in field or marsh. For the trials are the only means of demonstrating the great value of retrievers to hunters, and encouraging them to use them. Also, the trials are the proving ground for breeding stock, and enable better hunting dogs to be bred.

Some of these people get more excited about the dogs "biting" the live shackled ducks than about shooting the pigeons. Explain to them that these retrievers are very tender mouthed. They don't hurt the ducks. They carry them gently, and some of the old ducks that are used over and over actually get to enjoying the ride. One maiden lady refused to believe me when I told her this. I finally convinced her by getting one of my dogs out of the car, borrowing a fresh egg from the lunch wagon, and having the dog retrieve it to hand, without breaking it. After that the old gal relaxed, stuck around, and ended up enjoying the trial.

In every state, of course, the use of game-farm pheasants and ducks must be completely legal, and approved by the state division of fish and game. But beyond this, most of these state departments thoroughly appreciate the retriever's great contribution to conservation, and heartily encourage and support the retriever trials in every way.

If you encounter a "cruelty" screamer at a trial, you can make yourself useful by explaining all this to him. But if that doesn't satisfy him, and he still wants to make a noise, then he's just a nut. The chances are, he is also a hypocrite. Ask him if he's a vegetarian. Ask him if it's worse to shoot a pheasant than to club a bawling steer to death in the slaughterhouse. Or to stick a pig in the throat with a knife while it's fully conscious, and let it slowly bleed to death. Tell him that's how he gets his bacon and pork chops. Tell him to please go home.

SOME INSIDE STUFF TO WATCH

1. *Bird throwers.* (See Illustration 116.) The boys who throw the birds for the official guns to shoot can make a trial an even competition—or a crap game. There is a considerable art in throwing a bird so it will fly in the exact direction wanted. Pigeons are especially ornery and unpredictable, particularly in a strong wind, and are apt to turn most any way except the way they're supposed to go. But a good thrower can hurl each bird out by main force, far enough so the guns can kill it without messing it up, before the bird *can* turn. This takes a strong pitching arm, plus plenty of experience. Watch the falls. If all the dogs get falls of approximately equal length, you're not only watching some good guns—but some expert bird throwers. Sometimes an old hunter is inclined to sneer when he sees the birds thrown—presumably instead of *flushed*—to be shot. But obviously it would be impossible to get anything like equal falls for each dog by flushing the birds to fly wild in all directions.

2. *Official guns.* (See Illustration 116.) The old hunter who thinks it is unsporting to shoot thrown birds as "shooting fish in a bucket" would get the surprise of his life if he tried just once to shoot for a retriever trial. A pheasant kicked out of heavy cover gets away slowly. If he takes off into the wind, he hangs up there on a string. All the hunter has to do is knock him

down, any way and anywhere he can. It doesn't matter where the bird falls.

In the trials the birds are given an instant start at top speed. Usually they are hurled straight downwind. They are really going away from there. They must be shot at just the right distance—not at the most convenient distance for the gunners. The judges are ugly about this. They want equal falls for all dogs, so they can fairly judge and compare their performances. Furthermore they want no birds shot too close, smashed to pieces by a tightly bunched wad of shot, and turned into a mass of bloody raw hamburger. Just one of these to pick up can make a valuable young dog hard mouthed.

On the other hand, the birds must be cleanly killed. If the guns wait a split second too long, and let a cock pheasant ride slightly out of range, a strong running cripple is the likely result. If the dog fails on it, he's had a rough break. But if he works it out, and gets it, the judges can't fairly put him above a dog who did a faultless job on a dead bird. Not being crystal gazers, they have no way of knowing what the second dog might have done with a cripple. Perhaps if he'd had the opportunity, he would have done even better.

For most retriever trials the finest wing shots in the territory are drafted to do the shooting. Many of these men are champion skeet shots, who think nothing of breaking twenty-five straight targets, as well as being ardent hunters. Usually they shoot in pairs. In any trial I have anything to do with, they are requested to use 12-gauge open-bore skeet guns, and to swallow their pride and *both shoot* simultaneously at every bird, when it is out about twenty yards.

A few judges prefer to have just one gun shoot, with the other backing in case the first one misses. The theory is that they will try harder this way—that when both shoot together, they tend to become careless. My objection to the backing method is that by the time the backer can swing his gun on a missed bird, it is almost out of range. All in all, I personally have seen better shooting at trials with both guns shooting at once. And if you have the right men shooting, and coach them properly, they will both try on every bird. A man who doesn't appreciate that a trial is a serious contest for the dogs—and not a clambake for the benefit of the guns—has no business being out there.

Even the finest shots, shooting together, occasionally miss. This can be a tough break for a keen young dog, who watches a missed bird fly away and light in a distant field. He is all too likely to remember and go on a fruitless chase of that one, instead of marking and getting the bird subsequently killed for him. The very pressure not to miss, and the judges yapping about just where the birds should be dropped, and having to worry about not shooting the other gunners, or the gallery—can cause even a gunner with iron nerves to tighten up and get off his timing for a moment.

So watch the work of the guns. If they go on all day, killing birds cleanly, dropping them not too close and not too far—you're watching a superlative performance. And if you think it looks easy, just get out there and try it sometime.

3. *Importance of uniform cover.* One of the biggest headaches of every field-trial committee is trying to get adequate ground for the land tests, with uniform cover. If a bird falls on bare ground for one dog, while the next gets a fall in a patch of dense weeds, it is hardly an equal contest. But sometimes it is simply impossible to get even cover, particularly for the spring trials. Then it is interesting to watch how the judges make the best of it, skipping around from one place to another, trying to give all the dogs similar tests.

4. *Equal marking opportunities.* In a marking test, where dogs are scored on their ability to mark and remember one or more falls, it is obviously no contest unless all dogs have equal opportunities to *see* those falls. When hilly or rolling land must be used, good judges are careful to see that one dog is not expected to mark a bird that falls *over* a hill, while others have a clear view straight up a slope—or down—or on the level. Notice also whether the judges move on past a big tree or other obstruction that *might* interfere with a dog's view of the fall.

5. *Shot vs. shackled ducks.* In most of the Eastern trials live ducks are thrown and shot, just like the pheasants, for the water

tests. In the Middle West, and on the Pacific coast, live shackled ducks are still often used for the marked retrieves on water.

The Easterners argue that the shackled ducks are artificial, they have no blood scent, and do not simulate actual hunting conditions. Also, a live duck will occasionally squawk or flap a wing, and thus help a lucky dog find it quickly. All of this is true.

However, I still feel that under some conditions the shackled ducks are the lesser of two evils, and on the whole more uniform marking tests can be had with them. Mallards raised on a game farm are not nearly such dependable flyers as pheasants. There are always many of the ducks that, when thrown, drop like a rock. These are very hard to hit, and the best of guns frequently cripple them, particularly when it is necessary to try to shoot them from a boat. A cripple on water is much more serious than on the land. A dog can run down a crippled pheasant. But if a wing-tipped duck is out in a big body of deep open water, he can give the greatest retriever a bad time. He can swim just as fast as any dog, and he can dive deeper than any dog.

At this point I can hear the old duck hunters snorting, "What good is a retriever if he can't handle crippled ducks?"

It's a good question. The answer is that a good retriever can and does get at least nine out of ten cripples, under average duck-hunting conditions, even including those with nothing but a broken wing. In a fairly shallow marsh it's a cinch. The dog will quickly corner and catch the most vigorous cripple, and it can't dive deep enough to elude him. Even in a big lake, if you give the dog enough time, he can often drive the duck ashore, and then run it down.

Many Labradors will dive quite deep themselves after a duck. I once knocked down a blackjack that instantly dove in about eight feet of water. I sent Freehaven Jay after it, to the great distress of my guide. He was sure no dog could ever get that duck. But luckily the duck came up within ten feet of the dog, and immediately dove again. Suddenly one black Labrador completely submerged. Not even the tip of his tail was visible. He stayed under a long time. The guide was convinced I had lost a dog. I was beginning to wonder, myself. At last Jay surfaced, snorting like a whale. He had a very active blackjack in his mouth! To this day the guides at my old duck club in Illinois talk about that "submarine dog."

But that was hunting. A field trial is supposed to be an equal contest for all dogs. I'd have no objection to giving *all* dogs cripples, if someone could guarantee that each cripple would put on the same performance, no matter how tough it might be.

One time Freehaven Jay had done faultless work right up to the final series of a big Eastern trial. No other dog was close to him, and he appeared a cinch to win if he could just pick up two more ducks. Then two of the finest guns in the country fixed him up with a strong cripple. It was strong and it was the meanest duck I ever saw. It fell far out in a huge, deep lake, and the water was ice cold. Jay chased that ornery duck all over the lake. Whenever he got close, it dove in forty feet of water. He couldn't drive it ashore, and there was no other place to corner it in shallow water. He swam at top speed for *fifty minutes*, while I stood helplessly in the blind, and quietly had a stroke. At last, when I saw he was nearly exhausted, I called him in. No trial is worth drowning a dog.

So perhaps I'm prejudiced. But I've seen this happen to too many fine dogs, and I prefer shackled ducks, even if they occasionally give a dog a slight advantage by giving tongue or flapping a wing.

Another trouble with shooting thrown ducks is that they frequently turn and fly straight back at the gunners, no matter how skillfully they are thrown. This happened in several series at the 1948 National Championship Trial. Many of the ducks were consequently shot much too close—virtually shot to pieces.

In blind retrieves, of course, freshly killed ducks should always be used. The shackled birds are only practical for marking tests, and even then they must be handled correctly. A shackled duck falls so quickly that it will be down on the water before a dog has a chance to see it, if the gun is not fired until the bird is in the air. The shot must be fired *first,* and only then the duck should be thrown, giving the dog time to turn his head and see the fall.

This matter of shot vs. shackled ducks probably will be a lively topic of debate as long as trials are held. So pick your side, and when the trial is over and the post mortem begins, climb right up on that bar stool and start swinging.

Chapter 19

TYPICAL RETRIEVER TRIAL TESTS

TESTS VARY SOMEWHAT because of local conditions, but in general the experienced judges stick to the conventional, tried and true tests. If there is time to give enough of these, they offer plenty of opportunity for the best dog to reveal all of his desirable qualities and abilities. Too often, when a green judge attempts something tricky, it boomerangs, and he runs into complications that nobody could foresee.

In the early days of the sport in the Middle West we would sometimes see as many as six or seven different stakes in a two-day trial. But now that entries have grown so large, the American Kennel Club has made a rule that not more than two other stakes in addition to the Open All-Age may be included in a two-day trial. The favorite minor stakes seem to be the Derby and the Non-Winners. Many clubs now favor a Junior Stake instead of a Derby in the spring trials, because in the spring Derby dogs are little more than puppies.

But since this chapter is also to serve as a yardstick when you are buying a dog—to tell you what a retriever can fairly be expected to know and do at a given age—we will include a brief discussion of *all* the official stakes permitted by the American Kennel Club, even though you seldom see some of them any more at licensed trials.

It is customary to shoot pheasants for land work in Open All-Age Stakes, although any game bird may be used. Because pheasants are so very expensive, most clubs are obliged to use pigeons for the minor stakes. But occasionally a club shoots the works, and provides pheasants for all stakes. Before entering a trial, be sure to find out what birds your dog will have to retrieve. If he has been trained only on pigeons, you should give him a little practice on pheasants before asking him to pick up these much larger birds in a trial. The entry blank and premium list of a licensed trial always specify what birds will be used on land, and whether shackled or shot ducks on water. At an informal trial, you can be reasonably sure that only pigeons and shackled ducks will be used.

PUPPY STAKE

A Puppy Stake at a Retriever and/or Irish Water Spaniel field trial shall be for dogs of six months and not exceeding twelve months of age.

This stake is no longer favored, and you seldom see one in a licensed trial, because most good trainers are reluctant to start serious training so early. As we have previously said, many promising pups have been slowed down and even ruined by making them too steady too soon.

But the newer clubs sometimes have Puppy Stakes in their informal trials. Any reasonable judges would require puppies to do only the simplest single marked retrieves, on land and water, certainly not to exceed fifty yards in length. If the land cover is at all heavy, the retrieves should be much shorter. But I would prefer to work the puppies only in very light cover.

The AKC does not require puppies to be worked through decoys or from a blind, and while the judges can insist on both if they wish, I believe few experienced men would do so. They should also be very lenient on controlled breaks. If a puppy breaks even twelve or fifteen feet, and then is brought back under control by his handler, he should not be disqualified, although in fairness he must be penalized for unsteadiness.

I would not penalize a puppy very much for a sloppy hold, or for dropping a bird, or for a poor delivery. These are relatively minor faults anyway, and there is plenty of time to correct them after the baby grows up a bit.

In a Puppy Stake, good judges are looking for the largely undeveloped but important qualities that make the great dogs of the future. They are looking for natural marking ability, keenness to go and retrieve on land and water, nose, speed, and style. Those are enough. If a puppy is *too* steady, and too calm about the whole thing, I'm inclined to suspect him of laziness or lack of interest.

DERBY STAKE

A Derby Stake shall be for dogs whelped on or after the first day of January of the year preceding that year in which the stake is run.

A *spring* Derby should be nothing more than a Puppy Stake, as very few of the entries will be more than twelve months old.

It is a different matter in the fall, when the dogs entered may be as old as eighteen or twenty months. Even then most judges start out with a single retrieve on land, followed by one on the water. In medium cover, these should be about fifty yards or so, with a cross wind rather than a downwind.

In a Derby, as in all stakes except the Puppy Stake, the dogs must work at least once from a blind and through decoys. In a fall Derby (before it's over) I like to see the dogs do at least one double retrieve. In cover, I probably would have neither fall longer than forty yards. But before placing any dog, I'd want to see him go back for a second bird, and at least show that he had some idea there was another one out there.

Now please don't sue me if you enter your dog in a Derby and the judges start right off with a double retrieve with widespread falls of 75 or even 100 yards. There are many factors which make it necessary to lengthen falls, and vary the tests, under the conditions the judges are given with which to work. If there is no cover—just bare ground—the only way they can prove anything is to lengthen the falls. If scenting conditions are good, and for reasons of topography it is necessary to work directly into a brisk wind, then the falls must be lengthened even more. All of these conditions, and more, enter into the setting up of the tests. The quality of the competition also has much to do with the toughness of the tests.

Let's sum it up.

For a spring Derby, you're reasonably safe if you have your young hopeful ready only for the simple tests described under Puppy Stake, plus working from a blind and through decoys.

But for a fall Derby you'd best play safe and be prepared for a good deal more:

He *must* know about decoys, and working from a blind. He should be fairly steady, for although most judges won't throw him out for a controlled break, they *must* penalize for it. The dog should be going back for a second bird, say 50 yards in cover, and up to 100 yards on relatively bare ground. It will help a lot if he is beginning to understand about taking a line.

He should be thoroughly at home in the water, and accustomed to double retrieves of shackled ducks, up to fifty yards or so.

JUNIOR STAKE

A Junior Stake shall be for dogs which are not over two years of age on the first day of the trial at which they are being run.

If you enter your dog in a Junior Stake, he should be prepared to do fairly difficult double marked retrieves, on land and water. Depending on the quality of the competition, you might get falls up to 100 yards—even in fairly good cover—before the stake is over.

He will definitely work from a blind and through decoys, so he should be prepared for both of these. And he must be quite steady by now. While most judges won't throw out a junior dog for a controlled break, if he is otherwise doing good work, they may penalize for it severely enough that it would knock him out of a possible place.

By the time a dog is nearly two years old, he is expected to be doing about everything but blind retrieves and tests deliberately tempting him to switch birds. I've never yet seen one of the latter in a Junior Stake.

Usually the judges penalize a bit more for sloppy hold, dropping birds, poor delivery, and bad manners in a Junior Stake than in a Derby.

NOVICE STAKE

A Novice Stake shall be for dogs which never have won first place in a Novice Stake nor any place or certificate of merit in any other regular official field-trial stake at a licensed or member club trial. Wins in Puppy, Derby, or Junior Stakes excepted.

I haven't seen a Novice Stake at a licensed trial for years. It has been largely abandoned in favor of the Non-Winners Stake. However, if a club should have one, and I were judging it, the tests would be no more difficult than those of a Junior Stake. They might even be a little easier. For the quality of dog work in a Junior Stake is likely to be higher than in a Novice. Even though the latter is open to dogs of any age, they have never been able to get even a certificate of merit, and are not likely to perform in the same league with some of the hot youngsters coming up that are just under two years old and can still be run in a Junior Stake.

NON-WINNERS STAKE

A Non-Winners Stake shall be for dogs which have never won first, second, third, or fourth place in an Open All-Age or Limited All-Age Stake or won first place in a Non-Winners Stake at a licensed or member club trial.

This is the stake in which the hunters and their faithful meat dogs have their fun. It usually attracts a huge entry, and at most trials the judges are given only a half day in which to run it off. Therefore they frequently have no choice but to drop many dogs that complete the first series—but in mediocre fashion—in order to have time to give enough additional series so that the best dogs will be thoroughly tested. Probably the most difficult thing in judging is trying to guess how tough to make the first series in a Non-Winners.

The object is to plan a chore that will prove something, will separate the top dogs from the also-rans, but will not cause more than half the starters to fail. The judges' most haunting nightmare is that of losing all the dogs in the first series.

This fear is justified, because the quality of work in a Non-Winners is so unpredictable, and varies so greatly from trial to trial. Sometimes these experienced old meat dogs get hot and put on a show that looks like an Open All-Age. And sometimes they just plain stink.

So if you enter a Non-Winners, and have hopes of staying in to the end, you should have your dog prepared for *anything* but a blind retrieve. I have yet to see one of those pulled in a Non-Winners, but have seen just about everything else.

You may get a very severe steadiness test, with birds shot right in front of the dog. And with a large entry, the judges may even be obliged to drop dogs in the first series for partial breaks.

Be ready for double marked retrieves of almost any kind. In light cover, the falls might be as far as 150 yards. Another favorite is a *very* long single bird, for a marking test. Sometimes this bird is dropped *beyond* the edge of a field with cover on it, so the fall is out on bare ground, or freshly ploughed ground. This nearly always loses many Non-Winners dogs, who simply will not leave the cover and hunt the bare ground. If in all his recent practice your dog has been accustomed to finding birds only in cover, you'd better give him a little practice on this test.

Be prepared for long singles up to 300 yards, and try to have your dog sailing out on that line until his nose stops him, so he won't hunt short. Brush him up a bit on the matter of switching birds. You might get a test in which the dog is sent for a long marked bird. Then as he comes in with it, another bird is thrown and shot right in front of him, to tempt him to switch. This test is not used as much as it formerly was, but you'd better be ready for it.

You rarely encounter a "walk-up" test in a Non-Winners, so this will be described under Open All-Age, where it properly belongs. But it's easy to be ready even for this, and you might as well do so.

The dog will of course work from a blind and through decoys.

You can be reasonably sure you will get no handling test on a blind retrieve, and the dog will get a much higher score in the marking tests if he finds the birds without help from you. Just the same, it may come in very handy if he will obey hand and whistle signals. If he has failed to mark a bird, it is much better to handle him quickly and quietly to the fall—and at least have a fighting chance of staying in the trial—than to let him hunt all day, far from the vicinity of the fall, disturbing too much ground, and finally pick him up at the request of the judges. Then you *know* he's all through.

OPEN ALL-AGE STAKE

An Open All-Age Stake shall be for all dogs over six months of age.

This is the big-time stake that counts points toward the title of Field Trial Champion—*provided* there are at least twelve starters that are eligible for a Limited All-Age Stake. All clubs today allow at least one full day for it, and many provide a day and a half, so the dogs may be thoroughly tested.

The marking tests are not likely to be much more difficult than those described that you *might* encounter in a Non-Winners. You will probably get more of them, since more time is available for the Open Stake, and the entry is often smaller than in the Non-Winners.

To have a chance to go clear through the big stake, your dog must mark well, and do doubles, triples, or even four birds up to 100 yards in the heaviest cover. He must be absolutely steady. The judges have no choice but to throw him out if he makes a deliberate move to go before he is sent.

You should be prepared for a test tempting him to switch birds, and a "walk-up." The latter test simulates an ordinary hunting party driving a field for pheasants. Two or more dogs are on line at a time. At a word from a judge, the line moves forward, with guns and bird throwers walking also, out on the wings. Your dog must walk quietly at heel. Suddenly a bird is thrown and shot. The dog must *sit* at once—on your quiet command—

and stay until ordered by the judges to retrieve. Actually I don't think this is any more difficult for a jittery dog than sitting on a fixed line while his birds are shot out in front. If your dog is dependable about walking at heel, you'll have no trouble with a walk-up, but it wouldn't do any harm to practice it a little in advance.

In an Open Stake good judges will do their best to have at least four series, and sometimes five or six if time permits. The best dogs have a way of coming to the top, and automatically placing themselves, if given enough fair opportunities to do their stuff.

At least one series will be a handling test, on land or water or both. So unless your dog is quite responsive to the hand and whistle signals, you're wasting your entry fee in an Open All-Age Stake.

In setting up a handling test, the judges try to devise something that will really show them whether or not each dog can be handled—and how well he handles. When a dead bird is planted 100 yards or so straight out in front, it doesn't necessarily show the judges what they want to see. Many of the dogs will take a line, and romp straight out and stumble over the bird, without any handling being necessary. A dog cannot be penalized for this, even though he is suspected of being just lucky. But the judges still don't know whether he will handle.

Therefore they try to devise a handling test that is fair, yet will require the dog to respond to hand and whistle signals. Sometimes this is done by planting two dead birds, one of them out in front fifty yards or so. A cross wind is blowing from right to left. The second bird is planted much farther—100 yards or more—and slightly *to the left of the line of the first bird.*

Each handler is requested by the judges to get the far bird first. To do this, the dog must be sent on a line safely to the right, or upwind side, of the short bird. After he is well beyond it, the handler then stops him with the whistle, and directs him with hand signals back to the left, to the long bird.

I believe this type of test is fairer and usually proves more than having a long blind bird, with a marked bird in another direction that the dog gets first. It is true the marked bird pulls many dogs back to the vicinity of that fall, when they are sent out on the blind retrieve. And this makes it necessary for the dog to be handled. But a wise old campaigner with a good memory knows perfectly well he already has picked up the marked bird. He is likely to take a line, and go straight out and stumble over the blind bird—and still the judges don't know whether he can be stopped on the whistle and directed by hand signals.

Sometimes a disappointed handler whose dog fails sets up a beef that a certain test did not represent "hunting conditions." To my mind, this is the silliest of all complaints. Anything can happen when hunting. I can't conceive of a place I might not someday want to send a retriever for a fallen bird.

On the other hand, "hunting conditions" should not be used as an excuse for setting up a test that cannot be made approximately the same for every dog. Within that limitation, I feel that any retriever taking up the time of the judges in an Open All-Age Stake should be expected to do practically anything but answer the telephone and take a message.

LIMITED ALL-AGE STAKE

A Limited All-Age Stake shall be for dogs over six months of age that have previously been placed in an Open All-Age Stake (first, second, third, or fourth) or that have been placed first or second in a Derby, Junior, Novice, Non-Winners, or Amateur All-Age Stake at a licensed or member club trial.

This stake merely provides a means for a club, when its Open All-Age entry becomes too large to handle, to limit it to the qualified dogs. It keeps out the youngsters who aren't yet ready for the big-time competition, and some of the old-timers who never will be up to it.

In general the tests are the same as in the Open All-Age. The only difference is that with the limited entry, there may be time to run more series, and give the best dogs an even better chance to come to the top.

NATIONAL CHAMPIONSHIP STAKE

A National Championship Stake shall be for dogs over six months of age, which by reason of wins previously made qualify under rules approved by the board of Directors (of AKC). This stake shall be run not more than once in any calendar year by a club, or association, formed for this purpose and duly licensed by the American Kennel Club. The winner of such Stake shall become a Field Trial Champion of Record and shall be entitled to be designated "National Retriever Champion of 19—."

The next chapter is devoted to a complete report of the 1948 National Trial, including a description of each of the ten tests actually used. As you will gather, they were *some* tests.

Chapter 20

THE NATIONAL CHAMPIONSHIP TRIAL

THE ORIGINAL CONCEPTION of the National Championship Trial was to take the top twenty dogs or so of the year, run
them through at least ten series in three days, and then average
all the work and pick the winner. An ordinary Open Stake is
frequently decided after only four series. Some have had as few
as three.

It is possible for an erratic and unreliable dog to have luck,
and get through three or four tests without making a mistake.
But a dog who can put together ten faultless performances on
difficult tests over a three-day period has to have a good deal
more than luck. However, those of us who initiated the National
did not feel the winning dog would necessarily make no mistakes
in ten series.

Theoretically it would be possible for a dog to have one or
even two poor series, yet do such spectacular work in all the rest
that his *average* for the whole trial *might* surpass all his competition.

I've always hated to see good dogs thrown out of a trial after
a poor first series. How many times, on the opening day of
pheasant season, I've seen a dog do a perfectly miserable job
on his first bird—just through overexcitement—then settle down
and do beautiful work all the rest of the long day.

Now I prefer that dog to an uninspiring plodder who stumbles around at slow motion and manages to find all his birds, if that's *all* you can say for him.

This was the idea of the National Trial. With a small entry of top dogs, and three full days to run them—dogs would be definitely eliminated only for the crimes of breaking or hard mouth. Judges at their discretion could even carry along a dog after a complete failure to find a bird. *This* trial was going to be different. Instead of an elimination contest, it was to be just the opposite. The judges were to keep *all* the dogs in, all through the trial, unless a dog broke, was clearly guilty of hard mouth, or had done such perfectly stinking work that he obviously was unworthy of the title of National Champion, no matter what he might do for the balance of the trial.

I have been sorry to hear in recent years this plan has not been followed, and the National has been gradually slipping back to an elimination contest, although the Field Trial Committee still gives lip service to the original idea.

Let me quote from the official program of the 1948 National, held at Crab Orchard Lake, near Herrin, Illinois, December 3–4–5, 1948:

This is the Eighth Annual Championship Trial for Retrievers held under the auspices of the National Retriever Field Trial Club, Inc.

The dog winning this Trial is designated and regarded as the Champion Retriever for 1948. All the retriever dogs competing in this Trial have previously demonstrated their ability in other licensed Retriever Trials during the past year.

Most of the dogs competing are Field Trial Champions at the present time. This trial will bring forth the new Champion of Champions for the retriever breeds for the year 1948 and will be acclaimed by all as the outstanding Retriever of the year.

The entry in the National Retriever Trial is limited to twenty-one dogs which includes the retrievers that have placed highest in points in the licensed retriever trials during the year 1948 and also includes the winner of the 1947 National Trial and this previous winner qualifies automatically. The National Retriever Trial must have at least ten tests, five of which shall be on land and five in water, and during these tests the Judges give every dog competing every possible chance to continue in the trial for its full duration. The Judges take every precaution against having any unnatural tests which would be unfair to the dogs competing and all of the tests given are selected so as to resemble as near as possible actual hunting conditions.

You can decide for yourself, from the series by series account of the trial, whether every dog was given "every possible chance to continue . . . for its full duration."

Right now let me clearly state I intend no personal criticism whatever of the 1948 judges. They were: E. N. Dodge, Wayzata, Minnesota; A. T. Mickle, Waukesha, Wisconsin; and Joe Versay, Sheboygan, Wisconsin.

All three are thoroughly experienced amateur handlers and judges of the finest type, and their integrity and unselfish love of the sport are unquestioned. They worked hard and they put on a beautiful trial. While I mildly criticized the cover used in a couple of the land series, nobody realizes better than I do that judges are at the mercy of conditions, and must use the cover and other facilities provided for them by the field-trial committee.

I somewhat questioned one of the water tests, but that is a matter of opinion, and if retriever-happy people didn't honestly disagree occasionally on planning tests, there would be no need of having more than one judge in *any* trial.

I don't necessarily blame the judges for dropping dogs as rapidly as they did. They were merely following a trend that had been established in recent years, and for which they had ample precedent. There is no question they found the winner. He went through ten series with only one slight mistake that I was able to see. As things turned out, none of the dogs dropped earlier would have had a ghost of a chance.

But *if* the winner, and all the other top dogs, had run into serious trouble late in the trial, the judges might have wished they still had some of the dogs they dropped earlier, after only two poor performances.

It isn't likely in a National Trial that all the top dogs will fall down in two series, but it *can* happen. That is why I'd like to see the National judges get back to carrying all the dogs as far as they possibly can. And thus endeth my beefing.

It was still a wonderful trial, a spectacle of sparkling dog work to warm the heart of any hunting man.

Before we go on with the play by play report, here is the list of starters, showing the number of points won by each during 1948 only, and the number of series for which each dog was called back by the judges in the National Trial:

Dog	Owner	*1948* Points	*No.* Series
1. F.T.CH. MOTT PLACE CAPTAIN Black Labrador—Male	G. A. Bertsch Glasgow, Montana	13	5
2. F.T.CH. BRIGNALL'S GRINGO Black Labrador—Male	Clifford N. Brignall Long Beach, California	17½	10
3. F.T.CH. MARVADEL BLACK GUM Black Labrador—Male	Paul C. Bakewell III St. Louis, Missouri	9½	10
4. F.T.CH. GILMORE'S PEGGY Black Labrador—Female	Dr. L. M. Evans Sauk Rapids, Minnesota	22½	10
5. GOLDEN KIDD Golden—Male	Kingswere Kennels Winona, Minnesota	8½	8
6. TODD'S TARTAR Black Labrador—Male	Sandy Smith Woodstock, Illinois	8	5
7. MULLY GULLY GOO Black Labrador—Male	John Sturtevant Wausau, Wisconsin	8	5
8. F.T.CH. FIRELEIS HORNET Black Labrador—Male	Kingswere Kennels Winona, Minnesota	14½	8
9. BLACK PRINCE OF SAG HARBOR Black Labrador—Male	Mrs. Gerald M. Livingston New York, New York	6	8
10. MATCHMAKER FOR DEER CREEK Black Labrador—Male	Mr. & Mrs. Paul Bakewell III St. Louis, Missouri	6	1
11. ROYALS ROYAL OF STONEGATE Golden—Male	George W. Holmes Lincoln, Nebraska	6	8
12. MALARKEY'S OKANAGAN PAT Black Labrador—Male	Terrence M. Malarkey Portland, Oregon	15½	5
13. VICTORY JOY Black Labrador—Female	Dr. Wm. F. Carver Hollywood, California	5	2
14. GRANGEMEAD PRECOCIOUS Black Labrador—Male	Grangemead Kennels St. Charles, Illinois	5	2

Dog	Owner	1948 Points	No. Series
15. F.T.CH. BENGAL OF ARDEN Black Labrador—Male	Mrs. James M. Austin Old Westbury, New York	18	8
16. F.T.CH. BRACKEN'S SWEEP (1947 National Champion) Black Labrador—Male	Daniel E. Pomeroy Englewood, New Jersey	25	8
17. F.T.CH. BLACK PANTHER Black Labrador—Male	Carl W. Carlson Helena, Montana	22	7
18. GOLDWOOD FRISCO Golden—Male	Ambrose C. Lund White Bear Lake, Minnesota	9½	5
19. RIP OF WAKE Black Labrador—Male	Ben W. Stafford El Cajon, California	6½	5
20. F.T.CH. LITTLE PIERRE OF DEER CREEK Black Labrador—Male	Mr. & Mrs. Paul Bakewell III St. Louis, Missouri	30½	10
21. F.T.CH. KEITH'S BLACK MAGIC Black Labrador—Female	Daniel E. Pomeroy Englewood, New Jersey	11½	10

DESCRIPTION OF 1948 NATIONAL
FRIDAY, DECEMBER 3
(Fair and cold)

First Series: Land. Medium natural cover, knee high. Marking test. Two shot pheasants. Two dogs on line. Long bird on right, almost straight downwind, shot first—average fall, 110 yards. Then left bird shot, far to left, cross wind for dog on this one, average fall from dog, seventy-five yards. Wind, light. Scenting conditions, only fair.

Twenty-one starters. One dog broke. Fifteen retrieved both birds quickly, with no handling. Five needed some help from their handlers on one or both birds. Twenty completed, and were carried to next series.

Second Series: Water. Handling test. One dog at a time worked from end of point jutting into lake. Heavy bulrushes and flag grass along shore all around point. Blind retrieve: a dead duck was dropped out in open water, far to right, at least 150 yards. Cross wind, left to right. Two short marked diversion birds shot from point to fall in decoys to the left. This was also a severe steadiness test, as one of these short ducks was thrown right past the dog's nose.

From the gallery it was impossible to see what happened out on the point on the two short marked retrieves, but it appeared most of the dogs handled beautifully on the long blind retrieve in the open water. Twenty starters. Two failed on blind retrieve, and were picked up. Eighteen completed, and were called back for next series.

Third Series: Land. Very heavy and dense marsh grass cover—armpit high. Marking test. One dog on line, sat on road at edge of field. One judge with dog and handler. Two judges out with guns. A single pheasant shot straight out in front in that hellish cover. Average fall, perhaps seventy-five yards. Cross wind. Dog disappeared from road. Either he returned quickly with bird, or he didn't. Possibly the two judges out near the fall could follow some of the dogs by ear. But the judge on the road could have no more idea than the gallery where the dogs were or what they were doing—and for that series he was disfranchised.

I think possibly the judges were stampeded into using this too-high cover because it was getting late, there was barely time to complete a quick series before dark, and this was the only land cover offered by the committee that was nearby and could be moved to quickly. Of course, it may be that some of them really wanted this test. Certainly it represented perfectly normal "hunting conditions," and a retriever should be expected to find game in any kind of cover.

But in trial competition, I think the judges have a tough enough job comparing dog work when they can see what the dogs are doing.

Eighteen starters. Some got the bird very quickly. Others disappeared in the dense cover a long, long time, emerging at last with the bird. All eighteen finally completed, and were carried over for the next series the following morning.

SATURDAY, DECEMBER 4
(Cloudy and cold, clearing later)

Fourth Series: Land. Handling test. Two blind retrieves. Dead pheasants. Scant cover. Moved forward to fresh ground for each dog. Cross wind from right to left. Handlers instructed to get right bird first, approximately 100 yards. Then the other bird, far to the left, and almost straight downwind for dog, at least 150 yards.

Eighteen starters. All but two did splendid—and many perfectly spectacular—work. It was a thrilling test to watch—a perfect demonstration of "guided missiles." All eighteen completed and were called back for next series.

Fifth Series: Water. A difficult but perfectly fair marking and memory test. Dog worked from a blind and through decoys. Wind from right to left. A shot was fired, and a dead duck thrown to fall in heavy bulrushes on far shore, at least 150 yards away— to the left and at an angle across an arm of the lake. The wind was almost downwind from the dog to this fall. Then two diversion ducks were thrown and shot from up the shore to the right of the dog. These landed in a heavy clump of bulrushes, out in the water. Some of these short falls were quite difficult, and after hunting out both of those, it was a real indication of a remarkable memory if a dog then remembered the long fall across the water to the left, and swam across and got it quickly without help from his handler.

Eighteen starters. Six dogs did a very poor job, needed a great deal of handling. Eight showed some memory of long bird, did a fair job, but needed a certain amount of help. Only four showed positive memory, did a sparkling job with no handling, which is an indication of how tough this test proved to be. Eighteen completed.

At the conclusion of this series, with the trial only half over, the judges eliminated six dogs, to the great surprise of the gallery. It was perfectly evident that all of these dogs had at least two very poor series out of five, but some had done sparkling work in the other three tests, and conceivably might have gone on to win the trial had they stayed in—and *if* the top dogs had run into bad trouble in two or more of the later series. But possibly the judges felt none of these dogs worthy of the title National Champion, even if they did superb work from then on. This left only twelve starters for the sixth series.

Sixth Series: Water. But mainly a brambles test. To the gallery it looked very simple, almost like a test for Derby dogs. Across an arm of water only thirty yards or so wide a shot was fired and a dead duck thrown to fall back on shore about twenty yards—but what the gallery didn't realize was that it was deliberately tossed into a patch of heavy briars. The fall was not more than sixty yards from the dog in the blind. A very short duck was then thrown and shot to the left, from beside the blind, to fall in the edge of the water among the decoys. This was a mild marking test, but mainly a test of a dog's guts, and ability to take really punishing cover. Nearly all did well, going into the brambles boldly, and hunting out the far bird quickly. Only two showed any disposition to avoid the briars and hunt the easier cover away from the vicinity of the fall.

Twelve starters. All completed and were carried to next series.

Seventh Series: Land. Fairly thin cover, but enough of it was waist high so that the dogs, sitting down in it, had apparent difficulty marking the longer fall. The test used here is now commonly called an "over and under." Two shot pheasants. Long bird shot first, average fall eighty to ninety yards. Short bird then shot, *on the same line,* about half way out, or forty yards from dog. Wind quartering down and to the right of line of falls. Two dogs on line. Here again the judges separated, one out with far guns, the other two staying behind the line. I think they must have been amazed at the trouble many of the top dogs had with this test, some of them disappearing from view in the tall cover for a long time. In these cases the two rear judges could have no more idea what the dog was doing than the members of the gallery.

Twelve starters. One dog broke and was eliminated. Seven dogs failed to mark the long bird, disappeared far out into the big field, finally had to be whistled back in and handled endlessly to complete the test. Yet four dogs did manage to roll up both birds beautifully, and did faultless work. In a case like this, you can't help wondering how much luck was involved—whether those four dogs happened to sit in patches of lower cover, and thus had better marking opportunities than the others—or what? Eleven completed and were carried to next series the following morning.

SUNDAY, DECEMBER 5
(Cold, raining hard, blowing a near gale)

Eighth Series: Land. Short but good uniform cover—plenty to hide falls. Yet every move of every dog could be seen by gallery *and* judges. An ideal field for this test. A combination marking and handling test, with emphasis on handling. Two marked birds—one blind. One dog on line. Strong wind and rain at his back. The blind bird, a dead pheasant, was planted at a 45-degree angle to the left, at least 250 yards away, in the edge of a sparse hedgerow, containing some briars. Then the dog was called up to line, and a second pheasant shot to fall at a wide angle to right, 100 yards away. And a third bird was shot to fall out in front and slightly to the left, about sixty yards from dog.

This was a tough series, but beautiful to watch. Only two dogs hurt themselves badly here, although one of these appeared to be a leading contender up to this point in the trial. Three dogs did only a fair job of handling on the blind retrieve. But six of the eleven starters came up with break-taking, spectacular performances.

After this series, once again to the surprise of the gallery, the judges cut deep—dropping 6 dogs, which were however held "in reserve"—and calling back only 5 for the ninth series.

Ninth Series: Water. Rain now stopped but wind increased to a real gale. Whitecaps on lake. Many in gallery thought this a rather trick test. Dog sat on a point. Short bird, a duck, thrown and shot *first* from just to left of dog, to fall in fast water. Then the long bird—a dead duck—was thrown, with shot fired, across arm of lake, perhaps 125 yards away, to fall in light flag grass on edge of shore.

Handlers were instructed to get either bird first, as they chose. Normally a dog would take the last fall—the far bird in this case—first. But it was obvious that in the meantime the short duck would drift a long way down the lake in the fast water. Therefore, all of the handlers attempted quietly to give their dogs a line to the short duck first. Four of the five succeeded, and thus made the test look simple. The other dog ignored the handler's hand motion, did the normal thing, and retrieved the far bird first. Then of course she had to be handled on a long swim far down the lake for the first duck, which was drifting nearly as fast as a dog could swim. If I were obliged to judge such a test, I'm darned if I know how I would score this latter performance. I don't see how the dog could be faulted very much. She might be marked down slightly for ignoring the handler's line, originally. But then she did a perfect job on the far bird—and handled beautifully on the other, which had then drifted so far from the fall it had become a blind retrieve, and a tough one.

Five starters. Five completed and were called to final series.

Tenth Series: Water. Handling test. This was a fine test, a spectacular finale for the trial. Wind now blowing harder than ever. Really big waves on lake. A dead duck planted barely on edge of a point of land, far down and across the lake, at least 200 yards away. Wind blowing down and quartering to right. Then a shot was fired from boat, and a dead duck thrown in lake, far to the left and behind the dog, about seventy-five yards away.

Five starters. All completed. Only one did a poor job. Three did splendid work, handling beautifully across the rough water. And one, who proved to be the winner of the trial, put on a superb performance. He took a line from his handler, never deviated from it one foot, went straight across 200 yards of rugged water— somehow miraculously compensating for the strong sidedrift. No whistle blown, no hand signal given. The dog went ashore exactly on the duck! The gallery gasped.

THE WINNER

To the utter astonishment of our good friends in the East and the Middle West, the dog crowned National Champion Retriever for 1948 was:

Dog No. 2
BRIGNALL'S GRINGO
Field Trial Champion
Black Labrador—Male
Whelped: May 10, 1946
Sire: Freehaven Lucky
Dam: Victoria Crescent
Owner: Clifford N. Brignall
      Long Beach, California
Handler: Roy Gonia

This two-year-old youngster had stacked up a magnificent record in West Coast trials during 1948. But our Eastern friends, accustomed to thinking that the country west of the Rockies is populated exclusively by Hollywood characters, Indians, and desert rats—had not realized how rapidly the quality of our retriever competition had grown out here. They had discounted Gringo's record as being compiled in easy trials.

When he was announced as the new Champion I'm afraid I was guilty of a most undignified rebel yell. For his owner is not only a good friend of mine, and a leading member of our Southern California Retriever Club—but Gringo himself happens to be a grandson of both Freehaven Jay and Freehaven Molly.

I unblushingly mention the winner's ancestry to indicate why I couldn't have been happier about the outcome of the trial. Certainly I had no ax to grind in the mild criticisms I have voiced. As things turned out, none of the dogs that were dropped early could possibly have come close to Gringo. He scarcely put a foot down wrong in ten series. Just the same, I'd have liked to see some of those others in there pitching to the end—just in case.

Chapter 21

THE WHEELS IN A JUDGE'S HEAD

NEWCOMERS TO THE trials often wonder just what the judges are writing in those mysterious notebooks—and how they compare and evaluate and score the work of the different dogs. There are different methods of scoring, but all depend on the men who use them, and all seem to arrive at about the same result.

METHODS OF SCORING AND KEEPING NOTES

Some judges have elaborate score sheets in their notebooks, and on each performance they manage to check off a detailed list of items such as: manners, marking, memory, attention, sagacity, control, steadiness, nose, delivery, courage, perseverance, speed, style, etc. I tried something like this once, but found I was not nimble enough to keep up with it. I was so wrapped up in my bookkeeping work I had no time to watch the dogs.

I think the majority of experienced judges now use a much easier and simpler system. As each dog works, a running diagram is drawn, showing just where he went in relation to the falls. This can be done by simply moving your pencil while watching the dog. This is then supplemented by a few very brief notes—just enough to recall the entire performance later. A single grade, or score, is then jotted down for the over-all performance for that series. Some use A-plus for perfect, and grade down with A, B-plus, B, C-plus, etc. Others prefer 10, 9-plus, 9, 8-plus, etc.

A few men with whom I've judged give a separate grade or score for each bird but in my opinion this is a needless complication. In a double retrieve marking test for instance, the important thing is whether a dog remembers the *second* bird for which he is sent, and his performance on that one should count much more heavily than on the first one.

I use the 10-for-perfect method, giving a single score for each entire test. At any stage of the trial you can quickly total the scores of each dog, and get a *rough* idea of how they stand. This is often most useful when the judges are pressed for time, and must quickly decide whether another series is needed, or whether it is possible to place the dogs fairly without seeing further work and without resorting to a lot of hairsplitting on minor faults. If there are at least four top dogs whose total scores are well separated, you're reasonably safe to stop the trial. If several are very close, it's best to get in another series if this can possibly be done before dark.

But let me say right here that after the stake is over, careful judges *never* award the placings just on the basis of the total scores. The performances in each series of every dog which finished the trial are reviewed, discussed, and compared. Scores of one or more judges are sometimes then revised, to make them fair on a *comparative* basis.

In a long-drawn-out series you sometimes discover your scoring has become more lenient, or perhaps more severe, as time dragged on. I try to keep checking this during a series, leafing back through my book to compare what I gave previous performances with that of the current dog. But when all the notebook pages are spread out before you, you sometimes find you have slipped and given a bit higher grade to a dog whose actual work was slightly inferior to that of another. This always comes out in the final discussion, if sufficient time is given to it. On the whole, however, it is surprising how closely the offhand scores given in each series by two or three different judges usually agree with each other.

I am reproducing here a fairly typical page from my notebook. (See cut.) There is one such looseleaf page for each dog, with room for three series on each side. Dogs are identified and judged only by number.

Offhand this looks like the doodlings of a diseased mind, I grant you. But it makes sense to me. It clearly recalls to my mind even now, some six weeks later, every detail of that dog's performances in the first three series of the Open at the fall trial of the Women's Field Trial Club, November 12, 1948, at Westhampton Beach, Long Island.

The first series was on land, a marking test (M). In the diagram, X marks position from which dog was sent. The arrow shows wind direction. The circle labeled (1) is the first fall, a shot pheasant, approximately 100 yards. The circle labeled (2), on the right, is a short diversion bird, a fall of about 40 yards.

The diagram, plus the brief notes on the right side of the page, tell me something like this:

On the short bird (2) the dog had a perfect mark, hit it right on the nose. Did a fast, stylish job. There was nothing wrong with his pickup, delivery, or anything else, or mention would have been made of it in the notes. But of course this was the last fall, and merely a short diversion bird. An open all-age dog *should* do perfect work on it. The real test here is what he does on the other.

Not so good. He overran it quite badly on the upwind side. Then showed poor memory, because instead of correcting and hunting back to the downwind side of (1), he hunted much too much ground too far out and too far to the right. Then he hunted back almost to the second fall (the one he had already retrieved).

At this point the handler whistled, and handled him twice; he then got the bird quickly, but the main damage had been done. He had badly flunked his marking and memory test. However, he was a "goin' dog," an aggressive, hunting fool. Otherwise he might have drawn an even lower score than 4 on the series.

The second series was in water, a marking and memory test (M). From a point of land the first duck was thrown and shot to fall out in a salt-water cove, 150 yards from the dog. Then two

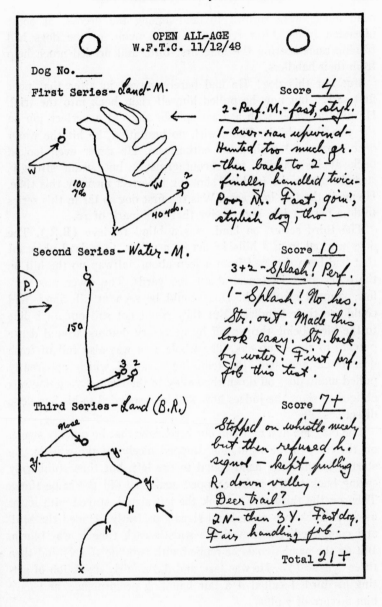

OPEN ALL-AGE
W.F.T.C. 11/12/48

Dog No.____

First Series—*Land-M.*   Score ___4__

2 - Perf. M. - fast, styl.

1 - over-ran upwind -
Hunted too much gr.
- then back to 2
finally handled twice -
Poor M. Fast, goin',
stylish dog, tho' —

100 yds.

W

40 yds.

X

Second Series — *Water-M.*   Score __10__

3+2 - *Splash! Perf.*

1 - Splash! No hes.
Str. out. Made this
look easy. Str. back
by water! First perf.
job this test.

P.

150

Third Series—*Land (B.R.)*   Score __7+__

Stopped on whistle nicely
but then refused h.
signal — kept pulling
R. down valley.
Deer trail?

2 N - then 3 Y. Fast dog.
Fair handling job.

Nose

Y.

Y.

Y.

N

N

X

Total __21+__

dead ducks were thrown to land among the decoys, as short diversion birds. After retrieving them, many of the dogs had trouble remembering the long first bird, and needed much help from their handlers.

But not this dog! He had barely stayed in after that poor first series, but now he pulled himself right back into the trial. He hit the water with a great splash, and did a perfect job on the two short birds. Then, with no hesitation, he hit the water once more, and with great enthusiasm. He never even looked back at his handler for encouragement, but swam strongly, straight out to the far bird, showing a perfect memory this time. He made the test look easy. Was the first dog so far in this series to do a perfect job, and receive that rare mark of 10.

The third series, on land, was a blind retrieve (B.R.). The dogs worked from a hillside, across a valley, to a dead pheasant that had been dropped from a jeep about halfway up the hill on the other side. Distance, about 200 yards. The cover was very low, stunted scrub oak. Dogs could be seen at all times, and could see their handlers. But they could not sail out on a line to the bird, being thrown off by necessary detours around dense patches of the scrub oak. The whole area was also full of fresh deer track and sign, the tempting scent of which apparently pulled many dogs off down the valley to the right. Every dog was obliged to show the judges how well he responded to his handler's directions.

The diagram and notes on our hero show that he quickly swung off the line, to the right, but stopped nicely on the whistle. He started to take the hand signal to the left, but then stubbornly swung back to the right. Stopped again, he did the same thing. Then on the third try, he took the left signal, stayed with it for a while. Took two more hand signals perfectly, winded the bird, and completed. He obeyed the whistle each time it was blown. But on the hand signals he replied with two "no's" (N) and then three "yes's" (Y). He was fast, and did a fairly quick job of getting his bird. I called it a fair handling performance, and gave him a score of 7-plus.

Well, that's enough I think to give a rough idea of how many judges score and keep notes. Some might score a point or so higher than I did on the first and third series described above, and some a bit lower. *But the relation of the scores to all the other dogs in the series would be about the same.*

Watching and scoring the work is easy, if the tests pan out as they are supposed to. By far the hardest part of the judging job is planning the tests, and trying to avoid unpleasant surprises. For when a series is once started, you must go through with it, no matter how it pains you. You can't call it off and do something else after the first dog has run.

PLANNING THE TESTS

A man judging a retriever trial is—or at least should be—looking for exactly the same sort of work he would like to see his own gun dog do, from the duck blind, or in the field. However, there is one important limitation in the trials that he must constantly remember.

Retrievers perform some spectacular and astonishing feats in the hunting field, but many of these don't make practical tests in a trial. Unless a test can be controlled so that each dog is given approximately the same job to do, it is useless for a trial competition.

For instance, one of the greatest values of a retriever is in tracking down, catching, and bringing to bag a strong running crippled pheasant. Nobody in his right mind would argue that. Yet I at least have never figured out a way to test competing dogs on cripples, and do it fairly for all dogs. A man who has judged trials and should know better recently made the serious proposal that every open all-age stake should include at least one series on running pheasants. He suggested the birds be brailed so they can't fly, a bit of fresh blood smeared on their legs to give them blood scent, then tossed in cover as a shot is fired.

I would be all for this test if there were any way to get these unpredictable cock pheasants to co-operate. But the first one might land running like a jack rabbit and be halfway out of the county in a very few seconds, and give a dog a really rough job of trailing. The next might crawl into a clump of dense cover, sit tight, and be picked up practically where he fell. Now if you were judging, how would you compare the work of two dogs doing such different jobs? It isn't fair to dog number two to penalize him because he had only a simple marked retrieve to do, if he did it well. You have no way of knowing what he would have done if given the same opportunity as dog number one.

A few people in the sport sometimes sneer at my "phobia" for having equal tests for all dogs. But these are usually not the people who have done much training and handling themselves.

If you have ever had a dog of your own knocked out of a trial by an unfair and avoidable "break of the game," you're inclined to develop a rabid sympathy for the dogs and their handlers—and to think it's important to give each dog the same opportunity. That's why experienced amateur handlers usually make the best and fairest judges.

Of course the top professional handlers would be splendid judges—but it is unfair to ask them to judge. The best ones usually have strings of field-trial dogs. They are obligated to the owners to run them in as many trials as possible. It's their business. If a pro is invited to judge a big trial, it's embarrassing to him to refuse. Yet if he accepts, and passes up running his dogs in that trial, it may be a real sacrifice to him. It might cost him qualifying a dog for the National. And it might even lose him one or more clients.

But whether he's amateur or pro, no matter how much experience he's had, a man often yearns for a crystal ball when he's trying to guess right in setting up a test.

On a given day, nobody knows how scenting conditions will be until after they've seen a few dogs work. When dogs can easily wind a bird from a distance of twenty-five or thirty yards, they often will make two long falls in the heaviest cover look almost too simple to bother with. But if scenting conditions should be nil, and a dog must stumble on a bird to find it, the same falls may cause many top dogs to fail miserably.

Sometimes scenting is fine in one field, and you are amazed to find it very poor in another, later in the day. This may be due to catnip or some other weed hidden in the cover, which gives off a strong odor. But sometimes when this happens, nobody has the slightest notion as to the cause.

Another judge's headache is the matter of wind. If in the middle of a series the wind dies entirely, or if its direction changes, the entire test is different for the later dogs. Good judges do their best to compensate for this, by shortening falls or changing direction of working the dogs, when the terrain and other factors will permit.

Sometimes on an overcast morning a series is started, and before it is over the clouds clear away. Then the remaining dogs may have to mark their falls directly against a blinding sun.

Tests occasionally backfire on the most careful and experienced judges, for no apparent reason. They may plan something which should be perfectly simple for open all-age dogs, yet have dog after dog go haywire and fail completely.

The judge's worst nightmare is having a test boomerang so badly that he loses *all* the dogs in the first series, or any series for that matter, of any stake. Even with a huge entry and being pressed for time, I believe any conscientious judge would hate to lose as many as half the dogs through failure in a first series.

Sometimes you hear people in a gallery feeling sorry for the judges because so few dogs fail. This is nonsense. Oh, I suppose there have been a few lazy, incompetent, or inexperienced judges who were happy to see dogs eliminate themselves, to make their own job easier.

But men who train and handle their own dogs are not likely to be planning tests with such an objective. They want to keep the good dogs in, as long as possible, for they know that's the only way to be sure of finding the best one at the end of the trial.

He can't win if he isn't still in there.

Such judges, in planning tests, are trying to make them just hard enough to give the dogs a chance to show *how well they can do them*, yet not to make too many of them fail. This is a bit like walking a tight rope. To accomplish it, a man needs experience, ingenuity, sympathy for dogs and handlers—and then he also needs a lot of luck in his guessing.

CONDUCT OF A TRIAL

Good judges won't stand for very much sloppy gunning. They will usually insist that a pair of gunners who miss more than one bird be relieved, instantly. They feel a trial is for the dogs, and not for the amusement of the local skeet shooters. If two men who are good shots take it seriously, and both shoot and both try on every bird, there is little excuse for a pheasant ever flying away.

When a bird is missed, it may sail a half mile before it goes down. The dogs on line have their eyes glued on it. If another bird is then shot, and one of these dogs sent, he is all too likely to take out cross country after the missed bird. After all, it was shot at by a pair of skeet champions, and it *could* be a cripple.

Therefore, careful judges do the best they can to cancel the effect of a missed bird by excusing the dogs from the line. Or they may give the handlers their choice of being called back later in the series, or just walking their dogs around for a moment, to get their minds off the long fall of the missed bird.

The fussiest judges usually won't allow a dog to be sent for a bird they think might be a runner. When in doubt, they excuse the dogs from the line, and have the bird picked up. They won't even permit a dog to take an unusually long fall. It *might* cause him to fail, unfairly. But even if he does a perfect job on it, he can't be scored higher than dogs who performed perfectly on the shorter falls they were given.

I think this procedure is the lesser of two evils. But picking up hair-trigger dogs after birds have flown and shots have been fired is at best a precarious business. It sometimes causes a dog to break later, even if he doesn't leave right now, as the handler gingerly reaches for his collar.

The best solution is to avoid the whole problem by insisting on good gunning.

In a marking test, the dogs should have equal opportunities to see their falls. Obviously it is unfair if one dog sits up high with a full view, and another is down in a depression, or behind a clump of brush, or attempting to mark a fall over a hill. When you see the line move on beyond such obstructions, or when you see a judge squat down beside a dog to determine just what the dog can see from *his* eye-level, you're looking at a man who is trying to run an equal contest for all.

Good judges keep a trial moving. If necessary they keep going straight through the daylight hours, with no time out for lunch or anything else. They expect the field-trial committee to have things organized, and are apt to be ugly about any unnecessary delay.

Their objective is to run enough series so every worthy dog in every stake is given sufficient opportunity to win or place if he is capable of it. Ordinarily, they want at least three series in a Derby, Junior, or Non-Winners Stake, and at least four in an Open All-Age. But the number needed will vary greatly in different trials. Recently at the Woman's Club Trial which I was privileged to judge with my good friend, Howes Burton, the Open dogs were hot, and there were forty-two of them. I never saw such beautiful dog work, and so much of it, in my life.

By Saturday night, after running four series in a day and a half, we felt it would be ridiculous to try to place the dogs. Too many were too close to perfection. We could have done it, but it would have meant resorting to some very fine distinctions on minor faults. Both of us felt we hated to award championship points on such hairsplitting.

The field-trial committee co-operated splendidly, secured other judges for the Amateur Stake on Sunday, and allowed us to go on with the Open. We kept running and running those marvelous dogs until, after seven series, they finally placed themselves.

If you see enough work, it's easy to place them. But nowadays, with entries growing so large at some of the trials, this matter of having enough tests in the available time is often the biggest problem the judges face.

GALLERY JUDGES

Many people in the galleries at trials keep brief notes of their own, and score each performance. Sometimes they disagree violently with the decisions of the judges, when the awards are announced. Usually these are soreheads, selfishly interested in a dog that failed to win.

I have heard of "raw decisions" that were supposedly obvious to every handler and gallery spectator, but I have never seen one. When I am a spectator or handler at a trial, and people ask me what dog is on top, I usually must honestly answer that I have no idea.

Very rarely does anyone at a trial actually see *all* the work of *every* dog—except the judges themselves. Certainly a handler can't. He must spend much of his time running back and forth to his truck, bringing up his dogs, while other dogs are performing.

Spectators who think they're seeing everything don't realize how much time they spend gossiping with friends, wandering back to the lunch wagon or for a bottle of beer, and how much of the work they thus actually miss.

Then, too, nobody but the judges is close enough to the dogs to see and hear everything that goes on. A dog may whine quite loudly on line without the gallery knowing it. He may be very unsteady, when the gallery is not in position to see it. He may rough his birds severely, yet not quite badly enough to be disqualified entirely for hard mouth. He may give up his birds so reluctantly that the handler has to pry them out of his mouth. The gallery misses many of these things, and they may have quite a bearing on the final placings in a close trial.

I have done my share of criticizing *tests*, or *trial procedure*. Indeed, I did some kibitzing of this type in the previous chapter. But I have yet to feel competent as a spectator to quarrel with the *final placings* of any judges, in any trial I've ever seen.

So my advice is to go ahead and score the dogs yourself. Be a gallery judge. It's fun, and makes the trial more interesting to watch. But for heaven's sake, be quiet about it. Most of the retriever people are good sports, and lose as gracefully as they win.

But if you try you can always find one or two of the other kind, ready to enter into a malicious whispering campaign about who "really should have won." This is almost as bad as beefing directly to the judges about their decisions. The chances are at least 1000 to 1 that you are wrong and the judges are right. Nobody but a sucker bucks odds like those.

Chapter 22

TIPS FOR THE AMATEUR HANDLER

MANY AMATEURS, when handling in a trial, are as nervous as if they were appearing for the first time before a huge audience in Hollywood Bowl. But even some of the older pros confess they've always had this same trouble, and probably always will. So if, when you take your dog on line, your hands shake and the bottom of your stomach falls into your shoes, don't worry about it. You have plenty of company.

Don't be afraid of the judges. They're only people. And don't hesitate to ask them questions, if you're not sure what you're supposed to do. They want to see your dog do the best job of which he is capable.

Your purpose as a handler is to help your dog to give his best performance. It is smart to start showing him at his best, right from the time your number is called to summon you up to the line.

WHEN YOUR DOG IS UNDER JUDGMENT

At just what instant does a dog start being under judgment? There is no clear-cut rule on this.

In Open All-Age stakes it is customary to bring the dogs up to the line off leash, walking at heel. And if a dog does not heel reasonably well, but wanders around sniffing bushes, or if he precedes the handler by fifteen or twenty feet to the line or into the blind, many judges will notice and penalize the dog for bad manners.

In minor stakes you are safe to bring the dog to the line on leash, unless you have been specifically instructed to have him at heel. But he should walk along quietly. It looks lousy if he drags you up there like a moldboard plow, and some judges might penalize for this, even in a lesser stake. After all, a retriever is supposed to be under quiet control at all times.

Anything not specifically covered in the rules is left to the discretion of the judges. Thus your best bet is to consider that you and your dog are under judgment from the time you are called up until you have left the line again and are *out of sight of the judges*.

When you reach the line, have your dog *sit* on the exact spot designated by the judges. If they have neglected to pick a position from which he has a fair chance to see his falls, they'll be glad to have you call it to their attention. Don't hesitate to ask if you can move your dog slightly to avoid an obstruction. But usually the judges will pick a better place for your dog than you know how to do yourself.

Remove the leash at once and stuff it entirely in your pocket, so none of it is showing. Do this without being told. In the old days a few of the trickier handlers tried to use exposed leashes to intimidate unsteady dogs.

Take plenty of time, within reason, to get your dog sitting so he is aimed correctly. He should be facing what will be the most difficult fall, usually the first bird shot. That's the one you want to be sure he sees and remembers. He'll turn his head to see the other one. But in maneuvering him into position, don't grab him and haul him around. Coax him around to where you want him by patting your leg and commanding "heel." Once you've taken off the leash, don't touch your dog. Judges must penalize for this, because some handlers have attempted all sorts of stunts and subterfuges to hold dogs steady, even to standing on their tails. Of course any handler seen actually holding his dog to keep him steady must be disqualified entirely.

KEEPING YOUR DOG STEADY

However, you should use every *legitimate* means to help your dog resist the temptation to break. At a trial, excited by the other dogs, the crowd, and general hubbub, he's much more likely to leave you than he is in training workouts at home.

Stand beside him—but *beside his head, not his tail*. Stand far enough forward so that when your arm hangs naturally by your side, your hand is beside the dog's nose. He can see it, and smell it, and it reminds him that pappy is there, too, when those squawking cock pheasants go up and the guns start going off. This is very important. Yet how often you see a careless handler standing back beside a dog's stern, and then being greatly astonished when the dog suddenly leaves.

Watch your dog every minute. Be ready to hiss softly, or even sharply to command "sit" if necessary, the instant you see those muscles bunching for a take-off. A young dog who has been reasonably well trained to obedience can be kept steady in a trial if his handler is on the ball, and doesn't go to sleep.

Most judges won't penalize much if you hiss once or twice, or even say "sit" fairly quietly. But if you overdo it, are constantly nagging, and making a good deal of noise about it, they must assume the dog is very unsteady, and penalize quite severely.

If your dog *should* get away from you, try to stop him and get him back, even if you have to bellow "no!" and "sit" repeatedly. Don't make the common mistake of shouting his name. He'll just go faster, thinking you're sending him. Stop him and get him back as quickly as you can. If he broke only eight or ten feet, you might even stay in a minor stake, for the judges don't *have* to throw a dog out for a controlled break except in an Open All-Age stake.

But if only for the good of the dog, try to stop him before he goes clear out and retrieves the bird. If he gets away with that once or twice, and learns that at a trial there's nothing the boss can do by way of just retribution, he's well on his way to becoming a chronic breaker. And that can really be tough to cure. It's much easier never to let him get away with a complete break even once.

Don't get excited and send your dog before a judge calls your number. Does this admonition seem silly? Well, you'll probably forget it, at least once. Nearly everybody does, and nothing makes a handler feel sillier. This, of course, is a technical break.

If a bird is missed and you are told to pick up your dog, be sure to reach for his collar very cautiously and slowly, at the same time commanding "sit." This is a ticklish moment. A sudden movement of your hand might cause the dog to break, thinking you are giving him a line to the fall. And the rule book says very definitely that you are still under judgment until you have left the line with your dog on leash.

MARKING YOUR FALLS

Mark your falls. You can't help your dog find them if you don't know where they are yourself. This sounds elementary, too, but it isn't easy. Most humans are very poor markers to start with.

Then, remember, to complicate things further, you must not take your eye off your dog. You have to watch him with one corner of your vision, and with the other mark your falls. This is quite a trick, and has a tendency to make a man walleyed.

Before you go up in line, study the background of the field, at the approximate place from which you'll work. Distant farm buildings, odd-shaped trees, and fence posts are very helpful for remembering the exact *line* of a fall. Have all these possibly useful objects in your mind before you go on line. Then, when your birds are shot, and you see them down out of the *corner* of one eye, you say something like this to yourself, "The left one is on a line with the fourth fence post to the left of that big dead elm. It is out just beyond the second patch of darker green in the cover."

Then you memorize other landmarks for the second fall. But the important one to be sure of is the *first* fall—the one your dog is most likely to have trouble remembering. However, the smart handler marks them all, whether it's two, three, or more birds.

GIVING YOUR DOG A LINE

Before you go up in line, be sure you know exactly what direction the wind is blowing. Then, when you send your dog for his first retrieve, give him a line with a very slight gesture of your hand, on the downwind side of the fall. This is just a bit of insurance. If the dog marked the fall, he should hit it on the nose anyway. But if he cuts it too thin, he might just miss it on the upwind side, and run on out of the county.

For his second retrieve, always take time to have him *sit* for a second or two, aimed the way you want him to go, and then give him a line for the fall. Don't ever get cocky about the dog's memory and grab the first bird from him, and just vaguely wave him back for the other. I did it once, and it cost me a win in an Open stake.

Now what sort of line you give on this second retrieve depends on the setup of the test. If the first bird retrieved was on the right, and the wind blowing across from *left* to *right*, then with the average dog you would give him a line straight at the left fall. His tendency will be to swing back to the right a little, because of the right fall he's just retrieved. This will keep him safely on the downwind side of the left fall. But a test set up this way is quite simple, and not likely to be encountered except in very minor stakes.

More likely the wind will be blowing from right to left. And then, when you send him for that second retrieve, you'd best play safe and give him a *false* line—far to the left of the actual fall. Then if he curves in toward the old fall, he still has a margin of safety to keep him on the downwind side of the bird he's after.

More handlers fumble on this matter of giving a smart line than anything else. Study this with your own dog, in practice. Some dogs curve toward the old fall much more than others. See how much he usually curves, and then when you're in a trial don't get rattled and forget to allow for it when you give him his line.

HANDLING IN MARKING TESTS

Most beginning handlers are whistle happy. If they've trained their dogs to handle, they can't wait to prove it. Usually, they're just penalizing their dogs. In a marking test, any dog that apparently needs a lot of whistle and hand signals to help him find birds he saw fall must be marked down severely.

So, when your dog is hunting the vicinity of a marked fall, let him alone. Keep your whistle in your pocket. Let him hunt it out on his own. Even if it takes slightly longer, he'll get a better score than if you help him.

But this doesn't mean, if he badly overruns the bird and starts aimlessly hunting the whole country far from any fall, that you should let him go on indefinitely. After a reasonable amount of such wild romping, the judges have no choice but to tell you to pick him up. If that happens, you *know* you're all through.

When he overruns, if he does not correct himself quickly and come back to the area of the fall, then you'd better whistle him in, stop him, and with hand signals put him on the bird as quickly as you can. If you get your birds fairly fast, you at least have a chance to stay in the trial for awhile. You can't possibly win if you're dropped in an early series.

But if you're not fairly sure he will respond to the whistle, then you'd better not blow it, no matter what he's doing. All you can do is stand there and suffer, silently praying that he will tire of romping the horizon and stumble over the bird on his way back in, before the patience of the judges is exhausted. For the only thing worse than handling on a marked fall is to attempt to do so, and have the dog refuse.

Always watch your dog. Don't ever turn your back on him, to address a pleasantry to the judges. He will invariably choose that moment to start running a rabbit over the hill, and that fleeting instant when you *might* have stopped him with the whistle will be gone forever.

In a marking test there may be a dense gallery crowded quite close behind you, and if you find it necessary to handle, your dog will have difficulty picking you out of the crowd. For this reason, most smart handlers wear a white shirt or windbreaker. It also helps sometimes to move forward, just two or three steps ahead of the line. Most judges won't object to this, within reason. Frank Hogan, the old maestro, used to keep inching forward until the judges told him he'd gone far enough. If you didn't watch him, he would suddenly be halfway out to the dog.

Another useful stunt, when your dog has difficulty seeing you against a gallery, is to move your whole body when you give a hand signal to left or right. Often this motion will help him find you.

In each series, watch carefully what happens to the dogs ahead of you. You can avoid many pitfalls this way. If most of the dogs seem to be having the same kind of trouble, assume that yours will, too, and try to compensate for it in your handling.

If your dog overruns a fall, and you think you'll have to handle, stop him before he gets beyond "range of control." Nearly every dog has one. He'll stop beautifully on the whistle and obey hand signals like a German soldier until he gets out a certain distance. After that, he suddenly goes "deaf." The distance at which this phenomenon occurs varies greatly with different dogs. You'll quickly discover what your dog's is, after he has defied you once or twice.

In a walk-up test, as you move forward, repeat the command "heel" quietly, and only as often as necessary to keep your dog at heel. Watch him with one eye, and keep the other on the boy who will throw the first bird. The instant the pheasant is thrown, stop and command your dog to sit. Be sure you stop beside his head, not his tail. From then on the procedure is usually the same as in a marking test from a stationary line. The other bird is then thrown and shot, you mark your falls, watch your dog, and send him only when his number is called.

HANDLING IN WATER TESTS

In a double retrieve on water, the judges sometimes permit the handler to step outside the blind to send the dog for the second bird. If they so instruct you, take advantage of it. You'll get no extra credit if you show off by sending the dog from inside the blind. And it is, of course, much easier to give him the line from outside than through the hole in the front of the blind.

If the judges don't tell you, play safe and ask them whether they wish you to stay in the blind for both birds.

On a blind retrieve across water, don't attempt to send your dog into the water at very much of an angle to the shore line. Send him straight in, get him well out past the decoys, and then when he is still within easy "handling range," turn him and handle him to the hidden bird—by water as much as possible.

When a dog has seen no fall—and sometimes even when he has—if you try to send him in at an angle to the shore, he very likely will start hunting down the shore instead of entering the water. If he once gets this notion in his head, he may give you a bad time.

Well, that's enough about handling. At least it is enough to get you started, so you won't look or feel as silly as I did during my early handling attempts.

Bless you, sucker, and good luck. Perhaps you too got into this thing quite innocently, just wanting to have yourself a meat dog to use for hunting. But after you've handled your retriever in his first trial, you'll be hooked. You'll have field-trial fever. And so far as medical science now knows, this disease is incurable.

INDEX

INDEX

231